Prentice Hall LITERATURE

PENGUIN EDITION

Unit One
Resources

Grade Nine

PEARSON

Upper Saddle River, New Jersey
Boston, Massachusetts
Chandler, Arizona
Glenview, Illinois

BQ Tunes Credits
Keith London, Defined Mind, Inc., Executive Producer
Mike Pandolfo, Wonderful, Producer
All songs mixed and mastered by Mike Pandolfo, Wonderful
Vlad Gutkovich, Wonderful, Assistant Engineer
Recorded November 2007 – February 2008 in SoHo, New York City, at
Wonderful, 594 Broadway

ISBN–13: 978-0-13-366449-2
ISBN–10:   0-13-366449-X

2 3 4 5 6 7 8 9 10   12 11 10 09

CONTENTS
UNIT 1

"If I Forget Thee, Oh Earth . . ." by Arthur C. Clarke

from Silent Spring by Rachel Carson

About the Unit Resources

The *Prentice Hall Literature Unit Resources* provide manageable, comprehensive, and easy-to-use teaching materials to support each Student Edition unit. You can use these resources to address your students' different ability levels and learning styles, customize instruction to suit your teaching needs, and diagnose and assess student progress. All of these materials are also available at *PHLitOnline*, a rich, online source of personalized instruction and activities.

Here is a brief description of each element of the *Unit Resources*:

UNIT-LEVEL FEATURES

Big Questions (grades 6–10)

Support for the Big Questions includes complete lyrics to BQ Tunes (engaging songs that incorporate Big Question Vocabulary; available on CD); unit-opener worksheets that practice Big Question Vocabulary, an Applying the Big Question chart, re-rendered from the Student Edition.

Essential Questions (The American Experience; The British Tradition)

Support for the Essential Questions includes unit-opener worksheets that focus on each Essential Question individually and a worksheet to support the end-of-unit Essential Question Workshop.

Skills Concept Maps

Each map presents a graphic look at the relationship between the literature and the skills taught in the unit, with space provided for students' notes.

Vocabulary Workshop, Writing Workshop, and Communications Workshop support

End-of-unit worksheets provide opportunities for students to practice vocabulary and gather and organize information for their Student Edition assignments.

SELECTION-LEVEL SUPPORT

Vocabulary and Reading Warm-ups

These exercises and easy reading passages provide selection vocabulary practice for students reading at one or two levels below grade level

Writing About the Big Question (grades 6–10)

These worksheets tie the Big Question to individual selections, while giving students additional practice using the Big Question Vocabulary.

Literary Analysis, Reading, and Vocabulary Builder

This series of worksheets provides extra practice on each of the main skill strands in the Student Edition. You can find more support for the Literary Analysis and Reading strands in the separate Graphic Organizers Transparencies component.

Integrated Language Skills

The Student Edition Integrated Language Skills features are supported by grammar worksheets and additional pages containing graphic organizers and questions to help students gather and organize information to complete their Student Edition Writing and Listening and Speaking or Research and Technology assignments.

Enrichment

These activities give opportunities for advanced students to focus more closely on topics related to the content or theme of the literature selection.

ASSESSMENT

Diagnostic Tests

The beginning of each Unit 1 Resources book features a Diagnostic Test. Thereafter, each even-numbered Benchmark Test ends with a 20-question diagnostic component called Vocabulary in Context. Teachers desiring a larger sample for measuring students' reading ability can find an additional 20 questions at *PHLitOnline*.

Benchmark Tests

Twelve Benchmark Tests, spaced evenly throughout the year, assess students' mastery of literary, reading, vocabulary, grammar, and writing skills. A diagnostic Vocabulary in Context, described above, ends each even-numbered Benchmark Test.

Open-Book Tests

For every selection or grouping of selections, there is an Open-Book Test featuring short-answer and extended-response questions and opportunities for oral response. Most Open-Book Tests also contain a question requiring students to represent information in a graphic organizer. These tests are available as a computer test bank on CD-ROM and at *PHLitOnline*.

Selection Tests

For every selection or grouping of selections, there are two closed-book Selection Tests (A and B) featuring multiple-choice and essay questions. Both tests assess essentially the same material; however, Test A is designed for lower-level students, and Test B is designed for students who are average and above.

ADDITIONAL SUPPORT IN *UNIT ONE RESOURCES*

Pronunciation Guide

A two-page student guide to understanding diacritical marks given in standard dictionary pronunciations; includes practice

Form for Analyzing Primary Source Documents

In support of Primary Sources features in *The American Experience* and *The British Tradition*, a form for analyzing various types of primary sources

Teaching Guides

To support fluency monitoring, Guide for Assessing Fluency; to support vocabulary instruction through music, a Guide for Teaching with BQ Tunes

Guide for Assessing Fluency

The students' *All-in-One Workbooks* feature a series of twelve expository and narrative reading passages to be used to assess reading fluency. The passages have lexiles of increasing difficulty within the grade level range. They are designed to test students' reading accuracy and pace. An optional question is provided to assess comprehension.

The following oral reading rates are recommended goals:

ORAL READING RATES	
Grade	Words per Minute
6	115–145 with 90% accuracy
7	147–167 with 90% accuracy
8	156–171 with 90% accuracy
9–10	180–200 with 90% accuracy

Instructional Routine

- Hold reading practice sessions. Choose an appropriate practice passage of about 250 words from the literature students are studying or from another source. You will find a lexile score for each literature selection in your *Teacher's Edition* Time and Resource Managers. You may also use as practice passages the Warm-ups in the *Unit Resources* books and, for grades 6–8, articles in the *Discoveries* series and *Real-Life Readings*.

- Students should read the passage once silently, noting any unfamiliar words. Have them define or explain those words before reading the passage aloud. (Students may add these words to a *Word Wall* later.)

- Then, have students work in pairs to rehearse their oral fluency. (Alternatively, you may lead the class in a choral reading of a single passage.)

- After students have read the passage(s) with understanding, they may time themselves or each other for practice before the formal timed readings are conducted.

Formal Fluency Assessment

- From the students' All-in-One Workbook, select a passage at the appropriate lexile level.

- Using an audio recorder, instruct the student to read the passage aloud at a normal pace. Alternatively, you may ask the student to read as you follow along, marking the text. Time the student for one minute.

- Note these types of errors: mispronunciations, omissions, reversals, substitutions, and words with which you have to help the student, after waiting two or three seconds.

- Mark the point in the passage that the student reaches after one minute.

- Use the formula below for determining accuracy and rate.

- Determine the rate by calculating the total number of WCPM (words correct per minute) and comparing the student's results against the goals indicated in the chart above.

- Analyze the results and create a plan for continued student improvement.

Guide for Assessing Fluency

Calculating Fluency

Use this formula to calculate reading fluency:

Total words read correctly (both correctly read and self-corrected) in one minute *divided by* total words read (words read correctly + errors) × 100 = % accuracy

$$\frac{\text{number of words read correctly}}{\text{number of words read}} \times 100 = \text{WCPM}$$

Example: $\frac{137}{145} \times 100 = 94\%$

Post-reading Comprehension Activity

A short test item allows you quickly to assess student comprehension. The items include these formats:

- matching
- fill-in-the-blank
- true/false
- short answer

If the student demonstrates difficulty in understanding the passage, you may remediate using selected leveled resources in the *Prentice Hall Literature* program. These components include the Vocabulary and Reading Warm-ups in the *Unit Resources*; the *Reading Kit* Practice and Assess pages, which are aligned with specific skills; and the scaffolded support for comprehension and other ELA skills in the *Reader's Notebooks: Adapted* and *English Learner's Versions.*

Pronunciation Key Practice—1

Throughout your textbook, you will find vocabulary features that include pronunciation for each new word. In order to pronounce the words correctly, you need to understand the symbols used to indicate different sounds.

Short Vowel Sounds

These sounds are shown with no markings at all:

a	as in at, cap	e	as in end, feather, very
i	as in it, gym, ear	u	as in mud, ton, trouble

Long Vowel Sounds

These sounds are shown with a line over the vowel:

ā	as in ate, rain, break	ē	as in see, steam, piece
ī	as in nice, lie, sky	ō	as in no, oat, low

A. DIRECTIONS: *Read aloud the sound indicated by the spelling of each item. Then write the word each spelling stands for.*

1. kap _____
2. kāp _____
3. tīp _____
4. klōz _____
5. tuf _____

6. ker _____
7. wird _____
8. swet _____
9. swēt _____
10. nīt _____

Other Vowel Sounds

Notice the special markings used to show the following vowel sounds:

ä	as in father, far, heart	ô	as in all, law, taught
o͞o	as in look, would, pull	o͞o	as in boot, drew, tune
yo͞o	as in cute, few, use	oi	as in oil, toy, royal
ou	as in out, now	ʉ	as in her, sir, word

B. DIRECTIONS: *Read aloud the sound indicated by the spelling of each item. Then write the word each spelling stands for.*

1. boi _____
2. kär _____
3. ko͞od _____
4. lo͞oz _____
5. kroun _____

6. wʉrk _____
7. lo͞or _____
8. kôt _____
9. myo͞o _____
10. rä _____

Pronunciation Key Practice—2

Some Special Consonant Sounds

These consonant sounds are shown by special two-letter combinations:

hw as in which, white

sh as in shell, mission, fiction

ŋ as in ring, anger, pink

ch as in chew, nature

zh as in vision, treasure

th as in threw, nothing

th as in then, mother

Syllables and Accent Marks

Your textbook will show you how to break a word into syllables, or parts, so that you can pronounce each part correctly. An accent mark (´) shows you which syllable to stress when you pronounce a word. Notice the differences in the way you say the following words:

bā´ bē   ō bā´   den´ im   dē nī´

Sounds in Unaccented Syllables

You will often see the following special symbols used in unaccented syllables. The most common is the schwa (ə), which shows an unaccented "uh" sound:

ə as in ago, conceited, category, invisible

'l as in cattle, paddle

'n as in sudden, hidden

Light and Heavy Accents

Some long words have two stressed syllables: a heavy stress on one syllable and a second, lighter stress on another syllable. The lighter stress is shown by an accent mark in lighter type, like this: (´)

C. DIRECTIONS: *With a partner, read aloud the sounds indicated by the symbols in each item. Say the words that the symbols stand for.*

1. kôr´əs
2. kəm pash´ən
3. brē *th*iŋ
4. ig nôrd´

5. mezh´ ər
6. des´ pər ā´ shən
7. im´ ə choor´
8. plunj´ iŋ

9. fər bid´ 'n
10. hwim´ pər
11. fun´ də ment´ 'l
12. rek´ əg nīz´

D. DIRECTIONS: *With a partner, read aloud the sounds indicated by the symbols in the following lines. Each group of lines represent the words of a small poem.*

1. ī ēt mī pēz wi*th* hun´ ē.

   iv dun it ôl mī līf.

   it māks *th*ə pēz tāst fun´ ē.

   but it kēps *th*em än *th*ə nīf.

2. dōnt wʉr´ē if yoor jäb iz smôl

   and yoor ri wôrdz´ är fyo͞o.

   ri mem´bər *th*at *th*ə mīt´ē ōk

   wuz wuns ə nut līk yo͞o.

BQ Tunes Activities

Use **BQ Tunes** to engage students in learning each unit's Big Question vocabulary and introduce the issue that the Big Question raises. You can access **BQ Tunes** recordings and lyrics at *PHLitOnline* or in *Hear It*, the Prentice Hall Audio Program. The lyrics are also provided in your **Unit Resources** books and in the students' **All-in-One Workbooks**. Below are suggested activities for using the songs with your class. Each activity takes 20–25 minutes. Students should have copies of the lyrics available.

Listening Exercise

OBJECTIVE: *To familiarize students with the song vocabulary and initiate discussion of definitions*

1. Instruct students to listen to the selected song, listing any words they do not know.
2. Play the selected song.
3. Afterward, ask students to raise their hands if they know the definitions of words they listed, and call on individuals to share their definitions. Write the words on the board as they are called out.
4. Then, ask students to share words for which they did *not* know the definitions, and call on them individually. Write the words on the board as they are called out.
5. Direct students to turn to the selected lyrics, and instruct students to infer definitions for the remaining words in the lyrics. If they experience difficulty, encourage them to work in pairs or direct them to a dictionary.
6. Play song again, and instruct students to read the lyrics to reinforce the exercise.

Vocabulary Game Exercise

OBJECTIVE: *To reinforce students' knowledge of Big Question vocabulary in the songs, and to initiate class discussion of definitions.*

1. Divide the students into two teams, each on one side of the room.
2. Play the selected song to the class. Then, play it again as students follow along reading the lyrics.
3. Afterward, read the song's lyrics aloud and, alternating sides, ask each team to define key words as they come upon them. Award a point for each correct definition.
4. Write the words on the board as they are defined, and keep score as the teams win points.
5. Declare the team with the most points the winners.
6. Review vocabulary missed by both teams, and field any questions the students may have.

BQ Tunes Activities

Writing Exercise, Stage 1

OBJECTIVE: *To build students' writing skills, leveraging newly acquired vocabulary*

1. Instruct students to write three contextual sentences, each using a single vocabulary word present in the selected song. The sentences *do not* have to be related to one another.
2. Allow 5 to 7 minutes for students to complete the task.
3. Afterward, ask random students to read what they have composed.
4. Then, ask the class if the sentences satisfied the "contextual" criteria, and discuss the responses.
5. Repeat with as many students as time permits.
6. Field any questions the students may have.

Writing Exercise, Stage 2

OBJECTIVE: *To build students' composition skills, leveraging newly acquired vocabulary*

1. Instruct students to write three contextual sentences, each using a single vocabulary word present in the selected song. The sentences *must* be related to one another, as in a paragraph.
2. Allow 5 to 7 minutes for students to complete the task.
3. Afterward, ask random students to read what they've composed.
4. Then, ask the class if the sentences satisfied the "contextual" criteria and the "relationship" criteria, and discuss the responses.
5. Repeat with as many students as time permits.
6. Field any questions the students may have.

BQ Tunes

Situation & Circumstance, performed by the Fake Gimms

Oooo . . .

I attempt to **convince**, to lead you to see,

To see things my way.

It's my **perspective**,

So, don't you agree?

I can take it out of **context**.

Twist the facts and the **evidence**.

Yea, I **distort** the **truth**.

So, won't you agree?

Now don't you agree?

I stand firm in my **belief**,

That things are exactly as I see them to be.

It's what I **perceive**.

And I'm sure you'll agree.

Now you're starting to see it my way.

You've got to question if it's **credible**.

Or if it's even capable of being believed or trusted.

No, it's not enough to make **assumptions**.

Got to check the facts, **verify**, confirm and make sure . . . Oooo . . .

The situation and the **circumstance**,

I **speculate**, I think about . . .

But can the truth be changed?

No, no it can't!

I hear the **skeptics** that say they do not believe.

They **manipulate**, shape it their own way.

But the truth cannot be changed.

Oooo . . .

Continued

I attempt to **convince,** to lead you to see,

To see things my way.

It's my perspective,

And I'm sure you agree.

Song Title: **Situation & Circumstance**
Artist / Performed by Fake Gimms
Vocals & Guitar: Joe Pfeiffer
Guitar: Greg Kuter
Bass Guitar: Jared Duncan
Drums: Tom Morra
Lyrics by the Fake Gimms
Produced by the Fake Gimms
Studio Production: Mike Pandolfo, Wonderful
Executive Producer: Keith London, Defined Mind

Name _____ Date _____

Unit 1: Fiction and Nonfiction
Big Question Vocabulary—1

The Big Question: Can truth change?

A story can differ depending on who tells it. Every person sees things in his or her own way. So, if you ask three witnesses about the same event, you may get three different versions of the truth. Each is a subjective version of the truth.

credible: believable or trusted

distort: to explain or report something that is incorrect or untrue

evidence: a fact, an object, or a sign that convinces you that something is true

manipulate: to fool people into thinking or acting a certain way

verify: to find out if something is correct or true

DIRECTIONS: *Continue the story, using each vocabulary word at least once.*

> "Your bicycle came out of nowhere!" Stuart said. "I was minding my own business and—boom! There you were!"
> "Actually," Carlotta replied, "you ran into the street after your soccer ball without looking. If you had looked, you would have seen me. Now, because of you, I swerved into that fire hydrant and damaged my bicycle. You owe me money for the damage."
> Just then, Stuart's older brother came by and asked, "What happened?"
>
> _____
>
> _____
>
> _____
>
> _____
>
> _____
>
> _____
>
> _____

1

Unit 1: Fiction and Nonfiction
Big Question Vocabulary—2

The Big Question: Can truth change?

Who you are and what your experience has been greatly affect the way you view a situation. Never assume that others experience things the same way that you do.

belief: a feeling that something is true or exists

circumstance: a fact or condition that affects a situation, an action, or an event

convince: to persuade someone to believe something

perspective: point of view

skeptics: people who question what others believe to be true

DIRECTIONS: *Fill in the dialogue below using all of the vocabulary words.*

Ms. Patty was new to Canyon High School. She was excited about the art class she would teach the ninth graders. For their first project, they would spread a canvas on the floor of the art room and then take turns throwing paint at the canvas. It would be a group work of art. What a great way for the class to get to know each other.

The class got underway, and it went really well! At least that's what Ms. Patty thought. Some others at the school were not so sure. . . . What did they have to say about Ms. Patty's project?

Mr. Langston, Principal

Ms. Grace, Teacher, with classroom next door

Mr. Tompkins, Janitor

Willa Burke, Art Student

2

Name _____ Date _____

Unit 1: Fiction and Nonfiction
Big Question Vocabulary—3

The Big Question: Can truth change?

We often form opinions based on situations and prior experience. The danger in this is that sometimes we jump to incorrect conclusions.

assumption: something that you think is true even though you have no definite proof

context: the situation, events, or information that are related to something, and that help you understand it better

perceive: to see or recognize something

speculate: to guess about the possible causes or effects of something

truth: the actual facts about something

DIRECTIONS: *Use the vocabulary words above to help Jason tell his mother that she may have jumped to an unfair conclusion.*

"I want the facts!" Jason's mother said. "How did this lamp break? And why is there an orangutan in our living room?"
Jason looked at her. She thought it was his fault, when, really, he knew nothing about it. . . .

_____

_____

_____

_____

_____

_____

Name _____ Date _____

Unit 1: Fiction and Nonfiction
Applying the Big Question

The Big Question: Can truth change?

DIRECTIONS: *Complete the chart below to apply what you have learned about the truth and whether or not it can change. One row has been completed for you.*

Example	A Statement of Truth or Fact	Evidence	How It Could Change or Why It Could Not	What I Learned
From Literature	In "The Cask of Amontillado," Fortunato insults Montresor.	Montresor says that Fortunato insulted him.	If Fortunato narrated the story, he might say he never insulted Montresor.	The truth can change, depending on who tells it.
From Literature				
From Science				
From Social Studies				
From Real Life				

Diagnostic Test

Identify the answer choice that best completes the statement.

1. I still have to dust the furniture and _____ the rug.
   A. vacuum
   B. laundry
   C. wrung
   D. dye

2. The comedy was unsucessful; instead of outright laughter, it elicited only a few _____ .
   A. slang
   B. gossip
   C. performance
   D. snickers

3. The neighbor's farm has bees living in ten _____ .
   A. corridors
   B. hives
   C. vaults
   D. alcoves

4. On the warm summer night, the children ran in the yard and caught _____ .
   A. cod
   B. nevertheless
   C. lemmings
   D. fireflies

5. The teacher wrote our homework assignment on the _____ .
   A. policy
   B. chalkboard
   C. tapestry
   D. fiction

6. The children made a bridge from blocks, but it was not steady and it _____ .
   A. paralyzed
   B. collapsed
   C. lingered
   D. rendered

7. After his nap, the little boy's hair was _____ .
   A. fringed
   B. gnarled
   C. tousled
   D. distilled

8. To shave his face, he had a brand-new _____ .
   A. razor
   B. amulet
   C. niche
   D. parchment

9. When the car sped through the icy puddle, my shoes were splashed by the _____ .
   A. haze
   B. drizzle
   C. slush
   D. underfoot

10. We couldn't find the costumes we wanted, so we had to make our own and _____ .
    A. improvise
    B. conceive
    C. fabric
    D. speculate

11. The house had been neglected for so long that we had to clean and _____ everything.
    A. auctioned
    B. vigorous
    C. incense
    D. scour

12. The prime minister of Pakistan was killed by an _____ .
    A. enlisted
    B. unsuspecting
    C. assassin
    D. administration

13. Never be late for an appointment—always be _____ .
    A. punctual
    B. reluctant
    C. unnoticed
    D. intentional

14. The chef said that copper skillets and _____ are best.
    A. flagons
    B. blenders
    C. saucepans
    D. cookbooks

15. When I dug my cactus out of the small pot to replant it, I used this _____ .
    A. trowel
    B. initiation
    C. tier
    D. throng

16. I need to talk with you for just a second, so please excuse my _____ of your conversation.
    A. termination
    B. interruption
    C. separation
    D. demonstration

17. Someone left the back door open, _____ allowing the dogs to run outside.
    A. vainly
    B. dispersing
    C. thereby
    D. accessible

18. I had a feeling that she would call today; just call it _____ .
    A. initiative
    B. impassive
    C. intuition
    D. indication

19. After I mashed the potatoes, I added some butter and green _____ .
    A. parsley
    B. bland
    C. brine
    D. hotshot

20. When my leg was scratched by a stick, my father treated it with _____ .
    A. salve
    B. brazier
    C. awash
    D. pinpricks

21. We live in an area that is not very populated but rather _____ .
    A. remote
    B. elsewhere
    C. random
    D. amid

22. Whenever I open a juice box, the juice_____ out of the straw.
    A. blots
    B. spurts
    C. suspends
    D. busted

23. If you throw a stick, the dog will run after it and _____ it.
    A. impose
    B. threat
    C. fetch
    D. beckon

24. After being ill for so long, he had lost weight and was_____ .
    A. acute
    B. gaunt
    C. void
    D. eroded

25. I selected my groceries and paid the_____ with a credit card.
    A. journalist
    B. cashier
    C. suitor
    D. patron

26. After the ball broke the window, the angry woman shouted at us_____ .
    A. unnecessary
    B. largely
    C. aimlessly
    D. scornfully

27. Along with my hot chocolate in the afternoon, I enjoy a warm_____ .
    A. pastry
    B. brewer
    C. vitamin
    D. marrow

28. We plan to stop for the night at some charming_____ .
    A. niche
    B. excursions
    C. homeland
    D. lodgings

Name _____ Date _____

29. When the race started, she was behind, but she soon_____ the leader.
   A. awaiting
   B. descent
   C. onward
   D. overtook

30. On this remote island, the explorers were attacked by_____ .
   A. corpses
   B. menacing
   C. coachmen
   D. cannibals

31. Do you have to pay to ride the ferry and, if so, what is the_____?
   A. fee
   B. inheritance
   C. intention
   D. attraction

32. With no planning, I decided to take this trip on a_____ .
   A. mere
   B. whim
   C. adventurous
   D. whirlwind

33. As the cold weather approached, the bear found a safe_____ in which to sleep.
   A. suite
   B. turret
   C. desolate
   D. cavern

34. If I tell you a secret, will you be_____ and not spread the news?
   A. involuntary
   B. discreet
   C. withstanding
   D. distinguished

35. After a long day of riding bikes in the hills, we turned_____ .
   A. headland
   B. straggled
   C. alternately
   D. homeward

36. All of my apple trees were slowly being killed by a _____ .
    A. blight
    B. specter
    C. persistent
    D. pyre

37. Although they both spoke the same language, they grew up speaking different _____ .
    A. wit
    B. rites
    C. dialects
    D. vantages

38. The lion proudly considered himself to be the _____ king of the jungle.
    A. drastic
    B. wistful
    C. distraught
    D. almighty

39. From one corner to the opposite one, draw a line _____ on this paper.
    A. diagonally
    B. horizontally
    C. artful
    D. punctually

40. Before I could run such a long race, I had to build up my _____ .
    A. delirium
    B. stamina
    C. faculties
    D. antidotes

Unit 1: Fiction and Nonfiction Skills Concept Map—1

Can truth change?

Literary Analysis:
Fiction and Nonfiction

Narration → includes → a plot → and → significant details

(demonstrated in this selection)

Selection name:

(demonstrated in this selection)

Selection name:

Basic Elements of Fiction
- Characters
- Plot
- Conflict
- Theme

Basic Elements of Nonfiction
- Factual
- Narrator
- Purpose
- Tone

Comparing Literary Works:
Point of View

as seen from

- third-person point of view
- first-person point of view

(demonstrated in these selections)

Selection names:
1.
2.

Reading Skills and Strategies:
Predictions

You can **predict what will happen next** → by → asking questions about text and events → and by → reading ahead to verify predictions

Words you can use to discuss the Big Question

Informational Text:
Cookbook

You can use signal words → to → read to perform a task

(demonstrated in this selection)

Selection name:

Student Log

Complete this chart to track your assignments.

Writing	Extend Your Learning	Writing Workshop	Other Assignments

***from* The Giant's House and "Desiderata"** by Elizabeth McCracken
Vocabulary Warm-up Word Lists

Study these words from The Giant's House *and* "Desiderata." *Then, complete the activities.*

Word List A

assumed [uh SOOMD] *v.* took for granted; supposed
  I <u>assumed</u> that the train would arrive on time, so I was surprised when it came late.

conclusions [kuhn KLOO zhuhnz] *n.* final judgments or decisions
  The committee considered all the evidence before announcing its <u>conclusions</u>.

exaggerate [eg ZAJ uh rayt] *v.* make something seem to be more than it is
  Political candidates sometimes <u>exaggerate</u> their accomplishments.

imposing [im POH zing] *adj.* large and impressive
  Weighing over 300 pounds, the wrestler was an <u>imposing</u> figure.

incomplete [in kuhm PLEET] *adj.* not having all its parts
  I felt my story was <u>incomplete</u>, but I couldn't quite figure out what was missing.

nutrition [noo TRI shuhn] *n.* process of eating the right food for good health
  Experts in <u>nutrition</u> planned the hospital menu.

previously [PREE vee uhs lee] *adv.* at an earlier time
  I had <u>previously</u> planned to be a doctor, but now I'm thinking about studying law.

resisting [ri ZIST ing] *v.* fighting against
  I am <u>resisting</u> the temptation to watch TV instead of doing my homework.

Word List B

adolescence [ad uh LES uhns] *n.* time between childhood and adulthood
  Young people leave childhood around age twelve, when <u>adolescence</u> begins.

continually [kuhn TIN yoo uhl lee] *adv.* repeatedly, over a long period of time
  The program we were watching was <u>continually</u> interrupted by commercials.

correspondence [kahr uh SPAHN duhns] *n.* exchange of letters between people
  Our <u>correspondence</u> began when my best friend moved to another state.

doubtful [DOWT fuhl] *adj.* filled with doubt; uncertain
  If you are <u>doubtful</u> about passing the test, you should probably study more.

fiction [FIK shuhn] *n.* books and stories about imaginary characters and events
  I like short stories better than any other form of <u>fiction</u>.

passionate [PASH uh nit] *adj.* showing strong emotion
  We enjoy math class because our teacher is so <u>passionate</u> about the subject.

persistent [per SIS tuhnt] *adj.* continuing stubbornly; lasting
  I cannot seem to get rid of this <u>persistent</u> cold.

prospector [PRAH spek tuhr] *n.* person who searches for gold or other precious minerals
  The modern <u>prospector</u> uses a metal detector to search for gold nuggets.

Name _____ Date _____

from The Giant's House and "Desiderata" by Elizabeth McCracken
Vocabulary Warm-up Exercises

Exercise A *Fill in each blank in the paragraph below with an appropriate word from Word List A. Use each word only once.*

When I was growing up, I always [1] _____ that I would be a professional athlete some day. I do not mean to [2] _____ my own abilities, but I was almost always the fastest and strongest kid in my class. I was very careful about what I ate because I knew that good [3] _____ was just as important as working out. By the time I reached high school, I had developed an [4] _____ muscular build. I knew my high-school experience would be [5] _____ until I joined a sports team, but I was foolishly [6] _____ trying out for track for fear that I might not be good enough. I had [7] _____ been embarrassed back in junior high school when I came in third from last in a track meet. I thought about how to overcome my fear of failure, but I reached no useful [8] _____. Fortunately, my friends talked me into trying out. Now I'm a top athlete in the state. I guess you can't succeed unless you are willing to take a chance!

Exercise B *Answer the questions with complete explanations.*

Example: Can a lazy <u>prospector</u> be successful?
A lazy <u>prospector</u> would not search energetically for precious minerals, so the chances of success would be small.

1. Can a third grader know what <u>adolescence</u> is like?
   _____

2. If you are <u>continually</u> failing math tests, what should you do?
   _____

3. Could you have a <u>correspondence</u> with someone who speaks another language?
   _____

4. If you were <u>doubtful</u> about someone's honesty, would you lend that person money?
   _____

5. Can a work of <u>fiction</u> include real historical characters?
   _____

6. If you were <u>passionate</u> about baseball, would you be likely to read a book about it?
   _____

7. Would a person with a <u>persistent</u> headache be likely to have a cheerful attitude?
   _____

Name _____ Date _____

from The Giant's House and "Desiderata" by Elizabeth McCracken
Reading Warm-up A

Read the following passage. Pay special attention to the underlined words. Then, read it again, and complete the activities. Use a separate sheet of paper for your written answers.

Alicia had always been the tallest kid in her elementary school class. People were always getting silly ideas and jumping to <u>conclusions</u> about her just because she was tall. "You are going to be a great basketball player some day," they would say, even though Alicia hated basketball. For years, she had been <u>resisting</u> the troubling notion that she was always going to stand out in a crowd.

Then, in the third grade, Alicia decided that being special was not necessarily such a bad thing. That is when she decided that her goal in life was to be the tallest girl in the world.

For a while, it looked as if Alicia were going to achieve her goal. Her <u>imposing</u> height was a constant topic of conversation at school. When she reached five feet six inches, classmates would <u>exaggerate</u> her height to their friends, stretching it to six feet!

Alicia enjoyed all the attention. She even read books about <u>nutrition</u> to see if she could find a special diet that would make her grow taller. Alicia <u>assumed</u> that she could just keep growing forever.

Then, something unexpected happened: Alicia stopped growing. She was still the tallest girl in her seventh-grade class, but a lot of the kids had begun catching up to her. Some of the girls were nearly the same height, and quite a few of the boys were even taller. By the time Alicia was in high school, hardly anyone talked about how tall she was. Instead, people were beginning to talk about how smart she was! Kids who had <u>previously</u> teased her about her height were now asking her to help them study for exams.

That is when Alicia realized that her self-image had always been <u>incomplete</u>. She had not just been the tallest girl in school. She had always been the tallest girl and also one of the smartest. An important part of who she was had been missing.

1. Underline the words that tell why people were jumping to <u>conclusions</u> about Alicia. What *conclusions* might people jump to about you? Why?

2. Underline the words that tell what Alicia had been <u>resisting</u>. Name something that you have been *resisting*.

3. Circle the word that tells what was <u>imposing</u>. Use a synonym for *imposing* in a sentence.

4. Circle the words that help explain what it means to <u>exaggerate</u>. Write a sentence in which you *exaggerate* one of your characteristics.

5. Underline the word that hints at the meaning of <u>nutrition</u>. What is *nutrition*?

6. Underline the words that tell what Alicia <u>assumed</u>. Write a sentence about something you *assumed* that turned out to be wrong.

7. Underline the words that tell what some kids had <u>previously</u> done to Alicia. Write a sentence using *previously*.

8. Circle the words in the paragraph that help explain <u>incomplete</u>. What might happen if a recipe you were using were *incomplete*?

from **The Giant's House and "Desiderata"** by Elizabeth McCracken
Reading Warm-up B

Read the following passage. Pay special attention to the underlined words. Then, read it again, and complete the activities. Use a separate sheet of paper for your written answers.

As young people enter <u>adolescence</u>, they usually want to learn more about themselves and where they came from. Nearly all of us have families that originated in Africa, Asia, or Europe. You probably know where your parents and grandparents were born, but can you trace your family tree back even further?

Searching for your family roots is like being a <u>prospector</u> panning for gold, and the results can be every bit as rewarding. People who research their family histories are called *genealogists*. They have a <u>persistent</u> desire to learn everything they can about their ancestors. They study old diaries, yearbooks, passports, and even personal <u>correspondence</u> to find out as much as they can about the people in their family. Of course, not every document can be taken at face value. A teenager's diary, for example, may contain almost as much <u>fiction</u> as fact!

The best place to begin your search is at home. You can learn a lot just by looking at your own birth certificate. Your parents' birth certificates will tell you when and where they were born as well as the names of their parents. Search for death certificates, newspaper clippings, military records, and other documents that might tell you more about grandparents, uncles, aunts, and other family members. Write down names, dates, and places. See how they all connect.

Next, talk to as many of your relatives as you can. Some <u>doubtful</u> people may be hesitant about revisiting the past, but most will be delighted to take a walk down memory lane. If you are <u>passionate</u> about your quest, people will sense your excitement and try to help you.

The next places to look are the library and the Internet. Ask a librarian to help you find census data, immigration archives, military records, and other useful documents. This information may lead you to family members whom you never even knew about. By <u>continually</u> searching for your family roots, over time you might even learn a few new things about yourself!

1. Circle the words that give a clue to the meaning of <u>adolescence</u>. What would you say is the age range of *adolescence*?

2. Underline the words that tell something a <u>prospector</u> might be doing. How is a genealogist like a *prospector*?

3. Underline the words that tell what is <u>persistent</u> in a genealogist. Write a sentence about something that is *persistent* in your own life.

4. Underline the words that tell why genealogists study personal <u>correspondence</u>. Give an example of your own *correspondence*.

5. Circle the word that means the opposite of <u>fiction</u>. What kind of *fiction* do you enjoy reading?

6. Circle the word that helps explain <u>doubtful</u>. Why might some people be *doubtful* about revisiting the past?

7. Circle a word that gives a clue to the meaning of <u>passionate</u>. Write a sentence about something you are *passionate* about.

8. Underline the words that give a hint to the meaning of <u>continually</u>. What does *continually* mean?

Unit 1 Resources: Fiction and Nonfiction

Elizabeth McCracken
Listening and Viewing

Segment 1: Meet Elizabeth McCracken
- Where does Elizabeth McCracken get inspiration for the characters she writes about in her books?
- If you were writing a fictional story, would you base your characters on real people or invent them entirely? Why?

_____

_____

_____

_____

Segment 2: Fiction and Nonfiction
- Why does Elizabeth McCracken enjoy writing fiction?
- Why do you think it is important for a fiction writer to also read nonfiction books?

_____

_____

_____

_____

Segment 3: The Writing Process
- Why is it important for Elizabeth McCracken to develop her characters?
- Which fictional character left a lasting impression on you? Explain.

_____

_____

_____

_____

Segment 4: The Rewards of Writing
- What advice does Elizabeth McCracken offer young writers?
- What do you "get out" of reading fiction?

_____

_____

_____

_____

Learning About Fiction and Nonfiction

The following chart compares and contrasts two types of prose literature.

Characteristics	Fiction	Nonfiction
Elements	Fiction tells about **characters,** *imaginary* people or animals. They participate in a **plot,** or a series of made-up events, that contains a **conflict,** or problem, to be solved. The plot takes place in one or more **settings.** The story conveys a **theme,** or idea about life.	Nonfiction tells about *real* people, animals, places, things, experiences, and ideas. Nonfiction can contain facts, opinions, and ideas.
Sample forms	short stories, novels, novellas	articles, autobiographies, biographies, essays, journals
Author's purpose	to entertain	to explain, inform, persuade, or entertain

A. DIRECTIONS: *Write* fiction *or* nonfiction *to identify the kind of literature described.*

_____ 1. a piece of literature that features a talking tiger

_____ 2. a piece of literature about travel to Japan

_____ 3. a piece of literature about the lessons two friends learn about themselves when they go to summer camp

_____ 4. a piece of literature that explains how a runner trains for victory

B. DIRECTIONS: *Read the paragraph. Then, answer the questions that follow.*

The modem on Alicia's laptop computer had been blown apart in the lightning storm. Try as she would, she could not connect to the phone line. But Alicia refused to give up. Opening the cover on her cell phone, she held the instrument firmly and pressed a silver-colored button for precisely three seconds. Within another three seconds, she was small enough to slither through the back of the laptop. She saw the modem glinting on the motherboard. She was ready to begin the repair job.

1. Does the preceding paragraph introduce a piece of fiction or nonfiction? _____

2. Explain your answer to Question 1.

_____

_____

from **The Giant's House** by Elizabeth McCracken
Model Selection: Fiction

A fictional story is told by a **narrator.** The narrator may or may not be a character in the story. If the narrator is part of the story, he or she tells the plot using **first-person point of view,** with pronouns such as *I, me,* and *our.* If the narrator stands outside the story, he or she tells it in **third-person point of view,** using such pronouns as *he, she,* and *them.*

In reading fiction, you need to distinguish between plot and theme. The **plot** is what happens. The **theme** is the message carried by the plot, the characters, and the setting.

A. DIRECTIONS: *The excerpt from* The Giant's House *is a piece of fiction. Answer these questions about the narrator of* The Giant's House.

1. Is the narrator of *The Giant's House* inside or outside the story? _____

2. Does the narrator use first-person or third-person point of view? _____

B. DIRECTIONS: *Study the following example, which distinguishes between the plot of a story and its theme. Then, in your own words, state the plot of* The Giant's House *and the theme that grows out of the plot.*

Plot of story: Maria practices her lines for the school play every day. She wants to bring her character to life, so she experiments in front of a mirror with different gestures, facial expressions, and tones of voice. On opening night, she turns in a first-rate performance, and the audience applauds warmly.

Theme of story: Hard work leads to success.

Plot of excerpt from *The Giant's House:*

_____

_____

_____

Theme of excerpt from *The Giant's House:*

_____

_____

_____

Name _____ Date _____

"**Desiderata**" by Elizabeth McCracken
Model Selection: Nonfiction

The author of a piece of nonfiction has one or more purposes for writing. The purpose or purposes relate to the kind of nonfiction the author is producing.

- The purpose of **narrative** nonfiction is to tell about a real-life event. Examples of narrative nonfiction include autobiographies and memoirs. Some narrative nonfiction is **reflective writing,** which gives the writer's thoughts and feelings about a personal experience, an idea, or a concern. Examples of reflective writing include reflective essays and journals.
- The purpose of **expository** nonfiction is to inform or to explain. Examples of this type of nonfiction include analytical essays and research reports.
- The purpose of **persuasive** nonfiction is to make the reader act or think in a certain way. Examples include editorials and political speeches.
- The purpose of **descriptive** nonfiction is to create mental images for the reader. Examples include character sketches and scientific observations.

DIRECTIONS: *Authors often have more than one purpose in mind when they write a piece of nonfiction. Here is a list of purposes:*

| to explain | to inform | to report a real-life event |
| to persuade | to entertain | to share thoughts and experiences |

What two purposes do you think Elizabeth McCracken might have had in mind when she wrote "Desiderata"? Support your answer with reasons and examples from the selection.

_____
_____
_____
_____
_____
_____
_____
_____
_____
_____
_____
_____
_____
_____
_____

20

from The Giant's House and "Desiderata" by Elizabeth McCracken
Open-Book Test

Short Answer *Write your responses to the questions in this section on the lines provided.*

1. You are reading a book that takes place in your own home town. It is about a teenager who has traveled there from the year 2510. Are you reading a work of fiction or a work of nonfiction? Explain.

_____

_____

_____

2. You are reading a magazine article that describes a humorous event from the author's own childhood. Is the article an example of narrative nonfiction or expository nonfiction? Explain.

_____

_____

_____

3. You have just finished the last chapter of a great book. Somehow, the author managed to keep the main character alive *and* wrap up a half dozen other story lines. What type of fictional work is the book? Explain.

_____

_____

_____

4. You are reading a book written by a woman who is running for president. In the book, she tells about her own life. She also describes what she will do to improve the country if she is elected. Is the book a work of fiction or a work of nonfiction? Explain.

_____

_____

_____

5. A conflict is a problem that needs to be solved. What conflict does James, a main character of *The Giant's House,* face? Provide a detail from the story that illustrates the conflict.

_____

_____

_____

6. *The Giant's House* is set in 1955. How might the story be different if it took place in current times? Fill in the chart, giving examples or details from the story in the left column. In the right column, note how those details might be different today. Then, on the lines below, briefly tell how the story would be different if it took place today.

Details From Story	How Different Today

_____

_____

7. In *The Giant's House,* the librarian, Peggy, loves to help people solve their research problems. How do you think she feels at the end of the story, when she is unable to find the answer James wants?

_____

_____

8. Why are Elizabeth McCracken's family letters and papers important to her? Support your response with an example from "Desiderata."

_____

_____

9. In "Desiderata," the author states, "I come from a family strong on documents." Explain how this family strength has influenced McCracken's writing.

_____

_____

10. In "Desiderata," does the author feel vindictive toward any of her relatives? Base your answer on the meaning of *vindictive.*

_____

_____

_____

Name _____ Date _____

Essay

Write an extended response to the question of your choice or to the question or questions your teacher assigns you.

11. Choose either the excerpt from *The Giant's House* or "Desiderata" and write an essay in response to this question: What important idea is the author trying to get across? Begin your essay by stating one of the author's important ideas. Then provide details, examples, and quotations from the text that illustrate the idea.

12. Choose two characteristics of fiction and two characteristics of nonfiction from the lists in the unit introduction. Then, in an essay, explain how these characteristics are present in *The Giant's House* and "Desiderata." Use details from the texts to support your ideas.

13. In *The Giant's House*, Peggy, the librarian, states, "Never jump to conclusions when trying to answer a reference question. Interview the patron." In an essay, analyze how successful Peggy is when she tries to help James. Does Peggy's rule help her discover something she otherwise might not have discovered, or does it cause unforeseen problems? Support your ideas with details and examples from the story.

14. **Thinking About the Big Question: Can truth change?** Near the end of "Desiderata," the author describes finding a letter in a chest-of-drawers that she inherited. This letter changed one of her unquestioned beliefs. In an essay, identify the belief, and then explain how the letter changed it.

Oral Response

15. Go back to question 4, 7, or 9 or to the question your teacher assigns to you. Take a few minutes to expand your answer and prepare an oral response. Find additional details in either *The Giant's House* or "Desiderata" that will support your points. If necessary, make notes to guide your response.

from **The Giant's House and "Desiderata"** by Elizabeth McCracken
Selection Test A

Learning About Fiction and Nonfiction *Identify the letter of the choice that best answers the question.*

_____ 1. Which statement is always true of fiction?
A. Essays and biographies are examples of fiction.
B. Fiction tells about real people and events.
C. Examples of fiction include short stories and novels.
D. Conflict is not an element of fiction.

_____ 2. Which statement is true about nonfiction?
A. Nonfiction deals with imaginary people and made-up events.
B. Short stories are examples of nonfiction.
C. Nonfiction is intended only for entertainment.
D. Nonfiction can contain facts, opinions, and ideas.

_____ 3. Which statement correctly describes a work of fiction in which the narrator is a character?
A. The conflict remains unresolved.
B. The plot is given in chronological order.
C. The work is in first-person point of view.
D. The work is in third-person point of view.

_____ 4. Which of the following groups contains ONE kind of fiction?
A. article, novel, essay
B. essay, biography, diary
C. journal, speech, autobiography
D. article, autobiography, research report

_____ 5. Which of the following is the definition of *plot*?
A. the relationships among the characters
B. the series of made-up events
C. the time and place of the action
D. the point of view of the narrator

Critical Reading

_____ 6. Who is the narrator of the excerpt from *The Giant's House*?
A. James
B. Astoria
C. Darla
D. Peggy

___ **7.** At the beginning of the excerpt from *The Giant's House*, James wants to find information on which of the following subjects?

    A. ornithology

    B. astronomy

    C. tall people

    D. medicinal plants

___ **8.** Which of the following statements most accurately describes Peggy in *The Giant's House* as she does research for James?

    A. She has an eccentric sense of humor.

    B. She is sympathetic and sensitive.

    C. She is skeptical and pessimistic.

    D. She is unhappy in her job as librarian.

___ **9.** Toward the end of the excerpt from *The Giant's House*, we learn the real goal of James's quest. What is he looking for?

    A. an illustrated book about the circus

    B. memoirs written by basketball players

    C. medical cures for tall people

    D. instructions for studying library science

___ **10.** The theme of a work of fiction is its overall message about human life or behavior. Which of the following sentences best states the theme of the excerpt from *The Giant's House*?

    A. Being a librarian is a challenging career.

    B. People with a physical abnormality may have a hard time emotionally.

    C. A search for information on a topic sometimes turns up unexpected results.

    D. Telling the truth is better than beating around the bush.

___ **11.** At the beginning of "Desiderata," we learn about the narrator. In what field has she been trained?

    A. photography

    B. genealogy

    C. library science

    D. physics

___ **12.** In "Desiderata," who is the nanny for the writer's mother and aunt?

    A. Dolly

    B. Blanche

    C. Grandmother

    D. Martha

____ 13. What kind of nonfiction is "Desiderata"?

      A. biography

      B. speech

      C. reflective essay

      D. research report

____ 14. From the author's treatment of her subject in "Desiderata," what is the best description of her?

      A. prickly and irritable

      B. cool and objective

      C. curious and thoughtful

      D. inconsistent and fickle

____ 15. At the end of "Desiderata," what does McCracken mean by calling her fiction "love letters to love letters"?

      A. She is writing about the ideal man she would like to marry one day.

      B. She was inspired to write fiction by family photos, diaries, and love letters.

      C. She is interested only in romantic plots for her fiction.

      D. She believes that celebrating the power of love is the most important objective of fiction.

Essay

16. In most fiction, a conflict (sometimes called a struggle, an anxiety, or a difficulty) sets the plot in motion and hooks the reader, who wants to learn the outcome of the conflict. Write an essay in which you identify and discuss at least two conflicts in the excerpt from *The Giant's House*. Before you write, consider the following questions: What conflict, or anxiety, does James experience? What conflict does the narrator feel as she researches James's condition? Is either of the conflicts resolved, or settled, in the excerpt? How do you think the characters might resolve their conflicts in the future?

17. In an essay, tell what her family documents, or archive, mean to author Elizabeth McCracken. Include a statement on at least one positive feeling and one negative feeling that McCracken shares about keeping a family archive. Indicate whether or not you would be interested in starting one.

18. **Thinking About the Big Question: Can truth change?** Near the end of "Desiderata," author Elizabeth McCracken tells the reader that she believed her grandfather was a quiet and careful man. In a brief essay, tell what she finds that changes her mind about him. Then, tell how the found item changes one of her unquestioned beliefs.

from **The Giant's House and "Desiderata"** by Elizabeth McCracken
Selection Test B

Learning About Fiction and Nonfiction *Identify the letter of the choice that best completes the statement or answers the question.*

____ 1. Which statement about nonfiction is true?
  A. It always includes imaginary characters.
  B. It has only made-up details.
  C. It presents facts, ideas, and opinions.
  D. It presents only facts.

____ 2. Which statement about fiction is true?
  A. It can include only real people.
  B. It cannot contain any facts.
  C. It may contain imaginary people.
  D. It cannot contain any details.

____ 3. Which statement is true about a work of fiction in which the narrator is a character?
  A. The work is in first-person point of view.
  B. He or she knows everyone's thoughts.
  C. The work is in third-person point of view.
  D. The work is not told from a point of view.

____ 4. Which of the following is the best description of *plot* in a piece of fiction?
  A. the message or insight about life
  B. the location in which a story takes place
  C. the series of made-up events
  D. the point of view

____ 5. Which of the following is an example of fiction?
  A. a novella about the Civil War
  B. a flattering biography about a despot
  C. an article about new planets
  D. an editorial about the arts

____ 6. Which of the following is NOT an example of nonfiction?
  A. a report that describes the feeding habits of giraffes
  B. a letter describing your impressions of giraffes in a zoo
  C. an explanation of how giraffes cope with predation on their young by lions
  D. a letter from a giraffe about its experience in the wild

Critical Reading

____ 7. Which statement is true about the excerpt from *The Giant's House*?
  A. Its narrator is not a character in the story.
  B. Its narrator is Peggy, a librarian.
  C. Its narrator is James's mother.
  D. Its narrator is James.

___ 8. At the beginning of the selection from *The Giant's House,* what conflict does James face?
   A. He owes money for overdue books.
   B. He is trying out for the basketball team.
   C. He is self-conscious about his height.
   D. He does not understand an assignment.

___ 9. Which statement best explains why a good librarian is much like a prospector?
   A. Both are fulfilled but not well paid.
   B. Both share faith in finding something.
   C. Both search for ideas.
   D. Both undergo rigorous training.

___ 10. Which of the search words yields the best results for Peggy in *The Giant's House?*
   A. stature
   B. anthropometry
   C. height
   D. giant

___ 11. According to the narrator of *The Giant's House,* where did most tall people work?
   A. on professional basketball teams
   B. in the circus
   C. at libraries
   D. in clothing shops

___ 12. In *The Giant's House,* who were the husband-and-wife pair of extremely tall people?
   A. James and Anna Swann
   B. Anna Swann and Captain Bates
   C. Jack Earle and Peggy
   D. Byrne and Anna Swann

___ 13. In *The Giant's House,* what does Peggy discover James's real concern to be?
   A. medical cures for exceptional tallness
   B. information about a professional giant
   C. the history of basketball
   D. genetic information about gigantism

___ 14. The tone of a work is the attitude the author takes toward the subject matter. Which of the following best describes the tone in the selection from *The Giant's House?*
   A. skeptical
   B. optimistic
   C. satirical
   D. poignant

___ 15. In "Desiderata," the title refers to which of the following?
   A. things a librarian needs to make an archive useful
   B. romantic emotions
   C. stories passed down orally from one generation to the next
   D. illusions cherished by family members about one another

___ 16. In "Desiderata," who wrote letters to God?
   A. Grandfather McCracken
   B. Grandmother McCracken
   C. Aunt Blanche
   D. Grandmother Jacobson

_____ 17. In "Desiderata," what inference can you make from what the author's mother and aunt said about Martha?
  A. The author's mother and aunt agreed that Martha was delightful.
  B. People can remember the same person in strikingly different ways.
  C. Martha was more intelligent than the family members gave her credit for.
  D. Nobody knew the real Martha.

_____ 18. According to "Desiderata," what is the major frustration that a keeper of family archives might feel?
  A. One may learn things one does not want to know.
  B. Most of the information one learns is trivial.
  C. The writing of older family members may be difficult to understand.
  D. One's knowledge of people remains incomplete.

_____ 19. In "Desiderata," what topic was most important to Grandmother Jacobson during the last two years of her life?
  A. death   C. luck
  B. love   D. health

_____ 20. In "Desiderata," which word best describes the author's attitude toward collecting family memorabilia?
  A. casual   C. melancholic
  B. indifferent   D. enthusiastic

Essay

21. In the excerpt from *The Giant's House*, both Peggy and James confront conflicts. In an essay, identify and discuss a conflict that challenges each character. Does the author resolve the conflicts in this excerpt? How do you feel about the author's decision?

22. In "Desiderata," Elizabeth McCracken divides her essay fairly evenly between describing the satisfaction she takes in reading the documents in her family archive and describing the frustrations that such an archive involves. In an essay, identify and discuss what McCracken sees as the "plus side" of investigating an archive and also the "minus side." Do you agree or disagree with McCracken's reflections? Support your evaluation with reasons.

23. McCracken tells us she based her fictional work *The Giant's House* on the real-life story of Robert Wadlow, who grew to be almost nine feet tall. Think back on the character of James. In an essay, tell whether the character is realistic or not, and hypothesize why someone would make up a character for a novel instead of writing a nonfiction book about an interesting real person.

24. **Thinking About the Big Question: Can truth change?** Near the end of "Desiderata," the author describes finding a letter in a chest-of-drawers that she inherited. This letter changed one of her unquestioned beliefs. In an essay, identify the belief, and then explain how the letter changed it.

Vocabulary Warm-up Word Lists

Study these words from "The Washwoman." Then, complete the activities.

Word List A

bloomers [BLOOM erz] *n.* old-fashioned women's underwear
Long skirts covered the <u>bloomers</u> worn by pioneer women.

clotheslines [KLOHZ lynz] *n.* lines or ropes for air-drying laundry
You can only hang laundry outside on <u>clotheslines</u> when the weather is good.

conceive [kuhn SEEV] *v.* to form an idea of something in the mind
The uneducated man tried to <u>conceive</u> of what it would be like to read.

contributed [kuhn TRIB yoo tid] *v.* gave; donated
Many people who love sports <u>contributed</u> money for the new athletic center.

devoted [di VOH tid] *adj.* loving; loyal
The young mother was so <u>devoted</u> that she sat up all night with her ill toddler.

endure [en DOOR] *v.* to put up with; to tolerate
My mother will simply not <u>endure</u> bad manners at the table.

impression [im PRESH uhn] *n.* idea or opinion of someone or something
The stranger's noble bearing made a favorable <u>impression</u> on the elders.

uttered [UHT erd] *v.* spoke or made a sound
I had no idea she was there because she never <u>uttered</u> a sound.

Word List B

accumulated [uh KYOOM yuh lay tid] *v.* collected or gathered over time
The backyard was full of bones that the dog had <u>accumulated</u>.

brittle [BRIT uhl] *adj.* fragile; easily broken
Please handle the fine china carefully as it is very <u>brittle</u>.

collapsed [kuh LAPST] *v.* fell down; weakened suddenly
No one knew the young athlete had heart problems until he <u>collapsed</u> during a game.

gaunt [GAWNT] *adj.* very thin, pale, and sickly
The soldier was <u>gaunt</u> after months as a prisoner of war.

gnarled [NARLD] *adj.* twisted and misshapen
The farmer's <u>gnarled</u> hands were evidence of a lifetime of hard work.

institution [in stuh TOO shuhn] *n.* established practice or custom
The <u>institution</u> of marriage is an important part of our culture.

shard [SHAHRD] *n.* broken piece
Even a <u>shard</u> of pottery from an ancient culture is valuable to an archaeologist.

straggled [STRAG uhld] *v.* hung in an untidy way
The sheepdog needed to be groomed when his long hair <u>straggled</u> over his eyes.

"The Washwoman" by Isaac Bashevis Singer
Vocabulary Warm-up Exercises

Exercise A *Fill in each blank in the paragraph below with an appropriate word from Word List A. Use each word only once.*

Last year my family took a trip to Italy. One of the things that made the biggest

[1] _____ on me was seeing people's laundry hanging on

[2] _____ outside their windows, even in big cities. Maybe this sounds

silly, but I just cannot [3] _____ of having your [4] _____

(as my grandmother calls them) on display for everyone to see. I know I could not

[5] _____ it. When we needed to wash some of our travel clothes, I

[6] _____ some of my vacation money to pay for using a dryer. My mother

never [7] _____ a word at the time. However, when we got home, she

announced that since I was so interested in laundry, she now expected me to be her

[8] _____ helper with the wash!

Exercise B *Decide whether each statement below is true or false. Circle T or F. Then, explain your answer.*

1. A <u>brittle</u> candy is soft and chewy.
   T / F _____

2. A person who has <u>collapsed</u> should get medical attention immediately.
   T / F _____

3. When a family moves, they may sell things they have <u>accumulated</u> but no longer want.
   T / F _____

4. A <u>gaunt</u> appearance is a sign of good health.
   T / F _____

5. Changing people's minds about an <u>institution</u> like free public education is easy to do.
   T / F _____

6. If you find a <u>shard</u> of glass, it is wise to watch out for more because something has been broken.
   T / F _____

7. A <u>gnarled</u> tree was most likely planted recently.
   T / F _____

8. A room where the curtains <u>straggled</u> over the windows would probably be very neat.
   T / F _____

Name _____ Date _____

"The Washwoman" by Isaac Bashevis Singer
Reading Warm-up A

Read the following passage. Pay special attention to the underlined words. Then, read it again, and complete the activities. Use a separate sheet of paper for your written answers.

In the 1800s in America, women did laundry washing it by hand and hanging it out to dry on long ropes, or <u>clotheslines</u>. By the 1850s, people might have noticed something new in the laundry of some women. It was a type of long pants that were gathered at the ankles and used as an undergarment. They were worn with a knee-length tunic, or loose dress. The pants became known as <u>bloomers</u>. They were named for a woman who actually had nothing to do with creating them.

Amelia Bloomer was a <u>devoted</u> believer in women's rights. She worked tirelessly to help women recognize that greater equality was possible through social reform. One of her challenges was to overcome the idea that since women had put up with being second-class citizens for generations, they would continue to <u>endure</u> that role. Bloomer succeeded in opening the eyes of many women through her newspaper, *The Lily*.

Bloomer was the first woman in America to publish a newspaper for women. Well-known activists, such as Elizabeth Cady Stanton, <u>contributed</u> to *The Lily*. They wrote articles that helped unify women in the fight for the right to vote.

Ironically, it is thanks to Bloomer's newspaper that her name became connected to the long, baggy underwear. In her articles, Bloomer supported the idea of women wearing clothing that gave them more freedom of movement, as pants can do. In time, the pants-and-tunic outfit became known as the "Bloomer Costume."

Many people could not <u>conceive</u> of such a change. Women had always worn skirts and dresses that swept the floor. Who could picture them wearing anything else? Eventually, Bloomer and others realized that they were sending the wrong <u>impression</u>. People mistakenly thought that clothing was what they cared about, while the more important issues were really their cause. So bloomers went the way of countless other fashion trends. They were "hot" for a while and then gone, and few <u>uttered</u> a word of protest.

1. Circle the words that give clues to the meaning of <u>clotheslines</u>. Explain if you have **clotheslines** at home and, if not, why.

2. Underline the words in this passage that tell what <u>bloomers</u> were. Explain whether that was a good name for them.

3. Circle the words that tell what Amelia Bloomer was <u>devoted</u> to, and then underline the sentence that explains what she did to show her commitment.

4. Circle the words that tell what role women had to <u>endure</u>. Define **endure**.

5. Circle the words that tell how Stanton <u>contributed</u> to *The Lily*. Write about something you have **contributed** to and what you did.

6. Circle the word that gives a clue to the meaning of <u>conceive</u>. Give a synonym for **conceive**.

7. Underline the phrase that explains the <u>impression</u> Bloomer and others were sending. Explain the **impression** you would like to make on people.

8. Underline the phrase that explains what was never <u>uttered</u>. Explain what action would be the opposite of **uttered**.

"The Washwoman" by Isaac Bashevis Singer
Reading Warm-up B

Read the following passage. Pay special attention to the underlined words. Then, read it again, and complete the activities. Use a separate sheet of paper for your written answers.

When the old woman died, her son was astonished to see how few items she had <u>accumulated</u> over a lifetime. She possessed practically nothing. No collections of knick-knacks, no closets stuffed with clothes—and yet, as the owner of the only laundromat in town, she had spent her life surrounded by garments.

He thought about his mother's pride in her laundromat. She had once caught a teenager with a <u>shard</u> of metal, using its sharp point to etch his girlfriend's name in a partition. He was a <u>gaunt</u> fellow who looked as if he never got enough to eat. She recognized artistry in the boy's scratchings. Rather than threaten, she hired him to produce a mural for the laundromat.

Some owners might drop by mainly to collect coins from the machines. Not his mother; to her the act of creating clean clothes was as significant as the most sacred <u>institution</u>. You would think she was talking about marriage or motherhood when she began singing the praises of the contemporary washing machine and dryer! Old-fashioned hand washing that required wringing until your <u>gnarled</u> fingers looked as twisted as the wet coils of cloth was not for her. Not for her, either, was a sagging outdoor line where carelessly hung sheets <u>straggled</u> over the ground. She had no nostalgia for the olden days.

She came to the laundromat faithfully every day. She pitched in to help sort people's wash; she advised on when to add fabric softener. She fluffed towels from the dryer and folded shirts, pants, and pajamas into towering but tidy piles. She probably should have stopped after she slipped on some sudsy water and took a dreadful fall. Her bones had grown <u>brittle</u> with age and were easily cracked. Nonetheless, she went on sorting and fluffing and folding—struggling more each day—until one evening she <u>collapsed</u>, her body simply worn out.

In truth, the son understood why his mother had so few possessions. Everything she truly needed she had found in her laundromat—conversation, companionship, and the satisfaction of serving others.

1. What is mentioned in the first paragraph that could be <u>accumulated</u>? Write the meaning of *accumulated*.

2. Circle the words that are clues to the meaning of <u>shard</u>. Describe how you should handle a *shard*.

3. Underline the phrase that gives a clue to the meaning of <u>gaunt</u>. Tell what you would do if you had a friend who looked *gaunt*.

4. Underline two examples of an <u>institution</u> mentioned in this passage. Would a laundromat be considered an *institution*? Explain.

5. Circle the word that gives a clue to the meaning of <u>gnarled</u>. Would something *gnarled* be attractive? Explain.

6. Underline what the passage says <u>straggled</u> over the ground. Explain why the phrase *"straggled* neatly" would not make sense.

7. Because her bones were <u>brittle</u>, what happened when the old woman fell? Give an antonym for *brittle*.

8. Underline the phrase that explains why the old woman <u>collapsed</u>. Can a person who has *collapsed* recover? Explain.

"The Washwoman" by Isaac Bashevis Singer
Writing About the Big Question

Can truth change?

Big Question Vocabulary

assumption	belief	circumstance	context	convince
credible	distort	evidence	manipulate	perceive
perspective	skeptics	speculate	truth	verify

A. *Use one or more words from the list above to complete each sentence.*

1. Andrew made a(n) _____ about his neighbor that prevented him from getting to know the truth about him.

2. The washwoman had a strong _____ that kept her going.

3. The _____ of the washwoman's life forced her to work.

4. Reading about the washwoman's life gives _____ that everyone's truth does not have to be the same.

B. *Follow the directions in responding to each of the items below.*

1. Describe a time when something you thought was true changed. It might be something you did or that you observed.

   _____

   _____

2. What happened in the situation you described above that made you realize truth wasn't what you thought it was? Use at least two of the Big Question vocabulary words.

   _____

   _____

C. *Complete the sentence below. Then, write a short paragraph in which you connect this experience to the Big Question.*

In **"The Washwoman,"** a Jewish family learns to appreciate a Gentile washwoman whose son has abandoned her. Complete this sentence:

A mother's relationship with her son _____ .

_____

_____

Name _____ Date _____

"The Washwoman" by Isaac Bashevis Singer
Literary Analysis: Narrative Essay

A **narrative essay** is a short piece of nonfiction in which the author tells a story about a real person or event. In a narrative essay, the author chooses to include **significant details** that help move the story forward or that help to make his or her point about the subject. For example, if Singer were writing a narrative essay about his own childhood, he would include the significant detail that his father was a Hasidic rabbi who presided over a rabbinic court. In the same essay about his childhood, however, he would not mention the fact that Anjelica Huston starred in the 1989 movie *Enemies, a Love Story,* which is based on one of Singer's novels. That would not be a significant detail for an essay about his childhood. As you read, notice how the author's choice of significant details influences your impressions of the people and events he or she describes.

DIRECTIONS: *Follow the directions to answer each numbered item.*

1. In no more than two or three sentences, summarize the essay's narrative, or story.

   _____

   _____

2. Now, look back over the essay. Find two significant details that Singer includes about (a) the washwoman's appearance, (b) what she says, and (c) what she does. Write the details exactly as Singer expresses them, enclosing the words and phrases in quotation marks.

   (a) Her appearance _____

   _____

   _____

   (b) What she says _____

   _____

   _____

   (c) What she does _____

   _____

   _____

   ---

3. Think about why Singer wrote this essay. What main point about the washwoman do you think he makes in this essay?

   _____

   _____

   _____

"The Washwoman" by Isaac Bashevis Singer

Reading: Ask Questions to Make Predictions

A **prediction** is an informed guess about what will happen later in a narrative. Predictions are based on details in the text and on your own experience. When **making and verifying predictions,** predict what will happen, and then read on to see if the prediction is correct.

- One way to make predictions is to pause periodically while reading and **ask questions** about text details and events. You can ask yourself questions such as *Why does the author mention this detail? How might it become important later on?* Then, look for the answers to those questions as you read ahead.
- As you read, use the following chart to record your predictions. Then, see how many of your predictions were correct.

DIRECTIONS: *In the left column are some of the major events in "The Washwoman." As you read, ask yourself questions about what may be the outcome or consequence of each event. Write your questions in the center column. In the right column, record your predictions. The first one has been done for you.*

Event	Question	Prediction
1. The frail old washwoman works hard to produce beautiful, clean laundry.	Will the Singer family be satisfied with her work?	The Singers will like her work and employ her for many years.
2. She has a rich son who does not see her or give her any money.		
3. The rich son gets married but does not invite her to the wedding.		
4. One very cold winter day, the washwoman staggers away under a huge bundle of laundry.		
5. Weeks pass, and she does not return.		

"The Washwoman" by Isaac Bashevis Singer
Vocabulary Builder

Word List

accumulated   atonement   forebears   obstinacy   pious   rancor

A. DIRECTIONS: *Follow the instructions to use each vocabulary word in a sentence.*

1. Use <u>rancor</u> in a sentence about unsportsmanlike conduct.

   _____

2. Use <u>obstinacy</u> in a sentence about a two-year-old.

   _____

3. Write a sentence about something a king inherited from his <u>forebears</u>.

   _____

4. Use <u>atonement</u> in a sentence about littering a public park.

   _____

5. Use <u>pious</u> in a sentence about an old family friend.

   _____

6. Write a sentence about a collection you have <u>accumulated.</u>

   _____

B. WORD STUDY The Old English prefix *fore-* means "earlier" or "in front of." Answer each of these questions using one of these words containing the prefix *fore-*: *foreshadow, forefront, foreboding*.

1. Why might you feel a sense of *foreboding* if a black cat crossed your path one gloomy night?

   _____

2. If your teacher pointed to you as an example of someone at the *forefront* of your class, how would you feel?

   _____

3. In a novel with a happy ending, what might the arrival of a rich stranger *foreshadow*?

   _____

Name _____ Date _____

"The Washwoman" by Isaac Bashevis Singer
Enrichment: Learning From Our Elders

Isaac Bashevis Singer describes how the washwoman went about her extremely difficult job with honesty and great dedication. Singer learned valuable life lessons from the older people in his community. People who have lived long lives often have interesting stories, ideas, and advice that can benefit younger people who take the time to listen to what they have to say.

DIRECTIONS: *Think about what you have learned from the older people in your life. Answer the following questions.*

1. Who are some interesting older adults (grandparents, neighbors, or community members) in your life? _____

    _____

    _____

2. Briefly, what are some of the most interesting experiences these people have shared?

    _____

    _____

    _____

3. What is one valuable lesson you have learned from an older person, either through observation or conversation? _____

    _____

    _____

    _____

4. How do you think older people are generally treated in your community? _____

    _____

    _____

    _____

"The Washwoman" by Isaac Bashevis Singer

Open-Book Test

Short Answer *Write your responses to the questions in this section on the lines provided.*

1. How does Isaac Bashevis Singer describe the washwoman in his essay "The Washwoman"? Why is the description important to the narrative?

_____

_____

_____

_____

2. Near the beginning of "The Washwoman," the author describes the work of laundering clothes. Identify one detail from this description.

_____

_____

_____

3. When the washwoman says to the mother that her son looks like Jesus, the author's mother, who is Jewish, whispers, "May her words be scattered in the wilderness." Why might the author mention this detail in "The Washwomen"?

_____

_____

_____

4. In the middle of "The Washwoman," the author's mother says that the washwoman's son is disloyal to his own mother and an insult to all mothers.Is the son disloyal to his mother? Use examples from the essay to explain your opinion.

_____

_____

_____

5. In "The Washwoman," the washwoman lives her life and does her work without rancor. Use the meaning of the word *rancor* to explain this statement.

_____

_____

_____

_____

6. Fill in the Venn diagram to show the characteristics that are exclusive to each woman in "The Washwoman" and the characteristics that are common to both women. Then write a statement telling how the author strongly portrays one of these characteristics in the essay.

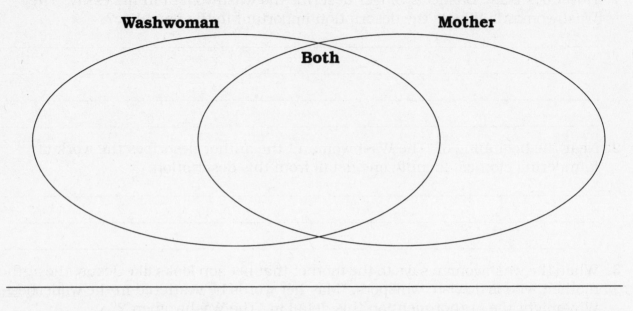

_____

_____

_____

7. In "The Washwoman," the author reflects that the washwoman's gnarled hands and whitened fingernails speak of "the stubbornness of mankind." Give two examples from the essay of the woman's "stubbornness."

_____

_____

8. Near the middle of "The Washwoman," the washwoman collects a very large load of laundry on a harsh winter day. What did you predict would happen to the woman and to the laundry? What details helped you make this prediction?

_____

_____

_____

_____

9. Near the end of "The Washwoman," the washwoman finally returns with the laundry. Did you or did you not predict her return? Describe her return from the perspective of your prediction.

_____

_____

_____

_____

10. At the end of "The Washwoman," the author muses that the washwoman's soul "passed into those spheres where all holy souls meet, regardless of the roles they played on this earth." Do you think the author's mother would agree with him? Support your response with an example from the essay.

_____

_____

_____

Essay

Write an extended response to the question of your choice or to the question or questions your teacher assigns you.

11. Review "The Washwoman," paying attention to important details. Then rewrite one incident from the washwoman's point of view. Explain how your details make your version different from Isaac Bashevis Singer's essay.

12. In an essay, tell what you believe Isaac Bashevis Singer learned from the women in "The Washwoman." Explain how this lesson might have affected him as he grew older. Use what you know about the author and his life in your essay.

13. At several key points throughout "The Washwoman," the author refers to the wash-woman as a Gentile, or a non-Jew. In an essay, identify two of these references, and explain how they help the author make his ultimate point at the end of the essay.

14. **Thinking About the Big Question: Can truth change?** In an essay, identify one truth by which the washwoman seems to live. Then consider whether this truth appears to change for her from the beginning of the essay to the end and how this truth affects her life. Support your ideas with examples from "The Washwoman."

Oral Response

15. Go back to question 1, 4, 7, or 8 or to the question your teacher assigns to you. Take a few minutes to expand your answer and prepare an oral response. Find additional details in "The Washwoman" that support your points. If necessary, make notes to guide your response.

"The Washwoman" by Isaac Bashevis Singer
Selection Test A

Critical Reading *Identify the letter of the choice that best answers the question.*

____ 1. Which phrase best describes the story Isaac Bashevis Singer tells in "The Washwoman"?
A. a true story that happened recently
B. a true story that happened long ago
C. a true story that he saw on TV
D. a fictional story that he imagined

____ 2. In Singer's essay, what does the mother mean when she calls the washwoman "a real find"?
A. She tells funny stories.   C. Her work is excellent.
B. Her son is rich.   D. She is a long-lost relative.

____ 3. Who is the narrator, the person who is telling the story?
A. the washwoman   C. a neighbor
B. the mother   D. Isaac Bashevis Singer

____ 4. Why is "The Washwoman" called a narrative essay?
A. It has a message, or theme.
B. It tells a story about a real person.
C. It gives the author's opinions.
D. It has a first-person narrator.

____ 5. Which character in "The Washwoman" does the narrator dislike?
A. the mother   C. the washwoman's son
B. the washwoman   D. the washwoman's daughter

____ 6. When you make a prediction about what will happen in a story, on what do you base your prediction?
I.   what you know about how the characters behave
II. what you know about how real people behave
III. what you know about the author's real life
IV. what has already happened in a story
A. I, II, III
B. I, III, IV
C. I, II, IV
D. II, III, IV

_____ 7. In Singer's essay, which word *best* describes how the mother treats the washwoman?

   A. rudely

   B. impatiently

   C. angrily

   D. kindly

_____ 8. What does the narrator most admire about the washwoman?

   A. her strength and sense of humor

   B. her love for her son and daughter-in-law

   C. her sense of duty and pride in her work

   D. her cheerfulness and cleverness

_____ 9. In "The Washwoman," which of the following is a significant detail that moves the story along?

   A. "She knew charms that went back to ancient times. . . ."

   B. "She also fed us rock candy against coughs. . . ."

   C. "Under the bundle tottered the old woman, her face as white as a linen sheet."

   D. "She blew on the coins and tied them in a kerchief."

_____ 10. What clues helped you to predict that the washwoman would come back with the laundry?

   A. The winter is long and very cold.

   B. The washwoman is thin and old.

   C. She is honest and dependable.

   D. Her son is rich.

_____ 11. Choose the quotation that explains what keeps the washwoman from dying when she is ill.

   A. "I do not want to be a burden on anyone!"

   B. "What good would such a long life be?"

   C. "The work becomes harder and harder . . . my strength is leaving me."

   D. "I could not rest easy in my bed because of the wash."

Vocabulary and Grammar

____ 12. Which phrase best describes what keeps the washwoman going despite her age and illness?

A. her obstinacy   C. her education

B. her rancor   D. her wealth

____ 13. If you were feeling *rancor* toward someone, what would you be feeling?

A. love   C. worry

B. hatred   D. upset

____ 14. Identify the noun in the following sentence.

This, however, did not prevent her from dedicating her life to us.

A. prevent   C. life

B. her   D. us

____ 15. What is the proper noun in the following sentence?

Fortunately, there was some money in the house and Mother counted out what she owed.

A. Fortunately   C. house

B. money   D. Mother

Essay

16. Singer provides many significant details in "The Washwoman" to describe the washwoman. Identify one character trait of the washwoman. Use details from the essay to show that the washwoman has this character trait.

17. What did you predict would happen to the washwoman when she disappeared for several months with the family's laundry? Explain the clues on which you based your prediction.

18. **Thinking About the Big Question: Can truth change?** One of the truths that the washwoman lives by is that it is better to bear a burden than to be a burden. In a brief essay, tell how her belief in this truth affects her actions. Then, tell whether this truth appears to change for her from the beginning to the end of the essay. Support your ideas with examples from the text.

"The Washwoman" by Isaac Bashevis Singer
Selection Test B

Critical Reading *Identify the letter of the choice that best completes the statement or answers the question.*

____ 1. In "The Washwoman," Isaac Bashevis Singer tells
   A. a fictional story he imagines.
   B. a true story that happened recently.
   C. a true story in a newspaper article.
   D. a true story that happened long ago.

____ 2. Which characteristic makes "The Washwoman" a narrative essay?
   A. In the essay, the author clearly states his attitude toward his subject.
   B. In the essay, the author tells a story about a real person.
   C. In the essay, the author discusses his feelings about the subject.
   D. In the essay, the author conveys a theme, or message.

____ 3. Why does the narrator's mother say that the washwoman is "a real find"?
   A. Her work is beautiful, yet she doesn't charge any more than the others.
   B. She is an unusual character who tells them entertaining stories about her youth.
   C. She found the washwoman accidentally by meeting her on the street.
   D. Her son is very rich, yet she remains humble and without rancor.

____ 4. The narrator expresses negative feelings about which character in "The Washwoman"?
   A. the washwoman
   B. the washwoman's son
   C. the mother
   D. the narrator

____ 5. When you make a prediction about what will happen in a story, on what do you base your prediction?
   I.   what you know about how the main character behaves
   II. what you know about how people in real life behave
   III. what you know about the author's real life
   IV. what has already happened in the story
   A. I, II, III
   B. I, III, IV
   C. I, II, IV
   D. II, III, IV

____ 6. What is the best interpretation of the following sentence from "The Washwoman"?
   These hands spoke of the stubbornness of mankind, of the will to work not only as one's strength permits but beyond the limits of one's power.

   A. The washwoman works as hard as she can but rests on holidays.
   B. The washwoman works just as hard as every other woman her age.
   C. The washwoman pushes herself to work beyond what she seems capable of.
   D. The washwoman learned to work very hard when she was a child.

_____ 7. What is the *main point* of the following passage, which describes what happens when the washwoman appears on a freezing day?

> Mother gave her a pot of tea to warm herself, as well as some bread. The old woman sat on a kitchen chair, trembling and shaking, and warmed her hands against the teapot.

A. The mother is kind to the washwoman.
B. The washwoman is always hungry and thirsty.
C. The mother and the washwoman are intimate friends.
D. It is important for the washwoman to have warm hands.

_____ 8. What is the *best* prediction based on the following sentence from "The Washwoman"?

> Someone had informed the son, and he had contributed money for a coffin and for the funeral.

A. The son will hurry to visit his dying mother.
B. The son contributes money, but he will not go to see his dying mother.
C. The washwoman will refuse to see her son when he arrives at her bedside.
D. The son will ask the narrator's mother to help the washwoman.

_____ 9. Choose the quotation that best explains what keeps the washwoman from dying when she is ill during the harsh winter.
A. "I do not want to be a burden on anyone!"
B. "What good would such a long life be?"
C. "The work becomes harder and harder . . . my strength is leaving me."
D. "I could not rest easy in my bed because of the wash."

_____ 10. In "The Washwoman," what clues helped you to predict that the washwoman would return with the laundry?
A. The winter is long and bitter cold.
B. The washwoman is tiny and old.
C. The washwoman is honest and reliable.
D. The washwoman's son is rich and just got married.

_____ 11. What attitude toward the washwoman does the author reveal in the following passage?

> I cannot imagine paradise without this Gentile washwoman. I cannot even conceive of a world where there is no recompense for such effort.

A. He feels responsible for the exhaustion that causes her death.
B. He feels she has wasted her life with her extraordinary efforts.
C. He feels she deserves to be given a proper funeral by her family.
D. He feels she deserves a final reward for her efforts on Earth.

_____ 12. Which of the following would be an appropriate addition to Singer's narrative essay?
A. a history of electric washing machines and dryers
B. the author's opinions about medical care for the elderly
C. a history of Warsaw, Poland, where the author grew up
D. anecdotes about the washwoman's relationship with her son when he was a boy

_____ 13. In "The Washwoman," which of these is a significant detail that moves the story?
  A. "She knew charms that went back to ancient times. . . ."
  B. "She also fed us rock candy against coughs. . . ."
  C. "Under the bundle tottered the old woman, her face as white as a linen sheet."
  D. "She blew on the coins and tied them in a kerchief."

_____ 14. What does the narrator most admire about the washwoman?
  A. the beautiful way she washes and irons the laundry
  B. her pride in her work and her sense of duty
  C. her ability to carry a heavy load of laundry a long distance
  D. her lack of anger toward her faithless son

Vocabulary and Grammar

_____ 15. An *atonement* is the act of making up for
  A. a good deed.   C. a wrongdoing.
  B. an absence.   D. an insult.

_____ 16. Which word best describes what keeps the washwoman going despite her illness?
  A. atonement   C. rancor
  B. obstinacy   D. kindness

_____ 17. If you were feeling *rancor*, how would you describe your mood?
  A. calm   C. lonesome
  B. cheerful   D. angry

_____ 18. The following sentence contains several nouns. Which one is a proper noun?

  My mother spoke a little Polish, and the old woman would talk with her about many things.

  A. mother   C. woman
  B. Polish   D. things

_____ 19. Which word in the following sentence is a proper noun?

  This did not prevent her from studying *The Duties of the Heart*, *The Book of the Covenant*, and other serious philosophic works.

  A. This   C. *The Duties of the Heart*
  B. her   D. philosophic works

Essay

20. In "The Washwoman," Isaac Bashevis Singer describes the old Gentile washwoman who does his family's laundry. What theme, or message about life or people, does he draw from the story he tells about the washwoman? How does he develop his theme?

21. Identify three characteristics of the washwoman that Singer clearly admires. For each characteristic, give one example from the essay to illustrate that characteristic.

22. **Thinking About the Big Question: Can truth change?** In an essay, identify one truth by which the washwoman seems to live. Then, consider whether this truth appears to change for her from the beginning to the end of the essay and how this truth affects her life. Support your ideas with examples from the text.

Study these words from "New Directions." Then, complete the activities.

Word List A

aroma [uh ROH muh] *n.* pleasant smell
From the <u>aroma</u> in the greenhouse, I knew that the jasmine was blooming.

assess [uh SES] *v.* to examine or judge
He is visiting both colleges to <u>assess</u> which one will be better for him.

balmy [BAHL mee] *adj.* mild
After weeks of freezing weather, a <u>balmy</u> day is a comfortable change.

blistering [BLIS ter ing] *adj.* very hot
The heat wave was <u>blistering</u> and getting hotter by the day.

pastry [PAYS tree] *n.* dough used in cooking
The hardest part of making a pie is making the <u>pastry</u> for the crust.

provisions [pruh VIZH uhnz] *n.* food and other basic supplies
There are no stores nearby, so bring all of the <u>provisions</u> you will need.

responsibility [ree spahn suh BIL uh tee] *n.* duty or job
My sister and I share the <u>responsibility</u> of watching our younger brother.

tempted [TEMPT id] *v.* attracted to or persuaded by something
They were <u>tempted</u> to go off their diet by the delicious desserts.

Word List B

dependent [di PEN duhnt] *adj.* not able to get along without
He must find a job because his three children are <u>dependent</u> on him.

disastrous [di ZAS trus] *adj.* causing suffering or loss
If both my parents lost their jobs, it would be <u>disastrous</u> for our family.

domestic [duh MES tik] *n.* a worker who does household chores
She is proud of her service as a <u>domestic</u> for families in town.

embarrassment [em BA ruhs muhnt] *n.* feeling of shame
Adding to her <u>embarrassment</u> at being late, she tripped and fell.

industry [IN duhs tree] *n.* hard work or great effort
Through <u>industry</u> and creativity, she became successful in her field.

presenting [pri ZENT ing] *v.* offering, giving, or explaining
The head coach is <u>presenting</u> awards to the top athletes at the banquet.

resolve [ri ZOLV] *n.* determination
You must combine talent with <u>resolve</u> to be a success in life.

unpromising [un PRAH mis ing] *adj.* unfavorable; not likely to go well
The season looked <u>unpromising</u> after the team's center sprained his ankle.

"New Directions" by Maya Angelou
Vocabulary Warm-up Exercises

Exercise A *Fill in each blank in the paragraph below with an appropriate word from Word List A. Use each word only once.*

Every day, a delicious [1] _____ filled Jenny's apartment building. She

was [2] _____ to knock on every door to find its source. Somewhere

was a great baker whose [3] _____ was making pies with flaky

[4] _____ crusts. When they emerged from the [5] _____

oven, their scent wafted everywhere. Jenny had no way to [6] _____

where that baker lived. Then, one day, she was making holiday cookies. The weather

was [7] _____ and the windows were open. Suddenly, there was a girl

at the door. "I smelled your cookies!" she said. "I'm baking, too, but I need some

[8] _____. May I borrow some flour and salt?" Jenny had met the "great

baker" who was soon a great friend!

Exercise B *Decide whether each statement below is true or false. Circle T or F. Then, explain your answer.*

1. If someone is <u>dependent</u> on you, he or she expects you to leave him or her alone.
   T / F _____

2. A situation that caused <u>embarrassment</u> is one you would enjoy experiencing again.
   T / F _____

3. A family that hires a <u>domestic</u> needs help around the house.
   T / F _____

4. The <u>disastrous</u> results of a tornado often include destroyed homes and cars.
   T / F _____

5. If you lack the <u>resolve</u> to solve a problem, you are likely to give up easily.
   T / F _____

6. A person who shows <u>industry</u> will get more done than a lazy person.
   T / F _____

7. An <u>unpromising</u> situation offers a good opportunity for success.
   T / F _____

8. <u>Presenting</u> a plan requires keeping it hidden.
   T / F _____

Name _____ Date _____

"New Directions" by Maya Angelou
Reading Warm-up A

Read the following passage. Pay special attention to the underlined words. Then, read it again, and complete the activities. Use a separate sheet of paper for your written answers.

"Not again," sighed Joe as he removed the sandwich from the wrapper. Today, it was peanut butter and pickle, which at least was an improvement on yesterday's baked beans on a roll. "Where does he come up with these concoctions?"

Joe and his brother Ben worked together and brought their lunch each day. Really, they had no choice. They had to supply their own <u>provisions</u> of food and anything else they needed. When you work in a forest cutting trees, lunch is pretty much your <u>responsibility</u>.

The problem was that Joe had two jobs, and it was the second job that made it necessary for Ben to prepare their work lunch. After getting home at night, cooking dinner, which he always did, and then letting himself be <u>tempted</u> by a little television—though he never gave in to watching for more than an hour—Joe went back to work.

Joe was a writer. What did he write about? Believe it or not, food! It was one of Joe's passions. He loved the smell of cooking and the way the <u>aroma</u> of a spicy dish filled the house. He loved the variety: Some foods were cooling and refreshing, and others so <u>blistering</u> hot that your tongue felt engulfed in a four-alarm fire.

Joe had never stopped to <u>assess</u> whether it made sense for him, a cookbook writer, to let Ben, a questionable cook, make lunch until he was forced to examine the situation.

It was a <u>balmy</u> day, and the lumbermen were working especially hard on the mild and pleasant morning. By lunchtime, Joe was starving. He unwrapped his sandwich and felt a stirring of dread—the filling looked suspiciously like dough. "Oh, it couldn't be!" he said aloud. Then he took a small taste. "BEN!" he screamed, as he swallowed the <u>pastry</u> he was planning to use for a pie!

That was the last time Joe let his brother make their sandwiches for lunch. As for Ben, he concluded the pastry sandwich was his best creation ever. It was the one that finally got *him* a good lunch every day.

1. Circle the phrase that is a clue to the meaning of <u>provisions</u>. What other **provisions** might lumbermen need?

2. Circle the word that names one <u>responsibility</u> of a lumberman. Write what **responsibility** means in this passage.

3. Circle words that are clues to the meaning of <u>tempted</u>. Explain what **tempted** Joe and how he responded.

4. Circle the word that means <u>aroma</u>. Describe what the **aroma** of a spicy dish might be like.

5. Circle the phrase that means the opposite of <u>blistering</u>. Write a sentence with an example of something that is **blistering**.

6. Underline the word that means <u>assess</u>. Describe something that you have had to **assess**.

7. Explain why lumbermen might work harder on a <u>balmy</u> day. Give an antonym for **balmy**.

8. Circle the word that means <u>pastry</u>, and explain why it would not make a good filling for a sandwich. Name a filling you would use with **pastry**.

Name _____ Date _____

"New Directions" by Maya Angelou
Reading Warm-up B

Read the following passage. Pay special attention to the underlined words. Then, read it again, and complete the activities. Use a separate sheet of paper for your written answers.

Sarah Breedlove, an African American woman better known as Madame C. J. Walker, founded her own business in the first decade of 1900. Within 15 years, she was a millionaire—the first black woman to attain that status.

Sarah Breedlove had humble beginnings. In fact, looking at her early life, she would appear to have an <u>unpromising</u> future. She was the daughter of former slaves in Louisiana who both died when she was a child. She was married at age 14, a mother by age 18, and widowed at age 20. Then she moved to St. Louis, Missouri, where she had brothers. There she found work as a <u>domestic</u> doing laundry for people. Sarah was not destined to be a servant for long; she had too much determination and <u>resolve</u>.

What propelled Sarah toward her road to success was what you might call a <u>disastrous</u> hair day! She developed a scalp problem and lost patches of hair. She was ashamed of her appearance and, in her <u>embarrassment</u>, she began mixing and experimenting with hair products to find a cure. In the process, she discovered the source of her future company.

In 1905, Sarah married Charles Joseph Walker. She took his name—initials and all—and began producing "Madame Walker's Wonderful Hair Grower." Soon she had a line of hair-care products for African American women and was <u>presenting</u> them door to door. She visited with women in their homes, demonstrating her products and always looking for new ways to sell them. Madame Walker was the picture of hard work and <u>industry</u>, and before long her business was thriving.

At the high point of her company's success, more than 3,000 people, many of them women, were <u>dependent</u> on her for employment, and she supported them with good jobs.

Madame C. J. Walker meticulously built her company, always maintaining a clear-cut set of standards that demanded honesty, quality, and effort. "If I have accomplished anything in life," she once said, "it is because I have been willing to work hard."

1. Underline sentences that explain why Sarah seemed to have an <u>unpromising</u> future. Tell what *unpromising* means.

2. Circle the word that gives the meaning of <u>domestic</u>. Give a synonym for *domestic*.

3. How did having <u>resolve</u> help Sarah? Explain how having *resolve* can help you.

4. Underline the sentence that describes how Sarah's day was <u>disastrous</u>. Tell what *disastrous* means.

5. Underline the sentence with clues to the meaning of <u>embarrassment</u>. Tell how *embarrassment* led to Sarah's success.

6. What was Madame Walker <u>presenting</u>? Use words from the passage to explain what she was doing when she was *presenting* door to door.

7. Circle words that are clues to the meaning of <u>industry</u>. Describe someone you know who is the picture of *industry*, and explain why.

8. Who was <u>dependent</u> on Madame Walker? What did she give? What did she get in return?

"New Directions" by Maya Angelou

Writing About the Big Question

Can truth change?

Big Question Vocabulary

assumption	belief	circumstance	context	convince
credible	distort	evidence	manipulate	perceive
perspective	skeptics	speculate	truth	verify

A. *Use one or more words from the list above to complete each sentence.*

1. If he could change one _____ of his school life, he thought it would change everything.

2. When we _____ that our lives are not going well, we should change them, just like Annie did..

3. For Annie, _____ is what she made it.

4. The _____ that truth cannot change is false.

B. *Describe a time when you or someone you know changed as a result of some change in life's circumstances. Write three or four sentences. Use at least two of the Big Question vocabulary words.*

_____

_____

_____

_____

C. *Complete the sentence below. Then, write a short paragraph in which you connect this experience to the Big Question.*

In "New Directions," Mrs. Annie Johnson finds herself on her own with two young children. Complete this sentence:

The truth about a person can change as a result of _____.

_____

_____

_____

_____

52

Name _____ Date _____

"New Directions" by Maya Angelou
Literary Analysis: Narrative Essay

A **narrative essay** is a short piece of nonfiction in which the author tells a story about a real person or event. In a narrative essay, the author chooses to include **significant details** that help move the story forward or that help to make his or her point about the subject. For example, if Maya Angelou were writing a narrative essay about her own childhood, she would include the significant detail that she and her brother Bailey spent much of their childhood living with their grandmother in Stamps, Arkansas. In such an essay about her childhood, however, she would not mention the fact that in 1993, at President Clinton's inauguration, she recited her poem "On the Pulse of Morning." That would not be a significant detail for an essay about her childhood. As you read, notice how the author's choice of significant details influences your impressions of the people and events he or she describes.

DIRECTIONS: *Follow the directions to answer each numbered item.*

1. In no more than two or three sentences, summarize the story that the author tells in the essay.

   _____

   _____

   _____

2. Now, look back over the essay. Find two significant details that Angelou includes about (a) Annie Johnson's appearance, (b) what she says, and (c) what she does. Write the details exactly as Angelou expresses them, enclosing the words and phrases in quotation marks.

   (a) Annie Johnson's appearance _____

   _____

   _____

   (b) What she says _____

   _____

   _____

   (c) What she does _____

   _____

   _____

   ---

3. Think about why Maya Angelou wrote this essay. What points or main ideas do you think she makes in this essay? _____

   _____

   _____

   _____

Name _____ Date _____

"New Directions" by Maya Angelou
Reading: Ask Questions to Make Predictions

A **prediction** is an informed guess about what will happen later in a narrative. Predictions are based on details in the text and on your own experience. When **making and verifying predictions,** predict what will happen, and then read on to see if the prediction is correct.

- One way to make predictions is to pause periodically while reading and **ask questions** about text details and events. You can ask yourself questions such as *Why does the author mention this detail? How might it become important later on?* Then, look for the answers to those questions as you read ahead.
- As you read, use the following chart to record your questions and the predictions you make from them. Then, see if your predictions were correct.

DIRECTIONS: *In the left column are some of the major events in "New Directions." As you read, consider what you think may be the outcome or consequence of each event. Write your questions in the center column. In the right column, record your predictions.*

Event	Question	Prediction
1. Annie Johnson's marriage ends, leaving her with two young sons.		
2. She needs to earn money to support herself and her family.		
3. She starts to sell her home-made meat pies to workers at the lumber mill and cotton gin.		
4. She is so successful selling pies that she builds a stall between the cotton gin and lumber mill.		

Name _____ Date _____

"New Directions" by Maya Angelou
Vocabulary Builder

Word List

amicably   balmy   conceded   meticulously   ominous   unpalatable

A. DIRECTIONS: *For each of the following items, think about the meaning of the italicized word, and then answer the question.*

1. What happens when two people settle an argument *amicably*?

   _____

2. If you were to clean a kitchen *meticulously*, what would it look like when you finish?

   _____

3. What kind of weather would you describe as *ominous*?

   _____

4. What task do you find most *unpalatable*?

   _____

5. Why might a politician have *conceded* the election?

   _____

6. What would the day be like if it were *balmy*?

   _____

B. WORD STUDY The Latin prefix *con-* means "with" or "together." Answer each of the following questions. Use one of these words containing the prefix *con-* in your new sentence: *converge, conceive, concur.*

1. Why would someone *concur* with an opinion when they don't really agree with it?

   _____

2. Why might three groups *converge* on the state capitol?

   _____

3. What method can you *conceive* of that will help you improve your writing skills?

   _____

Name _____ Date _____

"**New Directions**" by Maya Angelou
Enrichment: Women and Work

Women's Work in the Late 1800s and Early 1900s

In "New Directions," Annie Johnson examines job possibilities for herself and realizes that her choices are limited. In the late 1800s and early 1900s, job opportunities for all women—and especially African American women—were quite limited. Many women married simply because they had no way to support themselves. Once they were married, they often found themselves controlled by strict standards of behavior that their husbands and their communities expected of them.

The lives of women had been severely limited for centuries, but a few American women began to shake the old stereotypes of a woman's role. Susan B. Anthony (1820–1906) and Elizabeth Cady Stanton (1815–1902) pioneered the fight to give women the right to vote, receive equal pay, and take part in political movements. Nellie Bly (1867–1922) became one of the country's first female newspaper reporters. She went undercover to write articles that exposed various social problems, and she traveled around the world. Writers such as Kate Chopin (1851–1904) and Mary Wilkins Freeman (1852–1930) caused a scandal when they wrote novels and stories about women characters who challenged traditional roles. Each of these women, like Annie Johnson, worked to cut new paths for themselves and for women everywhere.

A. DIRECTIONS: *Imagine that Annie Johnson or one of the other women mentioned above could walk down the streets of your community today. How do you think she would feel about the changes she sees in the lives of women today? Which aspects of today's world might seem like progress? Where might she find need for improvement? Write complete sentences.*

1. **Progress:** _____

   _____

   _____

2. **Needs improvement:** _____

   _____

   _____

   _____

B. DIRECTIONS: *On a separate piece of paper, write a letter to Annie Johnson or one of the other women mentioned above. Explain how you think the work done by the woman whom you have chosen has been beneficial to women as a group and to society as a whole. If necessary, use the Internet, an encyclopedia, or another library source to find out more details about the work of the woman whom you have chosen.*

"The Washwoman" by Isaac Bashevis Singer
"New Directions" by Maya Angelou
Integrated Language Skills: Grammar

Common and Proper Nouns

A **noun** is a word that names a person, place, or thing. Nouns name things that can be seen and touched as well as those that cannot be seen and touched. Notice in the following chart that among the things nouns can name are ideas, actions, conditions, and qualities.

People:	Aunt Cele, Esteban, musicians, doctor
Places:	Sacramento, Lincoln Park Zoo, mountain, desert, park, lake
See and touch:	grass, dish, table, truck
Ideas and actions:	freedom, confusion, election, censorship
Conditions and qualities:	optimism, courage, shyness, bewilderment

A **common noun** names any one of a class of people, places, or things—for example, *day*, *river*, or *woman*. A **proper noun** names a specific person, place, or thing and always begins with a capital letter—for example, *Tuesday*, *Cuyahoga River*, or *Harriet Tubman*.

In the following example, the common nouns are underlined and the proper nouns are in boldface.

Example from "New Directions"

He did not tell her that he knew a <u>minister</u> in **Enid** with whom he could study and who had a friendly, unmarried <u>daughter</u>. They parted amicably, **Annie** keeping the one-room <u>house</u> and **William** taking most of the <u>cash</u> to carry him to **Oklahoma**.

A. DIRECTIONS: *In each numbered item, underline the common nouns and draw a circle around the proper nouns.*

1. The only Gentile in the building was the janitor. Fridays he would come for a tip, his "Friday money."

2. She lived on Krochmalna Street too, but at the other end, near the Wola section.

3. My mother spoke a little Polish, and the old woman would talk with her about many things.

4. The son had not invited the old mother to his wedding, but she went to the church and waited at the steps to see her son lead the "young lady" to the altar.

B. DIRECTIONS: *Write a three-sentence paragraph in which you describe the town where you live. Use at least three common nouns and three proper nouns in your paragraph. Remember that proper nouns are always capitalized.*

_____

_____

_____

_____

Name _____ Date _____

Integrated Language Skills: Support for Writing an Anecdote

Use the following cluster diagram to gather information for your **anecdote**—your very brief story. In the middle circle, write the name of a person whom you admire. In the surrounding circles, write several characteristics that you like and respect about that person. (You do not have to fill in all of the circles.) Then, make some notes about a specific event that shows what the person is like.

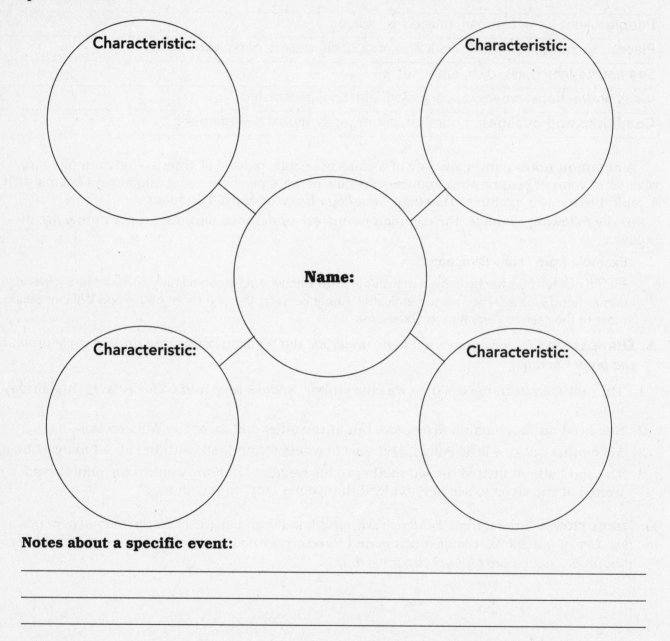

Notes about a specific event:

_____

_____

_____

_____

Now, write your anecdote. Describe in detail a specific event or action that illustrates what you admire about the person whom you have chosen. Be sure to tell what you learned from the person's actions.

Name _____ Date _____

"The Washwoman" by Isaac Bashevis Singer
"New Directions" by Maya Angelou

Integrated Language Skills: Support for Extend Your Learning

Listening and Speaking: "The Washwoman"

In the first column of the following chart, jot down some of the questions you plan to ask during your interview. Use the second column to take notes on your interviewee's responses.

Questions I plan to ask	How the interviewee responded
1. _____	1. _____
2. _____	2. _____
3. _____	3. _____
4. _____	4. _____
5. _____	5. _____

Listening and Speaking: "New Directions"

In the first column of the following chart, jot down some of the questions you would ask Annie Johnson during your interview. In the second column, write what you think she might reply.

Questions I would ask Annie Johnson	How Annie Johnson might reply
1. _____	1. _____
2. _____	2. _____
3. _____	3. _____
4. _____	4. _____
5. _____	5. _____

Name _____ Date _____

"New Directions" by Maya Angelou
Open-Book Test

Short Answer *Write your responses to the questions in this section on the lines provided.*

1. After reading the second paragraph of "New Directions," how would you characterize Annie's husband? Give one or two words you think best describe him, and cite a detail from the essay to support your thinking.

   _____

   _____

   _____

2. In "New Directions," Annie Johnson and her husband, William, have parted "amicably." What does this mean? What does it tell you about Annie?

   _____

   _____

   _____

3. What kind of a cook is Annie Johnson in "New Directions"? Answer this question with a detail from the essay. Then explain why you think the author included this detail.

   _____

   _____

   _____

4. In "New Directions," how does Annie go about making her plans? Why does she do it this way? Give an example from the essay to support your response.

   _____

   _____

   _____

5. When Annie first starts selling pies in "New Directions," business is slow. What prediction about Annie's success or failure did you make at this point in the essay? On what details did you base this prediction?

   _____

   _____

   _____

6. Explain whether the workers in "New Directions" found Annie's pies unpalatable. Tell why, and base your response on the definition of *unpalatable.*

   _____

   _____

Name _____ Date _____

7. Complete this Venn diagram with words or phrases that describe only Annie Johnson in "New Directions"; words or phrases that describe only her husband, William; and words or phrases that describe them both.

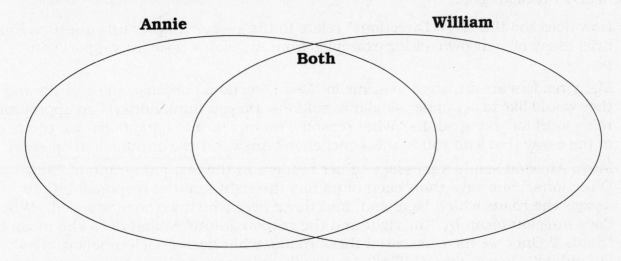

8. On what kinds of days and in what kinds of weather does Annie sell her pies in "New Directions"? Answer this question with a detail from the essay. What impression of Annie does this detail give you?

_____

_____

_____

9. When you learn in "New Directions" that Annie's stall eventually became a store, was your earlier prediction verified? If so, was her success exactly as you expected it to be? If not, how do you see Annie now?

_____

_____

_____

10. One of the main messages of "New Directions" is this: If you are unhappy with your life, you must change it by taking a risk and trying something new. Cite a passage from the essay that expresses this idea.

_____

_____

_____

Essay

Write an extended response to the question of your choice or to the question or questions your teacher assigns you.

11. How does the title "New Directions" relate to the essay? Answer this question in a brief essay of your own, citing examples from Angelou's essay to support your points.

12. Many readers are attracted to Annie in "New Directions" because she acts the way they would like to act under similar conditions. Do you think Annie is an appropriate role model for young adults? What reasons, examples, and quotations can you find in the essay that lead you to this conclusion? Answer these questions in an essay.

13. Maya Angelou sends a message to her readers in the last paragraph of "New Directions." She says that "each of us has the right and the responsibility to assess the roads which lie ahead, and those over which we have traveled." What does Angelou mean by "the right and the responsibility"? What does she mean by "roads"? Once we have assessed these roads, what does Angelou believe we should do? Do you agree? Why? Answer these questions in an essay.

14. **Thinking About the Big Question: Can truth change?** In an essay, identify one truth by which Annie Johnson in "New Directions" seems to live. Then consider whether this truth changes for Annie between the beginning of the essay and the end of the essay. If so, how? If not, can you imagine any life situation in which this truth might change for Annie? Support your ideas with examples from the text.

Oral Response

15. Go back to question 1, 3, or 8 or to the question your teacher assigns to you. Take a few minutes to expand your answer and prepare an oral response. Find additional details in "New Directions" that will support your points. If necessary, make notes to guide your response.

Name _____ Date _____

"New Directions" by Maya Angelou
Selection Test A

Critical Reading *Identify the letter of the choice that best answers the question.*

_____ 1. "New Directions" is a narrative essay. What does that tell you about Annie
Johnson?
    A. She is a real person.
    B. She is a made-up character.
    C. She is related to Maya Angelou.
    D. She is a character in a movie.

_____ 2. What quality does Maya Angelou most admire about Annie Johnson?
    A. her cheerfulness
    B. her appearance
    C. her firm purpose
    D. her curiosity

_____ 3. In "New Directions," which word describes Annie Johnson's husband?
    A. loyal
    B. hard-working
    C. loving
    D. dishonest

_____ 4. Why does Annie Johnson carry two pails of stones at night?
    A. She is testing her strength.
    B. She is selling them to the workers.
    C. She is selling them to a factory.
    D. She is in a weight-lifting contest.

_____ 5. In "New Directions," which of the following details is significant?
    A. Annie is very tall.
    B. Annie's marriage ends.
    C. Annie's husband is named William.
    D. Annie lives in Arkansas.

_____ 6. What does Annie Johnson do when she "cuts herself a brand-new path"?
    A. She cuts her lawn.
    B. She takes a job as a domestic.
    C. She finds a way to support her family.
    D. She gets a job fixing roads.

Unit 1 Resources: Fiction and Nonfiction
© Pearson Education, Inc. All rights reserved.
63

_____ 7. In "New Directions," what can you predict from the following sentence?

When she felt certain that the workers had become dependent on her, she built a stall between the two hives of industry. . . .

A. The stall will be a failure.

B. The stall will be a success.

C. Annie Johnson will move away.

D. Annie Johnson will remarry.

_____ 8. When Maya Angelou calls the lumber mill and cotton gin "two hives of industry," what is she comparing them to?

A. ant nests

B. bird nests

C. bee hives

D. crowded cities

_____ 9. In a narrative essay, such as "New Directions," what is the author's main purpose?

A. to persuade

B. to describe

C. to tell a story

D. to explain

_____ 10. Annie says she can "mix groceries well enough to scare hungry away." What does she mean?

A. She is a very bad cook.

B. She cooks fairly well.

C. She cooks fancy gourmet food.

D. She has never cooked in her life.

_____ 11. What does Maya Angelou mean by the word *roads* in the following sentence?

Each of us has the right and the responsibility to assess the roads which lie ahead, and those over which we have traveled. . . .

A. maps

B. superhighways

C. misfortunes

D. life directions

Vocabulary and Grammar

____ 12. In which sentence is the word *ominous* used correctly?

A. Those dark clouds are *ominous*.

B. She has an *ominous* head.

C. That pumpkin is *ominous*.

D. An *ominous* writer knows everything.

____ 13. Which word describes how Annie Johnson planned her business?

A. amicably

B. carelessly

C. ominously

D. meticulously

____ 14. Which word in the following excerpt is a proper noun?

Annie, over six feet tall, big-boned, decided that she would not go to work as a domestic and leave her "precious babes" to anyone else's care.

A. Annie

B. feet

C. domestic

D. babes

____ 15. Identify the common noun in the following sentence.

If the new choice is also unpalatable . . . we must be ready to change that as well.

A. new

B. choice

C. unpalatable

D. ready

Essay

16. In a brief essay, tell why you think Maya Angelou titled her essay "New Directions." Explain how the title relates to Annie Johnson's life story.

17. What message, or theme, does Maya Angelou draw from the story of Annie Johnson's life? In a brief essay, state the theme of "New Directions." Give two examples of how Annie's life story illustrates that theme.

18. **Thinking About the Big Question: Can truth change**? In "New Directions," Annie Johnson lives by a truth or a belief. She seems to believe that if a person isn't satisfied with life, they should "cut a new path," or move in a different direction. In an essay, tell whether this truth changes or does not change for Annie between the beginning and the end of Maya Angelou's essay. Support your ideas with examples from the text.

"New Directions" by Maya Angelou
Selection Test B

Critical Reading *Identify the letter of the choice that best completes the statement or answers the question.*

_____ 1. Because "New Directions" is a narrative essay, we know that Annie Johnson is a
   A. fictional character.
   B. real person.
   C. relative of Maya Angelou.
   D. character in a movie.

_____ 2. In "New Directions," which word best describes Annie Johnson's husband?
   A. deceptive
   B. annoying
   C. indifferent
   D. helpless

_____ 3. In "New Directions," why does Annie carry two five-gallon pails filled with stones?
   A. She is selling the stones to the cotton gin.
   B. She is gathering stones from a nearby quarry to repair her house.
   C. She is experimenting to see how heavy a load she can carry.
   D. She is training for a weight-lifting contest.

_____ 4. What does Annie Johnson do when she decides to "cut herself a brand-new path"?
   A. She cuts her lawn for the first time.
   B. She brings her children to a new school.
   C. She finds a way to support her family.
   D. She goes to work in a new lumber mill.

_____ 5. In "New Directions," which of the following is a significant detail?
   A. Annie is over six feet tall.
   B. Annie is determined not to leave her sons.
   C. Annie's husband is named William.
   D. Annie likes to travel.

_____ 6. What can you predict about Annie's cooking ability from the following sentence?
   She told herself that she wasn't a fancy cook but that she could "mix groceries well enough to scare hungry away and from starving a man."
   A. She is a terrible cook.
   B. She is an adequate cook.
   C. She is a gourmet chef.
   D. She has never cooked in her life.

_____ 7. When Maya Angelou says that Annie Johnson "balanced her appearances between the two hours of activity," she means that Annie
   A. sold her meat pies hot and freshly cooked to the two locations on succeeding days.
   B. appeared only at the cotton gin one day and only at the lumber mill the next day.
   C. sold her meat pies every morning at the cotton gin and every afternoon at the lumber mill.
   D. sold an equal number of meat pies at the two locations.

Name _____ Date _____

_____ 8. What can you predict from the following sentence in "New Directions"?

When she felt certain that the workers had become dependent on her, she built a stall between the two hives of industry and let the men run to her for their lunchtime provisions.

A. The stall will fail because it is too far from the lumber mill and the cotton gin.
B. The workers will be willing to travel to buy Annie Johnson's meat pies.
C. Annie Johnson will need to hire some helpers.
D. Annie Johnson will change her recipe for meat pies.

_____ 9. To what does Maya Angelou compare the lumber mill and the cotton gin?

She built a stall between the two hives of industry and let the men run to her for their lunchtime provisions.

A. ant nests
B. bird nests
C. bee hives
D. crowded cities

_____ 10. Which statement helps you predict that Annie Johnson will succeed?
A. "She made her plans meticulously and in secret."
B. "That same night she worked into the early hours boiling chicken and frying ham."
C. "She balanced her appearances between the two hours of activity."
D. "In years that stall became a store where customers could buy cheese, meal, syrup. . . ."

_____ 11. Which of the following best states the *main idea* of Maya Angelou's sentence?

If the future road looms ominous or unpromising, and the roads back uninviting, then we need to gather our resolve and . . . step off that road into another direction.

A. It is better to be safe and comfortable than to take unnecessary risks.
B. If you travel a lot, always carry a map in your pocket.
C. If you want to start a new business, you must figure out what people need.
D. If you are unhappy with your life, you must take a risk and try something new.

_____ 12. In a narrative essay such as "New Directions," the writer
A. persuades the reader to take action.
B. describes a personal experience.
C. tells a story about a real person or a real event.
D. discusses one or more current issues.

_____ 13. From Maya Angelou's advice at the end of "New Directions," you can predict that she
A. has changed directions in her own life.
B. has made no changes in her own life.
C. is afraid of taking risks.
D. is embarrassed when she makes changes.

_____ 14. In talking about Annie Johnson's life, Maya Angelou uses the words *roads* and *path*
A. figuratively.
B. literally.
C. optimistically.
D. pessimistically.

_____ 15. What quality does Maya Angelou most admire about Annie Johnson?
A. her appearance
B. her determination
C. her creativity
D. her curiosity

Unit 1 Resources: Fiction and Nonfiction

Vocabulary and Grammar

____ 16. In which sentence is *ominous* used correctly?
A. The tone of her voice was *ominous*.
B. She had *ominous* ideas about her future.
C. That movie is far too *ominous* for me.
D. An *ominous* writer knows everything.

____ 17. Which word best describes how Annie Johnson made her plans?
A. amicably
B. impetuously
C. ominously
D. meticulously

____ 18. How would Annie Johnson's life have been different if her meat pies were *unpalatable*?
A. She probably would have been able to open a bigger store.
B. She probably would have gotten a job as a domestic.
C. She probably would have gone to school and become a teacher.
D. She probably would have gotten a job in the cotton gin.

____ 19. Identify the proper noun in the following sentence.

When she told her husband, Mr. William Johnson, of her dissatisfaction with their marriage, he conceded that he too found it to be less than he expected, and had been secretly hoping to leave and study religion.

A. husband
B. Mr. William Johnson
C. dissatisfaction
D. marriage

____ 20. How many nouns are in the following sentence?

That same night she worked into the early hours boiling chicken and frying ham.

A. three
B. four
C. five
D. six

Essay

21. In an essay, explain the title of Maya Angelou's narrative essay "New Directions." In what way does this title relate to the main character, Annie Johnson, and what she accomplished in her life?

22. In a narrative essay, the writer tells a story about a real person or a real event and then reflects on its meaning. What message, or theme, does Maya Angelou draw from the story she tells? In a brief essay, state the theme of "New Directions" and give examples from Annie's life story to support that theme.

23. **Thinking About the Big Question: Can truth change?** In an essay, identify one truth by which Annie Johnson seems to live. Then, consider whether this truth changes for Annie between the beginning and the end of the essay. If so, how? If not, can you imagine any life situation in which this truth might change for Annie? Support your ideas with examples from the text.

"Sonata for Harp and Bicycle" by Joan Aiken
Vocabulary Warm-up Word Lists

Study these words from "Sonata for Harp and Bicycle." Then, complete the activities.

Word List A

concealed [kuhn SEELD] *v.* hid
　　The children <u>concealed</u> themselves in their secret hiding place.

corridors [KAHR i derz] *n.* passageways; halls
　　The new student wandered the <u>corridors</u> in search of his classroom.

crumbling [KRUHM bling] *v.* falling to pieces; breaking up
　　The yellowing pages of the old book were <u>crumbling</u> in her hands.

director [di REK ter] *n.* supervisor; head of a project or business
　　As <u>director</u> of the corporation, Ms. Gonzalez has a great deal of power.

doomed [DOOMD] *adj.* condemned; sure to meet a terrible fate
　　The poorly planned project was <u>doomed</u> from the start.

employees [em PLOY eez] *n.* hired workers
　　The <u>employees</u> joined together to ask their boss for better wages.

mocked [MAHKT] *v.* teased; made fun of
　　Jennie grew angry when the boys <u>mocked</u> her high-pitched voice.

tragic [TRAJ ik] *adj.* very sad; horrible
　　The audience wept when the play reached its <u>tragic</u> conclusion.

Word List B

admirable [AD muh ruh buhl] *adj.* deserving of praise
　　Patience and generosity are just two of his many <u>admirable</u> qualities.

agitated [AJ i tay tid] *adj.* disturbed; upset
　　When she failed the test, Alice became <u>agitated</u> and started to cry.

distinguished [dis TIN gwisht] *adj.* dignified; famous
　　We were impressed by the <u>distinguished</u> gentleman's elegant manners.

intention [in TEN shun] *n.* plan; purpose
　　It is my <u>intention</u> to leave the party as soon as possible.

premises [PREM i siz] *n.* building and surrounding property
　　If you do not belong here, please leave the <u>premises</u> immediately.

reluctant [ree LUHK tuhnt] *adj.* hesitant; unwilling to act
　　She was <u>reluctant</u> to confess that she had not finished her homework.

vainly [VAYN lee] *adv.* unsuccessfully
　　They tried <u>vainly</u> to complete the assignment before finally giving up.

witty [WIT ee] *adj.* cleverly amusing
　　Everyone laughed at Sam's <u>witty</u> observation.

Name _____ Date _____

"Sonata for Harp and Bicycle" by Joan Aiken
Vocabulary Warm-up Exercises

Exercise A *Fill in each blank in the paragraph below with an appropriate word from Word List A. Use each word only once.*

Firefighters saved many lives in the [1] _____ fire last week. The

[2] _____ of the company ordered all of his [3] _____ to

leave the office building just before the [4] _____ ceiling began to col-

lapse. Firefighters ran up and down the winding [5] _____, alerting

workers to alternate exits. Fallen rubble [6] _____ the main exit, so

workers could not see it. Fortunately, firefighters' alerts reached workers who were

trapped inside their offices. No longer were they [7] _____ to die in the

fire. Those who had [8] _____ the idea of weekly fire drills were no longer

laughing as they fled from the burning building.

Exercise B *Decide whether each statement below is true or false. Circle T or F. Then, explain your answer.*

1. Most people are annoyed by an *admirable* person.
   T / F _____

2. Students are likely to be *agitated* if they get too much homework.
   T / F _____

3. A *distinguished* actor would probably perform poorly on stage.
   T / F _____

4. If your *intention* is to do well in school, you will probably not spend much time
   studying.
   T / F _____

5. If the value of the *premises* goes up, the price of the building comes down.
   T / F _____

6. People who are *reluctant* to do a job usually show great enthusiasm.
   T / F _____

7. If climbers struggled *vainly* to reach the mountaintop, they never got there.
   T / F _____

8. No one thinks that a *witty* remark is amusing.
   T / F _____

Name _____   Date _____

"**Sonata for Harp and Bicycle**" by Joan Aiken
Reading Warm-up A

Read the following passage. Pay special attention to the underlined words. Then, read it again, and complete the activities. Use a separate sheet of paper for your written answers.

Ed Dawson had been sweeping the <u>corridors</u> of Northshore High School for nearly forty years. Being a janitor was hard work, but Ed did not mind. He knew some of the students <u>mocked</u> the janitorial staff behind their backs, but he did not worry about it. That is just the way some kids are, he told himself.

Today, though, Ed was angry. Although he <u>concealed</u> his anger well, the old janitor was raging inside. It was the new principal, Mr. Rush, who had angered him. Mr. Rush often dropped hints that Ed should retire and take it easy, but Ed just smiled and walked away. He may have been the oldest of the school's <u>employees</u>, but he knew he still had a few good years left.

However, today there had been a letter waiting for him in the office, and Ed was sure he was <u>doomed</u>. He had no doubt that the unopened envelope he had stuffed into his shirt pocket contained a letter of dismissal. *Your services are no longer required,* he knew it would say.

Well, Ed was not going anywhere until he gave Mr. Rush a piece of his mind. Would it really be so <u>tragic</u> if he were allowed to hold onto his job? And who was going to keep this <u>crumbling</u> old building from falling apart when Ed was gone? Sure, the other janitors could keep the boiler running, but Ed knew a few secrets about Northshore High that those youngsters would not figure out for years.

Now, as Ed sat fuming in the principal's office waiting for Mr. Rush to get off the phone, he figured he might as well read the letter before confronting the boss. He yanked the envelope out of his pocket and ripped it open.

Congratulations, the letter read. *You have been promoted to <u>Director</u> of Janitorial Services.*

Promoted! He quickly finished the letter.

"Well," said Mr. Rush, smiling as he hung up the phone. "I see you got my letter."

"Yes, sir," said Ed, looking Mr. Rush square in the eye. "Mighty skimpy raise, though, don't you think?"

1. Circle the words that tell where the <u>corridors</u> were. What does Ed have to do with the *corridors*?

2. Circle the word that tells who <u>mocked</u> the janitorial staff. How do you think they might have *mocked* them? Explain why they might do this.

3. Underline the words that mean the same as "he <u>concealed</u> his anger." Then, write what *concealed* means.

4. Circle the names of two of the school's <u>employees</u>. Who else, besides the principal and the janitor, might be *employees* at a school?

5. Underline the sentence that tells why Ed felt <u>doomed</u>. Why might someone your age feel *doomed*?

6. Would it really be <u>tragic</u> if Ed held onto his job?

7. Underline the words that describe how the building is <u>crumbling</u>. Then, write what *crumbling* means.

8. Circle the words that tell what Ed will become the <u>director</u> of. How does he feel about becoming a *director*, and why?

"Sonata for Harp and Bicycle" by Joan Aiken
Reading Warm-up B

Read the following passage. Pay special attention to the underlined words. Then, read it again, and complete the activities. Use a separate sheet of paper for your written answers.

Alexander Graham Bell (1847–1922) was a underlined{distinguished} scientist and educator who is best known today for inventing the telephone. As a young man growing up in Scotland, Bell showed a great talent for music. His underlined{intention}, however, was to follow in his father's footsteps and become a teacher of the deaf. It was an underlined{admirable} goal, and Bell began working with his father while still in his teens. In 1870, the family moved to Canada. The following year, Bell was offered a job in Boston teaching deaf children to speak. Although he was underlined{reluctant} to leave his loving family behind, Bell accepted the job. Before long, he became a professor at Boston University and opened his own school for the deaf. Parents soon flocked to Bell's underlined{premises} in the hope that he could teach their deaf children to communicate more effectively.

With the help of his partner, Thomas Watson, Bell began to work on an electrical device that would transmit sound over telegraph wires. The two men struggled underlined{vainly} for years in their efforts to get the device to work. Then, one day in 1876, Bell and Watson were working in separate rooms. Bell spilled some acid on himself. underlined{Agitated} by the accident, he said, "Mr. Watson, come here. I want you!" To the astonishment of both men, Watson heard Bell's voice through the device on his workbench.

Bell's telephone had become a reality!

Bell and Watson were soon giving demonstrations of the amazing new invention. It was not long before the first telephone company was established. Bell and his new wife then set sail for England to introduce the telephone to the people of Europe. When the French government awarded him a prize for his important work, Bell used the money to set up a laboratory devoted to helping the deaf. He continued to make many important contributions to science throughout his life.

In Bell's later years, some people who worked with him made the underlined{witty} observation that the great inventor actually disliked the telephone because callers constantly interrupted his experiments!

1. Circle the careers in which Alexander Graham Bell was underlined{distinguished}. Then, explain what he is best known for.

2. As a young man, what was Bell's underlined{intention}? Write what *intention* means.

3. Why was Bell's goal underlined{admirable}?

4. Explain why Bell was underlined{reluctant} to take a job in Boston. Then, tell what *reluctant* means.

5. Underline the words that identify Bell's underlined{premises}. Why did parents flock there?

6. Circle the verb that tells what Bell and Watson did underlined{vainly}. When did their luck change?

7. Why was Bell underlined{agitated}? Write about something that makes you *agitated*.

8. Do you think the observation at the end of the article is underlined{witty}? Explain.

Name _____ Date _____

"Sonata for Harp and Bicycle" by Joan Aiken
Writing About the Big Question

THE BIG ?

Can truth change?

Big Question Vocabulary

assumption	belief	circumstance	context	convince
credible	distort	evidence	manipulate	perceive
perspective	skeptics	speculate	truth	verify

A. *Use one or more words from the list above to complete each sentence.*

1. Disbelief at losing the competition served to _____ Mona's perception of the truth.

2. Hearing strange noises in the empty building might _____ us that it is true that ghosts exists.

3. If we allow ourselves to _____ on whether there are ghosts, we might have to consider the possibility of different truths.

4. Seeing a ghost in person may force even _____ to see new truths.

B. *Follow the directions in responding to each of the items below.*

1. Describe a situation when an unexpected event changed what you thought about someone or some thing.

   _____

   _____

2. How did the experience you described above change what you thought to be true? Write two sentences. Use at least two of the Big Question vocabulary words.

   _____

   _____

C. *Complete the sentence below. Then, write a short paragraph in which you connect this experience to the Big Question.*

   In "Sonata for Harp and Bicycle," miscommunication leads to tragedy and a curse on a building. Complete this sentence:

   You can change your own fate by _____ .

   _____

   _____

   _____

"Sonata for Harp and Bicycle" by Joan Aiken
Literary Analysis: Plot, Foreshadowing, and Suspense

Plot is the sequence of events in a narrative. It is structured around a **conflict,** or problem, and it can be divided into the following parts:

- **Rising action**—the central conflict is introduced
- **Climax**—the high point of intensity in the conflict
- **Falling action**—the conflict's intensity lessens
- **Resolution**—the conflict concludes and loose ends are tied up

Writers use a variety of techniques to keep readers interested in the plot. One of these, **foreshadowing,** is the use of clues to hint at events that will happen later in a story. Authors use this technique to create **suspense,** a feeling of tension that keeps readers wondering what will happen next.

Read the following passage from "Sonata for Harp and Bicycle," in which Jason Ashgrove has a conversation with his secretary, Miss Golden. They are working on advertising copy for a cereal called Oat Crisps:

> "What do you want for your birthday, Miss Golden? Sherry? Fudge? Bubble bath?"
>
> "I want to go away with a clear conscience about Oat Crisps," Miss Golden retorted. It was not true; what she chiefly wanted was Mr. Jason Ashgrove, but he had not realized this yet.

What possibility does the passage foreshadow? Do you think the story will make clear whether or not Miss Golden and Mr. Ashgrove have a romance?

A. DIRECTIONS: *Read the following passage, and identify details the author uses to create suspense. Underline the words in the passage that make you curious about the outcome.*

> Jason was frustrated. "You'll be sorry," he said. "I shall do something desperate."
>
> "Oh, no, you mustn't!" Her eyes were large with fright. She ran from the room and was back within a couple of moments, still drying her hands.
>
> "If I took you out for a coffee, couldn't you give me just a tiny hint?"
>
> Side by side Miss Golden and Mr. Ashgrove ran along the green-floored passages, battled down the white marble stairs among the hundred other employees from the tenth floor, the nine hundred from the floors below.

B. DIRECTIONS: *Identify two clues the author gives that foreshadow the story's ending. Did you expect the story's ending, or were you surprised? Describe your response, and tell why you reacted that way.*

Clue 1: _____

Clue 2: _____

My response to story's ending: _____

_____

Name _____ Date _____

"Sonata for Harp and Bicycle" by Joan Aiken
Reading: Read Ahead to Verify Predictions

A **prediction** is an informed guess about what will happen later in a narrative. **Making and verifying predictions** keeps you actively involved in the story you are reading.

- Notice details that may foreshadow future events. Make predictions based on those details, and then read on to verify your predictions. If a prediction turns out to be wrong, evaluate your reasoning to determine whether you misread details or whether the author purposely created false expectations in order to surprise you later in the story.
- Use a chart like the one shown to record your predictions and evaluate their accuracy. Analyze any inaccurate predictions to determine why they were incorrect.

The key to making accurate predictions is paying close attention to the story you read. In "Sonata for Harp and Bicycle," the author provides many colorful details about what will happen.

Aiken's Original: Jason turned and stared at Grimes Buildings.
Somewhere, he knew, there was a back way in, a service entrance.

Prediction: Jason is going to enter the Grimes Buildings through the back way.

DIRECTIONS: *Fill in the second and third columns of the following chart. Write your predictions based on the details in the first column. Then, read ahead to find out the outcome of your predictions, and record the outcomes.*

Details	My Prediction	Outcome
1. The bell stopped beside him, and then there was a moment when his heart tried to shake itself loose in his chest. He was looking into two eyes carved out of expressionless air; he was held by two hands knotted together out of the width of the dark.		
2. "We must remedy the matter, Berenice. We must not begrudge our new-found happiness to others."		
3. "We don't want our evening to be spoiled by the thought of a curse hanging over us," he said, "so this is the practical thing to do. Hang onto the roses."		

"Sonata for Harp and Bicycle" by Joan Aiken
Vocabulary Builder

Word List

encroaching   furtive   menacing   preposterous   reciprocate   tantalizingly

A. DIRECTIONS: *Write the letter of the word that is the best synonym for the numbered word.*

____ 1. furtive
     A. quiet   C. sneaky
     B. stolen   D. honest

____ 2. reciprocate
     A. refuse   C. respond
     B. return   D. renew

____ 3. tantalizingly
     A. with great care   C. in an angry way
     B. with a lot of noise   D. in a teasing way

____ 4. menacing
     A. hoping   C. threatening
     B. challenging   D. regretting

____ 5. preposterous
     A. ridiculous   C. pretentious
     B. resentful   D. angry

____ 6. encroaching
     A. despairing   C. retreating
     B. intruding   D. considering

B. WORD STUDY The suffix *-ate* means "to become or form." Write sentences using a word formed with the suffix *-ate*. Choose from among these words: *incorporate, activate, captivate*.

1. Use the word *captivate* to describe how you might react to a colorful sunset.

_____

2. Use the word *incorporate* to tell what you might do with information you gathered for a report.

_____

3. Use the word *activate* to describe what might happen if you pushed a mysterious button.

_____

"Sonata for Harp and Bicycle" by Joan Aiken
Enrichment: Sonata Form in Music

DIRECTIONS: *Read the following encyclopedia entry for the word* sonata. *Then, use the information to answer the questions that follow. Write your responses in the space provided.*

Sonata is a musical term. The word comes from the Italian word *sonare,* which means "to sound." Originally, the term *sonata* was used to describe any kind of instrumental music, as opposed to a vocal work. As musical structure became more formal, *sonata* came to mean a musical form that has four distinct sections, or movements. The first and third movements are slow; the second and fourth movements are fast. By the late seventeenth century, there were two primary types of sonata: the church sonata and the chamber sonata.

After the seventeenth century, the sonata evolved into a clearly defined three- or four-movement piece. The term *sonata* was used only when the performing instrument was a keyboard instrument (such as a piano or harpsichord) or another instrument accompanied by a keyboard instrument.

The most famous early writer of sonatas was Arcangelo Corelli (1653–1713). Other famous composers of sonatas were J.S. Bach (1685–1750), Wolfgang Amadeus Mozart (1756–1791), Ludwig Van Beethoven (1770–1827), Robert Schumann (1810–1856), and Johannes Brahms (1833–1897).

Other musical forms use the same three- or four-movement structure, but have different names. A sonata for a whole orchestra is called a *symphony.* A sonata for a solo instrument accompanied by the whole orchestra is a *concerto,* and a sonata for four musicians playing stringed instruments is called a *string quartet.*

1. Since the seventeenth century, what does the word *sonata* refer to?

   _____

2. What is the origin of the term *sonata?*

   _____

3. Describe the general structure of a sonata.

   _____

4. What is the name for a musical work in sonata form for a whole orchestra?

   _____

5. Why do you think Joan Aiken calls her story a sonata?

   _____

6. What two musical instruments might she be referring to in her title?

   _____

Name _____ Date _____

"Sonata for Harp and Bicycle" by Joan Aiken
Open-Book Test

Short Answer *Write your responses to the questions in this section on the lines provided.*

1. Suspense is a feeling of tension that makes readers wonder what will happen next. How does the author of "Sonata for Harp and Bicycle" create suspense in the first line of the story?

   _____

   _____

2. Skim the section near the beginning of "Sonata for Harp and Bicycle" in which announcements are made to the staff beginning at a quarter to five. Based on these announcements, what prediction did you make?

   _____

   _____

   _____

3. A conflict is a problem that needs solving. In "Sonata for Harp and Bicycle," what is Jason Ashgrove's main conflict? Why does Miss Golden say she can't help him?

   _____

   _____

4. On the top line below, briefly describe the climax of "Sonata for Harp and Bicycle." On each of the lower lines, write one event that is part of the story's rising action.

   Climax: _____

   _____ ↑↑ _____

   _____ ‖   _____

                        Rising Action

5. Would you describe William Heron's behavior in the building in "Sonata for Harp and Bicycle" as furtive? Why or why not? Base your answer on the definition of *furtive*.

   _____

   _____

6. Reread the section of "Sonata for Harp and Bicycle" in which Jason climbs up the fire escape. Identify a detail that foreshadows another event, and explain how it does so.

   _____

   _____

   _____

7. After learning the true story of the building's ghosts in "Sonata for Harp and Bicycle," why does Jason embrace Berenice so suddenly? Provide a detail that helps bring this embrace to life.

_____

_____

_____

_____

8. After Jason and Berenice reveal their love for each other, "Sonata for Harp and Bicycle" takes on a comic, upbeat tone. Give an example of this, and explain why you think the author made this change.

_____

_____

_____

_____

9. Review the section of "Sonata for Harp and Bicycle" in which Jason and Berenice reunite the ghosts. Then think about the prediction you made at the beginning of the story. Was your prediction correct? Somewhat correct? Not at all? Explain.

_____

_____

_____

_____

10. In your opinion, why does the author have Jason and Berenice parachute off the fire escape rather than climb down it at the end of "Sonata for Harp and Bicycle"? What other story details help to make this same point?

_____

_____

_____

_____

Essay

Write an extended response to the question of your choice or to the question or questions your teacher assigns you.

11. Jason has discovered the mystery of the Grimes Buildings and faces the same fate as William Heron. Write an essay explaining why Jason and Berenice must resolve Jason's dilemma. Use examples and details from "Sonata for Harp and Bicycle" to support your response.

12. In one sense, "Sonata for Harp and Bicycle" consists of two love stories that converge, or meet, at the end. Explain in an essay how these love stories are different and similar. In what way is each couple indebted to the other?

13. Tales of "unexplained" events and situations often capture people's interest. In an essay, explain the appeal of these tales and the reason they are enjoyed even when the outcome is predictable. Support your ideas with examples from "Sonata for Harp and Bicycle" as well as from other tales that you have read, heard, or seen on TV or in movies.

14. **Thinking About the Big Question: Can truth change?** In reading, as in real life, we make assumptions about characters when we first meet them. When William the ghost first appeared in "Sonata for Harp and Bicycle," what did you think of him? On what details did you base this conclusion? Did you revise this belief later on? Why or why not? What point about real life—not ghosts—might the author be trying to make? Answer these questions in an essay.

Oral Response

15. Go back to question 3, 4, 6, or 8 or to the question your teacher assigns to you. Take a few minutes to expand your answer and prepare an oral response. Find additional details in "Sonata for Harp and Bicycle" that will support your points. If necessary, make notes to guide your response.

Name _____ Date _____

"Sonata for Harp and Bicycle" by Joan Aiken
Selection Test A

Critical Reading *Identify the letter of the choice that best answers the question.*

____ 1. In "Sonata for Harp and Bicycle," what is Jason Ashgrove's job?
A. He is director of the company.
B. He is a security guard.
C. He writes advertising copy.
D. He is Miss Golden's secretary.

____ 2. In "Sonata for Harp and Bicycle," what does Aiken mean when she writes that every evening "the staff hustled like lemmings"?
A. They moved very slowly.
B. They looked like small rats.
C. They hurried in a huge group.
D. They waited for the bell.

____ 3. In Aiken's story, which detail leads you to predict that something very strange is going on?
A. Jason is a new employee.
B. Jason's office is very small.
C. Loudspeakers announce odd messages.
D. Church bells ring at five o'clock.

____ 4. In "Sonata for Harp and Bicycle," why must everyone leave exactly at five o'clock?
A. There are no lights in the building.
B. There is no heat in the building.
C. A law firm uses the offices at night.
D. The building is haunted.

____ 5. Early in Aiken's story, Jason asks Miss Golden what she wants for her birthday. What can you predict from this sentence?
    What she chiefly wanted was Mr. Jason Ashgrove, but he had not realized this yet.
A. Jason and Miss Golden will fall in love.
B. Jason will hate Miss Golden.
C. Miss Golden will marry someone else.
D. Miss Golden will quit her job.

_____ 6. In "Sonata for Harp and Bicycle," what does Jason find the first time he goes back into the building?
   A. He meets the Wailing Watchman.
   B. He meets Daisy.
   C. He meets Miss Golden.
   D. Nothing happens.

_____ 7. In the following sentence from Aiken's story, what is happening to Jason?
   He was looking into two eyes carved out of expressionless air; he was held by two hands knotted together out of the width of the dark.
   A. He is staring at Miss Golden.
   B. He is staring at a ghost.
   C. He is watching a movie.
   D. He is looking in a mirror.

_____ 8. What is the climax, the moment of greatest suspense, in "Sonata for Harp and Bicycle"?
   A. Miss Golden and Jason kiss.
   B. Daisy rides the bicycle.
   C. The watchman plays the harp.
   D. Daisy and William are reunited.

_____ 9. In "Sonata for Harp and Bicycle," why must Jason resolve the Wailing Watchman's problem?
   A. Jason will be fired if he does nothing.
   B. All who see the ghost die in five days.
   C. The Wailing Watchman is Jason's uncle.
   D. William Heron has asked him for help.

_____ 10. What happens when Berenice rings Extension 170 from the switchboard?
   A. No one answers the phone.
   B. William answers the phone.
   C. Daisy answers the phone.
   D. The switchboard disappears.

_____ 11. What is the best definition of the *resolution* of a story's plot?
   A. The central conflict is introduced.
   B. The conflict reaches its most intense moment.
   C. The conflict's intensity lessens.
   D. The conflict concludes and loose ends are tied up.

____ 12. In "Sonata for Harp and Bicycle," what can you infer from this sentence?

Each was left with a memory . . . of a bicycle bearing on its saddle a harp, a bottle of wine, and a bouquet of red roses, sweeping improbably down the corridor and far, far away.

A. Jason and Miss Golden get married and live happily ever after.

B. Daisy and William Heron reunite as ghosts and leave the building forever.

C. Daisy and William Heron continue to live as ghosts in the Grimes Buildings.

D. Neither Jason nor Miss Golden believes in ghosts.

Vocabulary and Grammar

____ 13. What is the best synonym for *furtive* in the following sentence?

A tiny furtive wedge of darkness beckoned him. . . .

A. sneaky   **C.** dark

B. solid   **D.** scary

____ 14. In which sentence is the word *reciprocate* used correctly?

A. The speaker tried to *reciprocate* everyone's questions.

B. We always try to *reciprocate* when someone invites us to dinner.

C. Please *reciprocate* your homework before it gets too late.

D. I have looked everywhere, but cannot *reciprocate* my book bag.

____ 15. In the following passage, which word is an abstract noun?

It was so narrow that at any moment, it seemed, the overtopping walls would come together and squeeze it out of existence.

A. narrow   **C.** together

B. walls   **D.** existence

Essay

16. As you read "Sonata for Harp and Bicycle," how did you feel? Were you amused, puzzled, frightened, worried—or something else entirely? Did your feelings change at different times in the story? What details or events do you think Joan Aiken meant to be scary or eerie? In a brief essay, tell how you felt as you read this story. Give specific examples of details and events that evoked the feelings you identify.

17. What did you predict Jason would do when he learns the truth behind the ghost story? Write an essay in which you describe your prediction. Use details from "Sonata for Harp and Bicycle" to support your prediction.

18. **Thinking About the Big Question: Can truth change?** When we first meet story characters, we begin to form ideas about them. What did you think of William the ghost when he first appeared in the middle of "Sonata for Harp and Bicycle"? What details led you to this first opinion of William? How did your ideas about William change as you read more of the story? Answer these questions in an essay.

"Sonata for Harp and Bicycle" by Joan Aiken
Selection Test B

Critical Reading *Identify the letter of the choice that best completes the statement or answers the question.*

____ 1. Which of the following best describes "Sonata for Harp and Bicycle"?
   A. a serious biographical narrative
   B. an exciting autobiographical excerpt
   C. an informational article
   D. a mysterious, romantic story

____ 2. In "Sonata for Harp and Bicycle," which detail leads you to predict that something strange is going on?
   A. The offices are quite small.
   B. The lighting is very dim.
   C. Loudspeakers announce odd messages.
   D. Church bells ring at five o'clock.

____ 3. What can you predict from the following first sentence of Aiken's story?
   "No one is allowed to remain in the building after five o'clock," Mr. Manaby told his new assistant, showing him into the little room that was like the inside of a parcel.

   A. We will find out why everyone must leave the building at five o'clock.
   B. We will find out the reason why the office is so small.
   C. The new assistant will soon quit his job or Mr. Manaby will fire him.
   D. Neither Mr. Manaby nor his new assistant will be important in the story.

____ 4. In "Sonata for Harp and Bicycle," why does everyone leave promptly at five o'clock?
   A. The building's design makes it too dark to see after five o'clock.
   B. It is company policy to keep all work areas neat.
   C. The directors refuse to pay for overtime.
   D. The office building is haunted.

____ 5. What can you predict from the fact that Jason asks Miss Golden to explain the five o'clock policy?
   A. Jason and Miss Golden will fall in love.
   B. Jason's curiosity will get him fired.
   C. The central conflict will be between Jason and Miss Golden.
   D. The plot will follow the mystery of the five o'clock policy.

____ 6. What is Jason doing in the following sentence from Aiken's story?
   He was looking into two eyes carved out of expressionless air; he was held by two hands knotted together out of the width of the dark.

   A. He is standing next to Miss Golden.
   B. He is standing next to a mirror.
   C. He is standing next to a ghost.
   D. He is standing next to a bicycle.

____ 7. How does Miss Golden guess that Jason had been in the Grimes Buildings after five o'clock?
A. She sees him climbing the fire escape.
B. Daisy tells her.
C. The Wailing Watchman tells her.
D. His dark hair has turned silver.

____ 8. When Miss Golden finally explains the mystery to Jason, why is it necessary that Jason and she resolve the problem of the Wailing Watchman?
A. Jason will be fired for being in the Grimes Buildings after dark.
B. All who see the ghost die within five days.
C. They must find a way to restore Jason's youth.
D. They cannot marry until the spirits are satisfied.

____ 9. In "Sonata for Harp and Bicycle," which event marks the climax, the moment of greatest suspense?
A. Miss Golden tells Jason the secret.
B. Jason goes back into the building.
C. Jason and Miss Golden reunite the ghosts.
D. Jason borrows a parachute from a friend.

____ 10. Which of the following marks the resolution of "Sonata for Harp and Bicycle"?
A. Jason and Miss Golden parachute from the fire escape.
B. Jason goes back into the Grimes Buildings through a fire escape.
C. Jason asks Miss Golden what she wants for her birthday.
D. Jason hears strange noises and a bicycle bell inside the empty Grimes Buildings.

____ 11. What is the best meaning of the following sentence from "Sonata for Harp and Bicycle"?
Darkness infested the building like a flight of bats returning willingly to roost.
A. A colony of bats lives in the building.
B. Darkness is like an illness.
C. The employees leave the building quickly.
D. The building quickly became dark.

____ 12. Which of the following explains what Aiken means by "the staff hustled like lemmings"?
A. The staff hurried in a huge mass.
B. The staff looked like a bunch of rats.
C. The staff moved dreamily.
D. The staff waited politely for the bell.

____ 13. In "Sonata for Harp and Bicycle," what is Berenice doing when she spoons "out coffee powder with distracted extravagance"?
A. She uses a tiny bit of coffee powder.
B. She uses a lot of coffee powder.
C. She spills the coffee powder.
D. She adds water to the coffee powder.

____ 14. Based on the following sentence from Aiken's story, what can you predict happens to Daisy?

Daisy did not long survive him but pined away soon after.

A. She moves away.

B. She dies.

C. She gets married.

D. She gets a job.

Vocabulary and Grammar

____ 15. If you are *tantalizingly* close to the end of a five-mile hike, approximately how many miles do you have left?

A. five miles

B. four miles

C. two miles

D. half a mile

____ 16. What is the best synonym for *reciprocate* in the following sentence?

When someone does you a favor, you are expected to reciprocate.

A. reply

B. repair

C. return

D. reconnect

____ 17. In the following sentence, which word choice is an abstract noun?

The bell stopped beside him, and then there was a moment while his heart tried to shake itself loose in his chest.

A. bell

B. moment

C. heart

D. chest

____ 18. How many nouns can you find in the following passage?

Jason stood undecided on the pavement, with the crowds dividing around him as around the pier of a bridge. He scratched his head, looked about him for guidance.

A. four

B. six

C. seven

D. nine

Essay

19. In "Sonata for Harp and Bicycle," you can be swept away by the author's witty, skillful storytelling. How does Joan Aiken move the tale along? In a brief essay, identify three or four of the points of rising action (the plot events that introduce the story's central conflict) in Aiken's story. Explain how they are linked together to build suspense.

20. Although Aiken's story is suspenseful, few would suggest that it is scary. Even though the tale includes eerie buildings, ghosts, a tense moment on a fire escape, and a daring plan, we sense all along that this is a lighthearted tale. In a brief essay, identify three ways in which the author signals that "Sonata for Harp and Bicycle" is a happy story.

21. **Thinking About the Big Question: Can truth change?** In reading, as in real life, we make assumptions about characters when we first meet them. When William the ghost first appeared in "Sonata," what did you think of him? On what details did you base this conclusion? Did you revise this belief later on, and why? What point about real life—not ghosts—might the author be trying to make? Answer these questions in an essay.

Vocabulary Warm-up Word Lists

Study these words from "The Cask of Amontillado." Then, complete the activities.

Word List A

enthusiasm [en THOO zee az uhm] *n.* intense interest; eagerness
We began the exciting new project with great <u>enthusiasm</u>.

injuries [IN juh reez] *n.* emotional or physical harm or damage
Untrue stories about famous actors are <u>injuries</u> for which they can sue.

nevertheless [nev er <u>th</u>uh LES] *adv.* however; in spite of
I like my boss very much; <u>nevertheless</u>, I need a job that pays more.

perceived [per SEEVD] *v.* saw; understood
We soon <u>perceived</u> that ninth grade would be fun, but lots of work.

render [REN der] *v.* give
I expect you to <u>render</u> the best service possible at this price!

revenge [ri VENJ] *n.* punishment to pay back an injury or insult
Many traditions teach that it is better to forgive than to seek <u>revenge</u>.

unnecessarily [uhn nes uh SER uh lee] *adv.* without need or cause
Getting detention for giggling in class seems <u>unnecessarily</u> harsh.

ventured [VEN churd] *v.* went ahead despite risk
Despite the storm, they <u>ventured</u> out on the tiny sailboat.

Word List B

colossal [kuh LAH suhl] *adj.* gigantic; huge
Cheating on the test would be a <u>colossal</u> mistake.

excessive [ek SES iv] *adj.* too much; unreasonable
Ten dollars for a hamburger seems <u>excessive</u> to me.

immediate [i MEE dee it] *adj.* without delay; at once; instant
Time is running out, so we need an <u>immediate</u> answer.

indication [in di KAY shuhn] *n.* something that points to; sign
A high fever and sore muscles could be an <u>indication</u> of the flu.

interruption [in tuh RUHP shun] *n.* break or stop in an action; disturbance
I would like to finish my homework without any further <u>interruption</u>.

succession [suhk SE shuhn] *n.* a series of people or things
A <u>succession</u> of cold, rainy days ruined our beach vacation.

tier [TEER] *n.* row or layer placed one above the other
We sat in the fourth <u>tier</u> of seats at the theater.

vigorously [VIG uh rus lee] *adv.* with strength or force; energetically
Brush your teeth <u>vigorously</u> at least twice a day to prevent cavities.

Name _____ Date _____

"The Cask of Amontillado" by Edgar Allan Poe
Vocabulary Warm-up Exercises

Exercise A *Fill in each blank in the paragraph below with an appropriate word from Word List A. Use each word only once.*

Even as a little boy, Jim showed great [1] _____ for playing football. Despite his size, he bravely [2] _____ out to play with the big kids. The older boys quickly [3] _____ that Jim had great potential as a football player; [4] _____, they delighted in teasing him about his size, which caused emotional [5] _____ for Jim. While they were never [6] _____ rough with him, they refused to [7] _____ him the credit he deserved. Jim got his [8] _____ a few years later, however, when he grew up to be the best high school quarterback in the state.

Exercise B *Revise each sentence so that the underlined vocabulary word is used in a logical way. Be sure to keep the vocabulary word in your revision.*

Example: The people seated in the third <u>tier</u> had the best view of the performance.
The people seated in the first <u>tier</u> had the best view of the performance.

1. The coach threw a party to celebrate the team's <u>colossal</u> defeat.

   _____

2. She was delighted by the <u>excessive</u> price of the dress that she wanted so badly.

   _____

3. I am in no hurry, so please give me an <u>immediate</u> reply.

   _____

4. The fact that it rained a lot last spring is an <u>indication</u> that it will rain a lot next spring.

   _____

5. I have had a <u>succession</u> of great teachers, so I have not enjoyed school at all.

   _____

6. Thanks to one <u>interruption</u> after another, the job was completed in record time.

   _____

7. After exercising <u>vigorously</u> for six months, my aunt managed to gain almost twenty pounds.

   _____

"The Cask of Amontillado" by Edgar Allan Poe
Reading Warm-up A

Read the following passage. Pay special attention to the underlined words. Then, read it again, and complete the activities. Use a separate sheet of paper for your written answers.

They say <u>revenge</u> is sweet, but trying to get even with an old friend can be a sour experience.

Back in the fifth grade, Becky and I had been as close as two friends can be. We shared just about everything in those days, from our love of classic rock to our endless <u>enthusiasm</u> for eating popcorn and watching old movies. Back then, neither of us ever had a bad word to say about the other.

Then, in the eighth grade, Roger Ellison moved to town.

If I had to <u>render</u> a picture of Roger in a single sentence, I would say he was the kind of boy every girl dreams about. He was smart, funny, and good-looking. I knew from the moment I saw him that we were meant to be together.

Then Becky got in the way.

True, Roger never showed the slightest interest in me. <u>Nevertheless</u>, I <u>perceived</u> Becky as a threat and felt betrayed when she started hanging out with Roger. That is when I began giving my old friend the cold shoulder. At first, I just looked for excuses not to eat lunch with her. (Come to think of it, that is when she started eating lunch with Roger and his friends.) We began talking to each other less and less at school. When she <u>ventured</u> to leave messages for me at home, I did not bother returning her calls.

By the time we got to high school, Becky and I seemed to have very little in common. Roger had moved away by then, but I continued being <u>unnecessarily</u> rude to my former best friend. Then one day I realized that the only <u>injuries</u> I had managed to inflict had been upon myself. I had sacrificed a true friendship for no good reason. I knew I had to apologize.

Becky was understanding and kindhearted enough to forgive me. Now we are friends again. I have promised myself never to seek revenge against anyone else. I have learned that it may cost more than it is worth.

1. Underline the words that mean the same thing as <u>revenge</u>. Was this plan for *revenge* successful? How can you tell?

2. Circle two things for which the girls shared <u>enthusiasm</u>. Name two things for which you feel *enthusiasm*.

3. Underline the words that tell what the narrator tries to <u>render</u>. Then, *render* a brief description of someone you know.

4. What does the narrator imply by using the word <u>nevertheless</u>?

5. Underline the words that tell what the narrator <u>perceived</u>. Explain why things that are *perceived* are not always true.

6. Underline the words that tell what Becky <u>ventured</u> to do. How was she putting herself at risk by doing so?

7. Circle the words that tell to whom the narrator was <u>unnecessarily</u> rude. Explain why this was *unnecessary*.

8. Circle the word that tells who suffered the <u>injuries</u>. What kind of *injuries* is the narrator talking about?

"The Cask of Amontillado" by Edgar Allan Poe
Reading Warm-up B

Read the following passage. Pay special attention to the underlined words. Then, read it again, and complete the activities. Use a separate sheet of paper for your written answers.

Have you ever been to a carnival?

I do not mean the kind of carnival with carousels and cotton candy. The kind of carnival I am talking about started in Italy more than a thousand years ago. These carnivals were days of feasting that led up to religious observances and fasting. In Rome and Venice, people would put on masks and dance down the street, moving <u>vigorously</u> to the lively music while dressed in strange and colorful costumes.

The carnival tradition soon spread throughout Europe. French colonists who settled in America brought these customs with them. Today, the largest and most famous carnival in the United States is the <u>colossal</u> Mardi Gras celebration held every year in New Orleans.

The first New Orleans Mardi Gras was an <u>immediate</u> success. A spectacular parade has been held just about every year since, without <u>interruption</u>. Each year, tourists flock from all over the country to view amazing floats and listen to lively marching bands. Men and women in fantastic costumes balance on the highest <u>tier</u> of multi-level floats and shower the crowd below with colorful beads and trinkets. It is truly a sight to see!

If you prefer quiet celebrations, however, you had better stay away. The noise level at Mardi Gras can be <u>excessive</u>. The <u>succession</u> of floats, bands, and marchers seems to go on and on. The crowds that line the parade route tend to get a little rowdy. The police are always ready to step in at the first <u>indication</u> of trouble, however.

After the parade, the party continues at fancy costume balls decorated in the official colors of the carnival: purple, which stands for justice; green, which stands for faith; and gold, which stands for power. While most tourists think of Mardi Gras as just an excuse to enjoy a party, some local people continue to honor the customs and traditions that reflect the carnival's ancient origins as a religious festival. Either way, everyone has a good time at Mardi Gras.

1. Describe how the people were moving <u>vigorously</u> to the music. Define *vigorously*.

2. Circle the word that gives a clue to the meaning of <u>colossal</u>. Name two other things that might be described as *colossal*.

3. Write a sentence telling how long it takes an <u>immediate</u> success to happen.

4. Underline what takes place every year almost without <u>interruption</u>. Explain what *interruption* means.

5. Circle the words that tell what <u>tier</u> the people stand on. Where else might you see a *tier*?

6. Underline the words that tell you what is <u>excessive</u>. Then, tell what *excessive* means.

7. Circle the words that tell what is in the <u>succession</u>. Give a synonym for *succession*.

8. What might be an <u>indication</u> of trouble at a parade? Give a synonym for *indication*.

Name _____ Date _____

Can truth change?

Big Question Vocabulary

assumption	belief	circumstance	context	convince
credible	distort	evidence	manipulate	perceive
perspective	skeptics	speculate	truth	verify

A. *Use one or more words from the list above to complete each sentence.*

1. Ericka tried to _____ people by telling falsehoods.

2. Fortunato wanted to believe Montresor's flattery, but the _____ was, Montresor only wanted to kill him.

3. Fortunato wouldn't believe what was happening to him until he saw _____ rising before him, one stone at a time.

4. When did Montresor _____ the truth of what was happening?

B. *Follow the directions in responding to each of the items below.*

1. List an example of a situation when you noticed the truth was being manipulated.

   _____

   _____

2. Why do people sometimes manipulate the truth? Explain your answer. Use Big Question vocabulary words in your answer.

   _____

   _____

C. *Complete the sentence below. Then, write a short paragraph in which you connect this experience to the Big Question.*

In "The Cask of Amontillado," a wronged man seeks revenge. Complete this sentence:

The truth about a person is a result of _____.

_____

_____

_____

_____

_____

"The Cask of Amontillado" by Edgar Allan Poe
Literary Analysis: Plot, Foreshadowing, and Suspense

Plot is the sequence of events in a narrative. It is structured around a **conflict,** or problem, and it can be divided into the following parts:

- **Rising action**—the central conflict is introduced
- **Climax**—the high point of intensity in the conflict
- **Falling action**—the conflict's intensity lessens
- **Resolution**—the conflict concludes and loose ends are tied up

Writers use a variety of techniques to keep readers interested in the plot. One of these, **foreshadowing,** is the use of clues to hint at events that will happen later in a story. Authors use this technique to create **suspense,** a feeling of tension that keeps readers wondering what will happen next.

Read the following passage, which is the opening paragraph of "The Cask of Amontillado."

> The thousand injuries of Fortunato I had borne as I best could, but when he ventured upon insult I vowed revenge. You, who so well know the nature of my soul, will not suppose, however, that I gave utterance to a threat. At *length* I would be avenged; this was a point definitely settled—but the very definitiveness with which it was resolved precluded the idea of risk. I must not only punish but punish with impunity.

In the opening paragraph, what details does Poe include that suggest something about the narrator's personality and his plans? The paragraph arouses our curiosity: What does the narrator plan to do, and how can he possibly get away without being punished?

A. DIRECTIONS: *Read the following passage, and watch for details the author uses to create suspense. Underline the words and phrases in the passage that make you curious about the outcome.*

> The wine sparkled in his eyes and the bells jingled. My own fancy grew warm with the Médoc. We had passed through long walls of piled skeletons, with casks and puncheons intermingling, into the inmost recesses of the catacombs. I paused again, and this time I made bold to seize Fortunato by an arm above the elbow.
>
> "The niter!" I said; "see, it increases. It hangs like moss upon the vaults. We are below the river's bed. The drops of moisture trickle among the bones. Come, we will go back ere it is too late. Your cough—"
>
> "It is nothing," he said; "let us go on. But first, another draft of the Médoc."

B. DIRECTIONS: *Identify two clues the author gives that foreshadow the story's ending. Did you expect the story's ending, or were you surprised? Describe your response, and tell why you reacted that way.*

Clue 1: _____

Clue 2: _____

My response to story's ending: _____

_____

"The Cask of Amontillado" by Edgar Allan Poe

Reading: Read Ahead to Make and Verify Predictions

A **prediction** is an informed guess about what will happen later in a narrative. **Making and verifying predictions** keeps you actively involved in the story you are reading.

- Notice details that may foreshadow future events. Make predictions based on those details, and then read on to verify your predictions. If a prediction turns out to be wrong, evaluate your reasoning to determine whether you misread details or whether the author purposely created false expectations in order to surprise you later in the story.
- Use a chart like the one shown to record your predictions and evaluate their accuracy. Analyze any inaccurate predictions to determine why they were incorrect.

The key to making accurate predictions is paying close attention to the story's details as you read. In "The Cask of Amontillado," the author provides many colorful details that serve as hints about what will happen.

Poe's original:	I took from their sconces two flambeaux, and giving one to Fortunato, bowed him through several suites of rooms to the archway that led into the vaults. I passed down a long and winding staircase, requesting him to be cautious as he followed. We came at length to the foot of the descent, and stood together upon the damp ground of the catacombs of the Montresors.
Prediction:	The narrator is going to do something terrible to Fortunato in the catacombs.

DIRECTIONS: *Fill in the columns on the following chart. In the second column, write your prediction based on the details in the first column. Then, read ahead to find out the outcome. How closely did your predictions match the outcomes? Record the outcomes in the third column.*

Details	My Prediction	Outcome
1. "Thus speaking, Fortunato possessed himself of my arm; and putting on a mask of black silk and drawing a *roquelaure* closely about my person, I suffered him to hurry me to my palazzo."		
2. "There were no attendants at home; they had absconded to make merry in honor of the time."		
3. It was in vain that Fortunato, uplifting his dull torch, endeavored to pry into the depth of the recess. Its termination the feeble light did not enable us to see. "Proceed," I said: "herein is the Amontillado. . . ."		

Name _____ Date _____

"The Cask of Amontillado" by Edgar Allan Poe
Vocabulary Builder

Word List

afflicted   explicit   precluded   recoiling   retribution   subsided

A. DIRECTIONS: *Write the letter of the word that is most nearly* opposite *in meaning to the Word List word.*

____ 1. precluded
   A. allowed   B. prevented   C. discouraged   D. interrupted

____ 2. retribution
   A. punishment   B. reward   C. criticism   D. response

____ 3. explicit
   A. distinct   B. clear   C. complete   D. vague

____ 4. afflicted
   A. invigorated   B. confused   C. sickened   D. worried

____ 5. recoiling
   A. retreating   B. forgetting   C. lurching   D. advancing

____ 6. subsided
   A. weakened   B. relaxed   C. intensified   D. begun

B. WORD STUDY The suffix *-tion* means "the act of." Rewrite each sentence. Use the underlined word plus the suffix *-tion* in the new sentence.

1. As I walked up the mountain, the trail began to <u>elevate</u> more and more.

   _____

2. The huge male lion will <u>protect</u> the rest of the group.

   _____

3. When he could not pay his rent, the landlord threatened to <u>evict</u> him.

   _____

4. The coach sent in a <u>substitute</u> player when John was injured.

   _____

Name _____ Date _____

"The Cask of Amontillado" by Edgar Allan Poe
Enrichment: Coats of Arms

When Fortunato says to the narrator, "I forget your arms," he is referring to the Montresor family's coat of arms. A **coat of arms** is a group of symbols and figures drawn on a shield. It serves as the special sign, or insignia, of a person or family.

During the Middle Ages, coats of arms were originally worn on a knight's armor to proclaim his loyalty to his lord. Later, they were adopted by noble families throughout Europe. The origins, history, and rules governing coats of arms come under the study of *heraldry*, which goes back to the twelfth century. Heraldry is a complex system that has a specialized vocabulary. Montresor's coat of arms, for example, includes a "foot d'or," or "golden foot," in a "field azure," which means on a sky-blue background. The "serpent rampant" is a snake standing up, as if on hind legs. The motto is written in Latin at the base of the coat of arms. In Montresor's coat of arms, the motto is, appropriately, "No one attacks me with impunity."

A. DIRECTIONS: *Answer the following questions on the lines provided.*

1. During the Middle Ages, why do you think noble families desired coats of arms?

   _____

2. What does Montresor's coat of arms suggest about him?

   _____

B. DIRECTIONS: *In the space provided, design your own family coat of arms. Include four symbols and figures that suggest something about your family's interests and background. Be sure to include a motto. If you prefer, you can design a coat of arms for yourself—not for your family. Hint: You do not have to draw well to design a coat of arms. Stick figures are acceptable.*

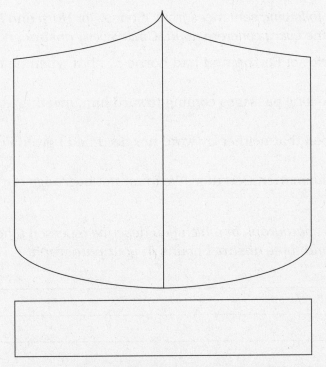

"Sonata for Harp and Bicycle" by Joan Aiken
"The Cask of Amontillado" by Edgar Allan Poe

Integrated Language Skills: Grammar

Abstract and Concrete Nouns

A **noun** is a word that names a person, place, or thing. Nouns name things that can be seen and touched as well as those that cannot be seen and touched. **Concrete nouns** refer to items that can be known by the senses—things that we can see, hear, taste, smell, or touch. **Abstract nouns** refer to ideas, qualities, states of being, and feelings—things that can be known only through the mind.

CONCRETE NOUNS
People: Sam Richman, sister, grandmother, Edgar Allan Poe, athlete, friend
Places: City Hall, Market Street, creek, school, Mount Rushmore
Things: raft, sidewalk, airplane, kittens, keyboard, water, lemons

ABSTRACT NOUNS
Ideas and actions: justice, independence, war, peace, reunion, trust
Conditions and qualities: strength, bravery, patience, optimism
Feelings and states of being: love, disappointment, friendship, fear

A. DIRECTIONS: *In the following sentences from "Sonata for Harp and Bicycle," and "The Cask of Amontillado," underline every concrete noun. Circle every abstract noun.*

1. The thousand injuries of Fortunato I had borne . . . but when he rentured upon insult I vowed revenge.

2. Jason could see two long passages coming toward him, meeting at an acute angle where he stood.

3. It must be understood that neither by word nor deed had I given Fortunato cause to doubt my good will."

4. "We must remedy the matter, Berenice. We must not begrudge our new-found happiness to others."

B. DIRECTIONS: *Write a paragraph in which you describe a person whom you know well. Use at least three concrete and three abstract nouns in your paragraph.*

_____

_____

_____

_____

"Sonata for Harp and Bicycle" by Joan Aiken
"The Cask of Amontillado" by Edgar Allan Poe
Integrated Language Skills: Support for Writing a Critique

Use the following chart to list the qualities that make a story suspenseful and that make the ending of a story satisfactory. Then, put a check mark in front of the qualities that you think apply to "Sonata for Harp and Bicycle" or "The Cask of Amontillado."

Qualities That Make a Story Suspenseful	Qualities of a Satisfactory Ending
❑ _____ _____ _____ _____	❑ _____ _____ _____ _____
❑ _____ _____ _____ _____	❑ _____ _____ _____ _____
❑ _____ _____ _____ _____	❑ _____ _____ _____ _____
❑ _____ _____ _____ _____	❑ _____ _____ _____ _____
❑ _____ _____ _____ _____	❑ _____ _____ _____ _____
❑ _____ _____ _____ _____	❑ _____ _____ _____ _____

Now, use your notes to write your critique in which you evaluate the ending of "Sonata for Harp and Bicycle" or "The Cask of Amontillado."

Name _____ Date _____

Integrated Language Skills: Support for Extend Your Learning

Listening and Speaking

DIRECTIONS: *Plan your retelling of the story by answering the following questions.*

1. From whose point of view will you retell the story?

   _____

2. What facial expressions will you use? Describe two facial expressions and the specific lines you will be saying as you use each expression.

   Expression: _____

   What I will be saying: _____

   Expression: _____

   What I will be saying: _____

3. What body movements, or gestures, will you use? Describe two body movements and the specific lines you will be saying as you use each body movement.

   Body movement: _____

   What I will be saying: _____

   Body movement: _____

   What I will be saying: _____

4. Where in the story will I change my intonation and voice to reflect the emotions of the narrator? List four situations that call for changes in voice. Describe your intonation and voice for each.

   a. _____

   _____

   b. _____

   _____

   c. _____

   _____

   d. _____

   _____

Name _____ Date _____

"The Cask of Amontillado" by Edgar Allan Poe
Open-Book Test

Short Answer *Write your responses to the questions in this section on the lines provided.*

1. In "The Cask of Amontillado," what is Montresor's attitude toward revenge? Use a quotation from the story to support your answer.

   _____

   _____

   _____

2. Early in "The Cask of Amontillado," Poe has Montresor repeat the line "I have my doubts" to Fortunato. In your opinion, why does he do this?

   _____

   _____

   _____

3. The word *explicit* means "clearly stated." In "The Cask of Amontillado," does Montresor make his plans explicit to Fortunato as they descend into the vaults? Explain, using the word *explicit* in your answer.

   _____

   _____

   _____

4. Once Montresor and Fortunato set out for Montresor's palazzo in "The Cask of Amontillado," what did you predict the outcome of the story would be? On what clues or details did you base this prediction?

   _____

   _____

   _____

5. Review the section of "The Cask of Amontillado" in which Montresor leads Fortunato through the crypts. Name the mood Poe creates in this scene, and list five sounds or objects that help convey this mood.

   _____

   _____

   _____

6. In "The Cask of Amontillado," Montresor and Fortunato have a conversation about "the brotherhood." In it, Fortunato produces an object. Reread this conversation. Then explain how the object foreshadows another story event.

   _____

   _____

   _____

7. Reread the paragraph near the end of "The Cask of Amontillado" in which Fortunato begins screaming and Montresor answers those screams. What does Montresor's behavior in this paragraph tell you about his state of mind? Did this behavior cause you to revise your earlier prediction about the story's outcome? Explain.

_____

_____

_____

8. On the top line below, briefly describe the climax of "The Cask of Amontillado." On each of the lower lines, write one event that is part of the story's rising action.

Climax: _____

_____   _____

_____   _____

Rising Action

9. Review the climax and falling action of "The Cask of Amontillado," and then return to the first line of the story. According to Montresor, what was Fortunato's initial crime? In your view, does the punishment fit the crime? Why or why not? What does this say about Montresor?

_____

_____

_____

10. Consider the last two lines of "The Cask of Amontillado." Based on what you know from the story, will Montresor be caught and punished for his crime? Why or why not?

_____

_____

_____

Essay

Write an extended response to the question of your choice or to the question or questions your teacher assigns you.

11. In "The Cask of Amontillado," Fortunato is dressed in motley, and Montresor wears a "mask of black silk." In an essay, explain why these costumes are appropriate for the roles that Fortunato and Montresor play in the story. Use details from the story to support your ideas.

12. Reread the last paragraph of "The Cask of Amontillado," noting Montresor's comment that his "heart grew sick." Some critics think Montresor is expressing regret for the murder of Fortunato, while others believe he is merely nauseated by the dampness and the smell of the crypt. What do you think makes Montresor's heart ill? What reasons and examples from Poe's story can you find to support your position? Answer these questions in an essay.

13. Review Montresor's description of Fortunato in the second paragraph of "The Cask of Amontillado." According to Montresor, in what ways is Fortunato a respectable man? In what ways is he a fake? What kind of a person do you think he is? Consider also whether Montresor himself is a reliable judge of character. Do you believe his description of Fortunato is objective? Answer these questions in the form of an essay.

14. **Thinking About the Big Question: Can truth change?** In an essay, explain how "the truth" changes for Fortunato over the course of "The Cask of Amontillado"— and why he is unable to perceive the *real* truth in the first place. When the reality of his situation becomes apparent to him, how does he respond? In your view, is this response appropriate? How so? Use information from the story to support your ideas.

Oral Response

15. Go back to question 5, 7, 9, or 10 or to the question your teacher assigns to you. Take a few minutes to expand your answer and prepare an oral response. Find additional details in "The Cask of Amontillado" that will support your points. If necessary, make notes to guide your response.

Name _____ Date _____

"The Cask of Amontillado" by Edgar Allan Poe
Selection Test A

Critical Reading *Identify the letter of the choice that best answers the question.*

____ 1. In "The Cask of Amontillado," who is the narrator, the person who tells the story?
   A. Luchesi
   B. Montresor
   C. Fortunato
   D. Amontillado

____ 2. Which word best describes the mood, or atmosphere, of Poe's story?
   A. humorous
   B. silly
   C. serious
   D. suspenseful

____ 3. With whom does Montresor have a conflict in "The Cask of Amontillado"?
   A. himself
   B. Fortunato
   C. Luchesi
   D. no one

____ 4. According to the following sentence from "The Cask of Amontillado," what has Fortunato done to Montresor?

   The thousand injuries of Fortunato I had borne as I best could, but when he ventured upon insult I vowed revenge.

   A. He has stabbed him.
   B. He has robbed him.
   C. He has insulted him.
   D. He has stolen his wife.

____ 5. What can you predict from the following sentence spoken by Montresor?

   At *length* I would be avenged; this was a point definitely settled. . . .

   A. Montresor will not do anything.
   B. Montresor will apologize.
   C. Montresor will carry out his revenge.
   D. Montresor will be murdered.

____ 6. In "The Cask of Amontillado," why does Fortunato go into the vaults?

A. to meet Montresor's ancestors

B. to find some peace and quiet

C. to attend a meeting of masons

D. to prove his wine expertise

____ 7. Why does Montresor tell his servants not to leave his house?

A. He knows they will do the opposite.

B. He is afraid of being robbed.

C. He wants them to enjoy the carnival.

D. He is punishing them.

____ 8. Why do you think Montresor chose the catacombs as the setting for his revenge?

A. It is his favorite place in his house.

B. It is filled with ghosts.

C. No one will find Fortunato there.

D. Fortunato is afraid of bones.

____ 9. In "The Cask of Amontillado," which event is the climax of the plot?

A. Montresor meets Fortunato on the street.

B. Montresor brings Fortunato home.

C. Montresor walls up Fortunato.

D. Montresor confesses his crime.

____ 10. Which statement proves your prediction that Montresor will succeed?

A. I looked at him in surprise.

B. The vaults are insufferably damp.

C. For half a century, no mortal has disturbed them.

D. The wine sparkled in his eyes and the bells jingled.

____ 11. What can you infer about Fortunato from the following sentence from "The Cask of Amontillado"?

He [Fortunato] turned towards me, and looked into my eyes with two filmy orbs that distilled the rheum of intoxication.

A. He is drunk.   C. He is blind.

B. He is crying.   D. He is suspicious.

Vocabulary and Grammar

____ **12.** Which word best describes the subject of "The Cask of Amontillado"?

    A. retribution   **C.** friendship

    B. recovery   **D.** danger

____ **13.** In which sentence is the word *explicit* used correctly?

    A. Sam is an *explicit* person.   **C.** In *explicit* weather, stay home.

    B. Nora gave us *explicit* directions.   **D.** She has *explicit* talent.

____ **14.** Which word is an abstract noun in the following passage?

    The wine sparkled in his eyes and the bells jingled. My own fancy grew warm with the Médoc.

    A. wine   **C.** bells

    B. eyes   **D.** fancy

____ **15.** How many nouns are in the following sentence?

    As I said these words I busied myself among the pile of bones of which I have before spoken.

    A. one   **C.** three

    B. two   **D.** four

Essay

16. In an essay, describe the basic plot of "The Cask of Amontillado." Identify one event that takes place during the rising action. Then, describe what event occurs during the climax, or high point, of the story. Finally, identify the resolution, or conclusion.

17. Authors help us to understand the characters in a story by showing us what they say and do. Sometimes, they tell us what a character thinks, too. Each character has character traits, or qualities. For example, Fortunato is too trusting; he believes Montresor's story about the Amontillado. In a brief essay, identify one character trait of Montresor. Give two examples from the story to support the character trait you mention.

18. **Thinking About the Big Question: Can truth change?** Early in the story "The Cask of Amontillado," Fortunato believes he is going with Montresor to judge a cask of wine. But this truth eventually changes for Fortunato. What is the truth? When does this truth change? How does Fortunato respond when he discovers the real truth? Use information from the story to support your ideas in a brief essay.

"The Cask of Amontillado" by Edgar Allan Poe
Selection Test B

Critical Reading *Identify the letter of the choice that best completes the statement or answers the question.*

____ 1. Who is the narrator in "The Cask of Amontillado"?
  A. Luchesi
  B. Montresor
  C. Fortunato
  D. Amontillado

____ 2. What motivates Montresor to vow to take revenge upon Fortunato?
  A. Fortunato has threatened him.
  B. Fortunato has insulted him.
  C. Fortunato has ruined his business.
  D. Fortunato has stolen his wife.

____ 3. In "The Cask of Amontillado," what is the central conflict?
  A. the narrator vs. Fortunato
  B. the narrator vs. society
  C. the narrator vs. Luchesi
  D. the narrator vs. himself

____ 4. What can you predict from the following quotation from "The Cask of Amontillado"?
  At *length* I would be avenged; this was a point definitely settled—but the very definitiveness with which it was resolved precluded the idea of risk.
  A. Montresor is weak and will be afraid to take any action.
  B. Montresor is rash and will make mistakes, and he will therefore be caught.
  C. Montresor is indecisive and will hesitate to take any action.
  D. Montresor is cautious and will make his plans carefully.

____ 5. What is the main idea of the following sentence from "The Cask of Amontillado"?
  A wrong is unredressed when retribution overtakes its redresser.
  A. The person who avenges a wrong must be punished.
  B. The person who avenges a wrong must not be punished.
  C. No wrong can ever truly be avenged.
  D. The person who suffers a wrong should not try to get revenge.

____ 6. Which aspect of the carnival season is most important to Montresor's plan?
  A. Hundreds of people attend the carnival events.
  B. It is a time of wild madness and excess.
  C. People wear fantastic costumes in the streets.
  D. People catch colds from the damp weather.

____ 7. When the narrator tells Fortunato, "I was silly enough to pay the full Amontillado price without consulting you in the matter," to what is he appealing?
  A. Fortunato's intelligence
  B. Fortunato's vanity
  C. Fortunato's humility
  D. Fortunato's sympathy

____ 8. Why does Fortunato go into the vaults in "The Cask of Amontillado"?
   A. to find some peace and quiet
   B. to avenge Montresor's wrong
   C. to prove his wine expertise
   D. to attend a meeting of masons

____ 9. In Poe's story, why does Montresor give his servants "explicit orders not to stir from the house"?
   A. He wants them to protect the house.
   B. He wants them to entertain Fortunato.
   C. He wants them to leave the house.
   D. He wants them to clean the house.

____ 10. What can you infer from the following sentence from "The Cask of Amontillado"?
   He turned towards me, and looked into my eyes with two filmy orbs that distilled the rheum of intoxication.

   A. Fortunato does not see well.
   B. Fortunato is weeping.
   C. Fortunato is drunk.
   D. Fortunato is frightened.

____ 11. Why does Montresor repeatedly warn Fortunato about the bad air in the vaults?
   A. He is sincerely concerned about Fortunato's well-being.
   B. He wants to make sure that Fortunato does not suspect his motives.
   C. He hopes Fortunato will prevent him from committing the planned murder.
   D. He wants to warn Fortunato that his death is near.

____ 12. Which event is the climax, or highest point of intensity, of "The Cask of Amontillado"?
   A. Montresor meets Fortunato.
   B. Montresor takes Fortunato into the vault.
   C. Montresor walls Fortunato in.
   D. Montresor confesses his crime.

____ 13. Which event foreshadows the resolution of "The Cask of Amontillado"?
   A. Montresor tells Fortunato he has bought a large barrel of Amontillado.
   B. Fortunato wears a parti-striped dress.
   C. Montresor drinks to Fortunato's health with a bottle of Médoc.
   D. Fortunato asks Montresor if he is a mason.

____ 14. Which statement best verifies your prediction that Montresor will succeed?
   A. "Enough," he said; "the cough is a mere nothing; it will not kill me."
   B. For the half of a century no mortal has disturbed them.
   C. We continued our route in search of the Amontillado.
   D. "Then you are not of the brotherhood."

_____ 15. When you make a prediction about what will happen in a story, on what do you base your prediction?

      I. what has already happened in the story

      II. what you know about the author's life

      III. what you know about how the main character behaves

      IV. what you know about how people in real life behave

    A. I, II, and III

    B. II, III, and IV

    C. I, II, and IV

    D. I, III, and IV

Vocabulary and Grammar

_____ 16. Which word best describes the subject of "The Cask of Amontillado"?

    A. succession   C. affliction

    B. termination   D. retribution

_____ 17. Choose the sentence in which *precluded* is used correctly.

    A. The arrival of Hurricane Frances *precluded* Sandra's flying to Chicago.

    B. Husam carefully *precluded* his books and lunch in his back pack.

    C. Gloria *precluded* everyone in her invitation to her birthday party.

    D. The stores *precluded* all of their merchandise for the sale.

_____ 18. In this passage from "The Cask of Amontillado," which word is an abstract noun?

    It was about dusk, one evening during the supreme madness of the carnival season, that I encountered my friend.

    A. dusk   C. madness

    B. supreme   D. friend

_____ 19. How many nouns (both common and abstract) can you find in this passage?

    He had a weak point—this Fortunato—although in other regards he was a man to be respected and even feared. He prided himself on his connoisseurship in wine.

    A. three   C. six

    B. five   D. eight

Essay

20. In "The Cask of Amontillado," Poe uses descriptive details to create a specific mood, or atmosphere. In a brief essay, identify the story's mood. Then, tell which key details create that mood and in which scenes the mood is most strongly expressed.

21. In an essay, describe the basic plot of "The Cask of Amontillado." Identify one event that takes place during the rising action. Then, describe what event occurs during the climax of the story. Finally, identify the resolution.

22. **Thinking About the Big Question: Can truth change?** In an essay, explain how "the truth" changes for Fortunato over the course of "The Cask of Amontillado"—and why he is unable to perceive the *real* truth in the first place. When the reality of his situation becomes apparent to him, how does he respond? In your view, is this response appropriate? How so? Use information from the story to support your ideas.

"Checkouts" by Cynthia Rylant
"The Girl Who Can" by Ama Ata Aidoo
Vocabulary Warm-up Word Lists

Study these words from "Checkouts" and "The Girl Who Can." Then, complete the activities.

Word List A

approved [uh PROOVD] *adj.* accepted as good
Elena bought only supplies that were on the <u>approved</u> list.

attractive [uh TRAK tiv] *adj.* pleasing to look at; charming
The street vendor pointed to an <u>attractive</u> display of jewelry.

discussion [dis KUH shuhn] *n.* conversation; the act of exchanging ideas
The <u>discussion</u> about getting a dog went on for two hours.

fascinating [FAS uh nay ting] *adj.* extremely interesting
Jerome thinks his hobby of rock collecting is <u>fascinating</u>.

items [EYE tuhmz] *n.* single things in a group
Jose packed sixteen <u>items</u> of clothing for the weekend.

kilometers [kuh LAHM uh terz] *n.* units of length equal to 1,000 meters
The distance between the two houses is two <u>kilometers</u>.

photographs [FOH tuh grafs] *n.* pictures made with a camera
Sunita took both color and black-and-white <u>photographs</u> of her dog.

transition [tran ZISH uhn] *n.* act of changing from one form or condition to another
The <u>transition</u> from caterpillar to butterfly is quite remarkable.

Word List B

anticipation [an tis uh PAY shuhn] *n.* act of expecting something to happen
Jake held his breath in <u>anticipation</u> of the surprise.

emphasize [EM fuh syz] *v.* to point out for special notice; stress
Inez wanted to <u>emphasize</u> her rule that guests in her house remove their shoes.

intuition [in too ISH uhn] *n.* knowledge of something without reasoning
Myra's <u>intuition</u> told her that the area was dangerous.

lowland [LOH lend] *n.* land that is lower than the area around it
The <u>lowland</u> was known for its mild weather.

resulting [ri ZUHL ting] *adj.* caused as an effect of something else
The heavy rains and their <u>resulting</u> floods caused great damage.

sheen [SHEEN] *n.* shine
The <u>sheen</u> on the silver was almost blinding.

solitary [SAHL uh ter ee] *adj.* done or experienced alone
The prisoner spent a month in <u>solitary</u> confinement.

tedious [TEE dee uhs] *adj.* long, dull, and boring
Paul had the <u>tedious</u> job of folding napkins at the restaurant.

"Checkouts" by Cynthia Rylant
"The Girl Who Can" by Ama Ata Aidoo
Vocabulary Warm-up Exercises

Exercise A *Fill in each blank in the paragraph below with an appropriate word from Word List A. Use each word only once.*

Karen walked more than three [1] _____ to get to the store that was

having the big sale. She had a list of ten [2] _____ of clothing that she

wanted to buy. She had recently made the difficult [3] _____ from coun-

try living to city living, and she wanted to get the clothes to go with her new lifestyle.

She had studied many [4] _____ in fashion magazines, searching for the

right look. According to the fashion critics, the clothes Karen wanted were on the one

and only [5] _____ list of things that every stylish girl wore. After a

brief [6] _____ with the salesclerk, Karen tried on a beautiful jacket

with a fur collar. Gazing in the mirror, Karen wondered if it made her look

[7] _____. She found it quite [8] _____ that the fur was

fake. It looked so real!

Exercise B *Answer the questions with complete explanations.*

Example: Would time seem to go fast if you were doing a tedious job?
   No, a job that is tedious *would be so boring that time would drag.*

1. Name a time when you followed your <u>intuition</u>, and it turned out that you
   were right.

   _____

2. Describe one <u>solitary</u> pursuit that you enjoy.

   _____

3. What would you have to do to bring out the natural <u>sheen</u> of a pet's coat?

   _____

4. Would you be likely to be climbing mountains if you visited a <u>lowland</u>?

   _____

5. What might be the <u>resulting</u> aftermath of a tornado in your city?

   _____

6. What event do you look forward to with great <u>anticipation</u>?

   _____

7. Describe a quality or trait you have that you would like to <u>emphasize</u>.

   _____

"Checkouts" by Cynthia Rylant
"The Girl Who Can" by Ama Ata Aidoo
Reading Warm-up A

Read the following passage. Pay special attention to the underlined words. Then, read it again, and complete the activities. Use a separate sheet of paper for your written answers.

We all go to the local supermarket to buy groceries, dairy products, and household goods, all in one place. However, not all of us know the <u>fascinating</u> history of the supermarket.

The word *supermarket* was first used in the late 1920s in the United States, but early stores were nothing like today's high-volume outlets. How did we get from small general stores to mega-supermarkets where you can even have <u>photographs</u> developed? Several important developments mark this <u>transition</u>.

In 1910, the Great Atlantic and Pacific Tea Company opened the so-called economy store format. On their shelves, they placed <u>attractive</u> displays of such <u>items</u> as tea, coffee, and canned foods. This company kept its prices fairly low by selling in high volume while keeping their profits low. In addition, this company was "cash only." Over the coming years, the "cash and carry" idea grew in popularity. In recent times, of course, credit cards have become an <u>approved</u> method of payment.

Any <u>discussion</u> of the history of the supermarket must include mention of two major developments: the introduction of the motor vehicle, and the invention of the home refrigerator. Both of these products allowed people to buy large quantities of food at one time.

As "one-stop shopping" became popular, store chains began competing for customers. The competition led to lower prices.

Because customers needed space to park their cars, businesses began to locate new stores on the outskirts of town, where land was cheaper. Often, these stores sprang up <u>kilometers</u> away from the expensive downtowns.

By the 1930s, the supermarket concept had taken hold. Convenient parking, self-service, and low prices have kept shoppers flowing to these stores for more than seventy years. We can only imagine how the supermarket concept will change over the *next* seventy years!

1. Circle the word that tells what is <u>fascinating</u>. Name one topic that you find *fascinating*.

2. Underline the words that tell what can be done with <u>photographs</u> in supermarkets. Describe two of your favorite *photographs*.

3. Circle the words in the paragraph that explain the <u>transition</u> that is being discussed. Define *transition*.

4. Underline the word that tells what is <u>attractive</u>. Describe something in a store window that you would regard as *attractive*.

5. Circle the words that name <u>items</u>. Use *items* in a sentence.

6. Underline the words that tell what was <u>approved</u>. What does *approved* mean?

7. Circle the words that tell what is under <u>discussion</u>. What was the topic of a recent *discussion* you had?

8. Underline the words that explain what the stores were located <u>kilometers</u> away from. Name something that is just a few *kilometers* away from your home.

"Checkouts" by Cynthia Rylant
"The Girl Who Can" by Ama Ata Aidoo
Reading Warm-up B

Read the following passage. Pay special attention to the underlined words. Then, read it again, and complete the activities. Use a separate sheet of paper for your written answers.

Training for a marathon can be a very <u>solitary</u> pursuit. The runner must spend many hours all alone, putting one foot in front of the other for long distances. Whether training on hills or in the <u>lowland</u>, it can be a <u>tedious</u> and tiresome process.

Many people think that the greatest challenge for a marathon runner is to make it to the *finish* line. After all, 26 miles and 385 yards is a very long run! Another school of thought says that the greatest challenge for the marathon runner is to make it to the *starting* line. Training errors <u>resulting</u> in injuries often prevent runners from ever getting to compete in their chosen event.

The athlete who becomes injured during training might make any of a number of training errors. For example, some runners, in <u>anticipation</u> of success, follow the "more is better" line of thought. They build up their mileage too quickly. Soon, they suffer breakdown and injury.

Another common training error is not being consistent. Some runners miss several workouts in a row. Then, recognizing that they are behind in their training, they run too much in an effort to catch up.

Even though experts <u>emphasize</u> that consistency is important, you should not be a slave to your training schedule. You must pay attention to what your legs are communicating to you. Suppose that you usually run five or six easy miles during the middle of the week. However, on one particular Wednesday, your muscles feel fatigued or sore. Your <u>intuition</u> should tell you to take an extra day off. You can save your legs for the long weekend run. Also, remember to incorporate rest days into your training schedule prior to hard workouts such as a long run or a race.

Follow tips like these, and you just may find yourself at the finish line, showing off the <u>sheen</u> on your gold medal!

1. Underline the word that tells what is <u>solitary</u>. Use *solitary* in a sentence.

2. Circle the word that contrasts with <u>lowland</u>. Is a *lowland* likely to have mountains? Explain.

3. Underline the word that gives a hint to the meaning of <u>tedious</u>. Name an activity that you regard as *tedious*.

4. Circle the words that explain why training errors <u>resulting</u> in injuries are so annoying to runners. Use *resulting* in a sentence.

5. Why might <u>anticipation</u> of success cause injury? What does *anticipation* mean?

6. Underline the words that tell what experts <u>emphasize</u>. If you were giving training advice to a runner, what would you *emphasize*?

7. Circle the words that explain what your <u>intuition</u> should tell you. Use *intuition* in a sentence.

8. Underline the words that tell what has a <u>sheen</u>. Describe something else that might have a *sheen*.

Name _____ Date _____

Writing About the Big Question

Can truth change?

Big Question Vocabulary

assumption	belief	circumstance	context	convince
credible	distort	evidence	manipulate	perceive
perspective	skeptics	speculate	truth	verify

A. *Use one or more words from the list above to complete each sentence.*

1. Ana was so shy, she could not _____ herself to even say hello.

2. The checkout boy and the girl were _____; neither believed the other could be interested.

3. If Ned and Ana would just say "hi," they could _____ their interest in each other.

4. The girl's fear will _____ what she thinks is true as easily as a lie.

B. *Follow the directions in responding to each item below.*

1. Describe a situation in which you didn't expect much of yourself but were surprised.

   _____

   _____

2. Think about the experience you described above. How did it change what you think about yourself? Use at least two of the Big Question vocabulary words.

   _____

   _____

C. *Although the characters in the stories seem sure of certain things, when circumstances change, new possibilities—and new question—emerge. Complete the sentences below. Then, write a short paragraph in which you connect this experience to the Big Question.*

People may have assumptions about others or themselves based on _____.

Those beliefs can be changed when _____.

_____

_____

_____

"**Checkouts**" by Cynthia Rylant
"**The Girl Who Can**" by Ama Ata Aidoo
Literary Analysis: Point of View

Point of view is the perspective from which a story is narrated, or told.

- **First-person point of view:** The narrator is a character who participates in the action of the story and uses the first-person pronouns *I* and *me.*
- **Third-person point of view:** The narrator is not a character in the story but is a voice outside the action. The narrator uses the third-person pronouns *he, she, him, her, they,* and *them* to refer to all characters. There are two kinds of third-person points of view. In the **third-person omniscient** point of view, the narrator knows everything, including the thoughts and feelings of all the characters. In the **third-person limited** point of view, the narrator sees the world through a single character's eyes and reveals that character's feelings and thoughts. The narrator can describe what other characters do or say but not what they feel or think.

A story's point of view affects what readers are told and what they must figure out. It may also affect which characters they identify or sympathize with and which characters they do not.

DIRECTIONS: *To understand point of view, readers must examine its effects on the telling of the story. It is sometimes useful to consider how a different point of view would affect the telling of the story. Answer the following questions to analyze the point of view in "Checkouts" and "The Girl Who Can."*

1. In "Checkouts," imagine that the author uses the first-person point of view with the girl as narrator. Review the description of the scene in which the bag boy drops and breaks the jar of mayonnaise. How would this scene be different if it were written from the first-person point of view?

   _____

   _____

   _____

   _____

   _____

2. Suppose that "The Girl Who Can" were told in the third-person omniscient point of view. Review the final scene in the story, in which Nana carries the trophy cup home on her back. How would this scene be different if it were told in the third-person omniscient point of view?

   _____

   _____

   _____

   _____

   _____

"Checkouts" by Cynthia Rylant
"The Girl Who Can" by Ama Ata Aidoo
Vocabulary Builder

Word List

comprehension   dishevelment   fertile   humble   perverse   reverie

A. DIRECTIONS: *Revise each sentence so that the underlined vocabulary word is used logically. Be sure not to change the vocabulary word.*

1. Sunk in <u>reverie</u>, the six-year-old twins had surprised expressions on their faces.

_____

2. She brags endlessly about her accomplishments in a <u>humble</u> manner.

_____

3. Hours of careful grooming resulted in Sam's state of <u>dishevelment</u> at the party.

_____

4. May's sister took a <u>perverse</u> pleasure in making her laugh.

_____

5. The soil is so extremely <u>fertile</u> that nothing can be grown in it.

_____

B. DIRECTIONS: *Answer the following questions in the space provided.*

1. How would a person with a <u>humble</u> attitude behave?

_____

_____

2. Describe the appearance of a <u>fertile</u> piece of land.

_____

_____

3. How would you feel if you were sure of your <u>comprehension</u> of a complex topic?

_____

_____

Name _____ Date _____

"Checkouts" by Cynthia Rylant
"The Girl Who Can" by Ama Ata Aidoo
Writing to Compare Literary Works

Use a chart like the one below to make prewriting notes for your essay of comparison and contrast.

Points of Comparison/Contrast	"Checkouts"	"The Girl Who Can"
Who is the narrator in each story?	_____ _____	_____ _____
What is the point of view?	_____ _____	_____ _____
What do we learn of the thoughts and feelings of the girl and of Adjoa?	_____ _____ _____ _____ _____ _____ _____	_____ _____ _____ _____ _____ _____ _____
How do other characters react to the girl and Adjoa?	_____ _____ _____ _____ _____ _____ _____ _____	_____ _____ _____ _____ _____ _____ _____ _____

Name _____ Date _____

"Checkouts" by Cynthia Rylant
"The Girl Who Can" by Ama Ata Aidoo
Open-Book Test

Short Answer *Write your responses to the questions in this section on the lines provided.*

1. At the beginning of "Checkouts," how does the girl feel about her family's move to Cincinnati? Why? Provide a detail from the story that shows the girl's feelings.

   _____

   _____

   _____

2. Reread the paragraph in "Checkouts" beginning "And when finally . . ." Use the following chart to compare the boy's and girls' actions with what you or someone you know might do in the same situation. Then explain your opinion of the characters' behavior.

Boy's Behavior	Girl's Behavior	My Behavior

   _____

   _____

3. An omniscient narrator knows the inner thoughts and feelings of all the characters in a story. Provide two details from "Checkouts" that show that its narrator is omniscient.

   _____

   _____

   _____

   _____

4. In "The Girl Who Can," how does Nana view women and their role in the world? Give an example from the story to support your response.

   _____

   _____

   _____

   _____

5. In spite of Nana's strong opinions, Adjoa loves her grandmother. Give one detail or quotation from "The Girl Who Can" that reflects this feeling.

_____

_____

6. At the end of "The Girl Who Can," does Nana feel that Adjoa's legs are perverse? Explain your answer based on the definition of *perverse*.

_____

_____

7. Identify the point of view from which "Checkouts" is told, and the point of view from which "The Girl Who Can" is told. How do the pronouns in each story help you identify its point of view?

_____

_____

_____

8. In "Checkouts," the omniscient narrator lets us know what the bag boy thinks and feels. How do we learn about Nana's thoughts and feelings in "The Girl Who Can"? Give an example from the story.

_____

_____

_____

9. In which story do you feel that you get to know the main character best: in "Checkouts," or in "The Girl Who Can"? Explain.

_____

_____

_____

10. Both the girl in "Checkouts" and Adjoa in "The Girl Who Can" view adults in similar ways. Explain, giving examples from each story to support your ideas.

_____

_____

_____

Unit 1 Resources: Fiction and Nonfiction
117

Essay

Write an extended response to the question of your choice or to the question or questions your teacher assigns you.

11. Imagine that it is twenty years in the future. Both the girl in "Checkouts" and Adjoa in "The Girl Who Can" are adults. Given what you know about the girls' childhoods, what will their adult lives be like? Where will each woman have made her home? Will she have a family? What kind of work will she do? Write an essay in which you describe each woman's future life.

12. Choose either "Checkouts" or "The Girl Who Can," and change its point of view. You may either change the point of view completely, or you may substitute a different character as first-person narrator. In an essay, describe the new point of view, and then explain how you think this new point of view would change the story. Finally, decide whether you prefer the story with its original point of view or with the new one, and explain why.

13. Both the girl in "Checkouts" and Adjoa in "The Girl Who Can" pursue a challenging goal. In an essay, identify each girl's goal, and explain whether each girl succeeds in reaching it. What do you think accounts for each girl's success or failure? Consider the girls' personality traits, their living situations, and their relationships with other characters.

14. **Thinking About the Big Question: Can truth change?** What truth changes for Nana in "The Girl Who Can"? How might this change cause Nana to see *all* people differently? Explain in a short essay.

Oral Response

15. Go back to question 3, 8, or 9 or to the question your teacher assigns to you. Take a few minutes to expand your answer and prepare an oral response. Find additional details in "Checkouts," "The Girl Who Can," or both selections (depending on the question) that will support your points. If necessary, make notes to guide your response.

"Checkouts" by Cynthia Rylant
"The Girl Who Can" by Ama Ata Aidoo
Selection Test A

Critical Reading *Identify the letter of the choice that best answers the question.*

____ 1. At the beginning of "Checkouts," why is the girl unhappy?
  A. She has lost her job.
  B. She has lost her boyfriend.
  C. Her parents have punished her.
  D. Her parents have forced her to move.

____ 2. Which of the following literary elements identifies the perspective from which a story is told?
  A. point of view
  B. character
  C. plot
  D. setting

____ 3. In "Checkouts," why does the girl like to shop for groceries?
  A. She hopes to meet someone at the supermarket.
  B. She loves to get bargains.
  C. She wants to be alone with her thoughts.
  D. She wants to help her parents.

____ 4. In "Checkouts," Cynthia Rylant uses third-person omniscient point of view. Which of the following accurately identifies this point of view?
  A. The reader learns about the thoughts and feelings of only one character.
  B. The reader can learn about the inner thoughts and feelings of all the major characters.
  C. The narrator is an important character in the story.
  D. The narrator uses first-person pronouns such as *I, me,* and *my.*

____ 5. In Cynthia Rylant's story, why do the bag boy and the girl not speak to each other when they meet a second time?
  A. She is angry with him.
  B. She has lost interest in him.
  C. He has lost interest in her.
  D. People do not always act on their desires.

_____ 6. What is the setting of "The Girl Who Can"?
   A. Africa   C. Australia
   B. South America   D. Asia

_____ 7. Who is the narrator of "The Girl Who Can"?
   A. a seven-year-old girl
   B. a young mother
   C. a villager who is a minor character in the story
   D. a person outside the story

_____ 8. Why does the grandmother criticize Adjoa's legs in "The Girl Who Can"?
   A. She thinks they are too fat.
   B. She thinks Adjoa may have a serious illness.
   C. She thinks the girl's legs are too spindly.
   D. She thinks Adjoa should walk more gracefully.

_____ 9. At the beginning of "The Girl Who Can," what does Nana think of the village school?
   A. It is a waste of time.
   B. It is very important.
   C. The school should hire a better teacher.
   D. Only bright children should attend school.

_____ 10. In "The Girl Who Can," how does Nana change at the end of the story?
   A. Nana admits that Adjoa's legs may be useful after all.
   B. Nana quarrels with the schoolteacher.
   C. Nana stops criticizing Adjoa's father.
   D. Nana never goes outside of her home.

_____ 11. Which of the following do "Checkouts" and "The Girl Who Can" have in common?
   A. They are both tragic stories.
   B. Both stories take place in the countryside.
   C. Young people are major characters in both stories.
   D. Both stories use flashback.

_____ 12. In which story (or stories) does the writer's choice of point of view allow the
   reader to learn the main character's thoughts and feelings?
   A. in "Checkouts"
   B. in "The Girl Who Can"
   C. in both of the stories
   D. in neither of the stories

Name _____ Date _____

Vocabulary

____ 13. When she is in the supermarket, the girl in "Checkouts" is lost in a <u>reverie</u>.
How would you describe the way she looks?
A. neat   C. angry
B. confused   D. dreamy

____ 14. The soil near the river delta is very <u>fertile</u>. Which of the following words would
you use to describe the soil?
A. muddy   C. rocky
B. productive   D. dry

____ 15. In "Checkouts," the girl is attracted by the bag boy's <u>dishevelment</u>. Which of the
following is an antonym (a word that means the opposite) of *dishevelment*?
A. messiness   C. gracefulness
B. tidiness   D. clumsiness

Essay

16. "Checkouts" and "The Girl Who Can" reveal important differences between the effects
of a writer's choice of point of view. Consider these sentences from the stories:

> I knew from her voice that my mother was weeping inside.—"The Girl Who Can"
> He believed he must have looked the fool in her eyes.—"Checkouts"

In an essay, identify the point of view of each story. Which point of view lets the
reader know more about the main character? Which point of view allows the reader
to know more about all of the characters? Use examples from the stories to support
your views.

17. In an essay, compare and contrast the main character of "Checkouts" and of "The
Girl Who Can." How would you describe each of these characters, and how do the
authors reveal their characteristics? Does the author describe them directly, or do
we learn about them from their actions, thoughts, and words? Consider also how
the author's choice of point of view affects what the reader can know about each
character.

18. **Thinking About the Big Question: Can truth change?** At first, the character Nana
in "The Girl Who Can" believes women should have thick, sturdy legs and solid hips
to support the weight of pregnancy. How does this truth about women's legs change
for Nana by the end of the story? How might this change cause Nana to see all people differently? Answer these questions in a short essay.

"**Checkouts**" by Cynthia Rylant
"**The Girl Who Can**" by Ama Ata Aidoo
Selection Test B

Critical Reading *Identify the letter of the choice that best completes the statement or answers the question.*

_____ 1. When "Checkouts" opens, the girl is wretchedly unhappy because
   A. she has been fired from her part-time job.
   B. she has broken up with her boyfriend.
   C. her parents confine her to the house.
   D. her parents have forced her to move.

_____ 2. The perspective from which a story is narrated is called its
   A. point of view.
   B. atmosphere.
   C. metaphor.
   D. characterization.

_____ 3. When the narrator of "Checkouts" says, "But it is difficult work, suffering, and in its own way a kind of art," she means that the girl is
   A. becoming ill after the move.
   B. trying to adjust but failing.
   C. exaggerating her grief.
   D. hoping to become an artist.

_____ 4. The girl in "Checkouts" likes to shop for groceries because
   A. she can be relaxed and just let her mind wander.
   B. she hopes to meet a new friend in the grocery store.
   C. she sincerely enjoys helping her parents.
   D. she wants to make her parents regret their decision.

_____ 5. When the narrator of "Checkouts" says that the girl feels it is not safe for her parents to share "such strong, important facts about herself," she means that
   A. the girl's parents do not care about their daughter.
   B. the girl feels that her parents would not understand her.
   C. the girl feels that her parents might stop her from going to the supermarket.
   D. the girl's parents are totally unaware of the dangers of the new city.

_____ 6. Which point of view does Cynthia Rylant use in "Checkouts"?
   A. first-person
   B. third-person limited
   C. third-person omniscient
   D. objective

_____ 7. When the bag boy and the girl in Rylant's story meet again, they do not speak. Why not?
   A. She is furious with him for not having called.
   B. People sometimes do not act on their desires.
   C. They decide that they dislike each other intensely.
   D. They realize that a relationship between them will not work.

____ 8. In "The Girl Who Can," which of the following is the setting?
A. a large city in South America
B. a tropical rainforest
C. a large village in Ghana, Africa
D. a city in South Africa

____ 9. Which point of view does the author use in "The Girl Who Can"?
A. first-person
B. third-person limited
C. third-person omniscient
D. objective

____ 10. Which of the following identifies Nana in "The Girl Who Can"?
A. the narrator's mother
B. the narrator's older sister
C. the narrator's grandmother
D. the teacher at school

____ 11. From her comments about Adjoa's legs, you can infer that the grandmother is very
A. shy.
B. traditional.
C. liberal.
D. nearsighted.

____ 12. According to the narrator, what does Nana think about school for Adjoa?
A. School is a waste of Adjoa's time.
B. School is extremely important for everyone.
C. The teaching standards in Adjoa's school should be improved.
D. School costs the parents too much.

____ 13. The ending of "The Girl Who Can" is ironic because
A. Nana changes her opinions about Adjoa's legs.
B. Adjoa's mother appreciates the school better.
C. Adjoa wins a trophy as the best all-around athlete.
D. Adjoa finally understands the ways of adults.

____ 14. In which story (or stories) does the point of view enable the narrator to reveal the thoughts and feelings of all of the major characters?
A. in "Checkouts"
B. in "The Girl Who Can"
C. in both stories
D. in neither story

____ 15. Which of the following statements BEST contrasts "Checkouts" with "The Girl Who Can"?
A. The two stories have sharply different moods.
B. One story has a child as narrator; the other has an omniscient narrator.
C. The writer's style in "The Girl Who Can" is more formal than that of "Checkouts."
D. "Checkouts" is a comic story; "The Girl Who Can" is tragic.

_____ 16. In "Checkouts," Rylant's choice of point of view lets us know what the bag boy thinks and feels. How do we learn about Nana's thoughts and feelings in "The Girl Who Can"?
   A. directly from the omniscient narrator
   B. directly from Nana as first-person narrator
   C. indirectly through Nana's actions and words
   D. indirectly through a description of her physical appearance

_____ 17. In which story (or stories) does the main character pursue a challenging goal and achieve a great triumph?
   A. in "Checkouts"
   B. in "The Girl Who Can"
   C. in both stories
   D. in neither story

Vocabulary

_____ 18. Which word describes how the girl in "Checkouts" looks when she is lost in a reverie?
   A. tidy   C. dismal
   B. dreamy   D. animated

_____ 19. The village in "The Girl Who Can" is in very fertile lowland. Fertile soil is best described as
   A. arid.   C. rocky.
   B. productive.   D. eroded.

_____ 20. If your actions appear perverse to others, how might they react to you?
   A. critically   C. indifferently
   B. admiringly   D. humorously

Essay

21. Choose one of the stories ("Checkouts" or "The Girl Who Can") and change its point of view. Either change the point of view completely or substitute a different character as first-person narrator. Write an essay in which you speculate on how the story would change; give three examples. Then, decide whether you prefer the story with its different point of view or whether you prefer the point of view the author chose. Explain why.

22. Cynthia Rylant and Ama Ata Aidoo use very different perspectives, or points of view, to tell their stories. In an essay, analyze how the authors' choice of point of view is closely linked to the total effect in the stories. Identify each story's point of view and then tell its effect. Give examples from the stories to support your points.

23. **Thinking About the Big Question: Can truth change?** What truth changes for Nana in "The Girl Who Can"? How might this change cause Nana to see *all* people differently? Explain in a short essay.

Name _____ Date _____

Narration: Autobiographical Narrative

Prewriting: Gathering Details

Create a timeline to record the detailed events of your narrative by writing down the first incident related to your subject and recording subsequent incidents in the order in which they occurred.

Event 1	Event 2	Event 3	Event 4	Event 5	Event 6

Drafting: Providing Elaboration

Use the chart to write your responses to the questions. Include vivid details that show readers what happened in your narrative and how you felt.

Questions:	Your Response:
What specific details can you add about the place where your narrative occurs?	
What clear descriptions can you provide about the people in your narrative?	
What descriptions can you include about the events occurring in your narrative?	
What personal thoughts can you add about the events in your narrative?	

Writing Workshop
Possessive Nouns: Integrating Grammar Skills

Revising to Correct Use of Possessive Nouns

Possessive nouns show ownership or belonging. They are used to modify other nouns and function as adjectives in sentences. Follow these rules to form possessive nouns:

For most nouns, add an apostrophe and *s*.	the pen of my aunt ⟶ my *aunt's* pen
If the singular noun ends in *s*, add an apostrophe and *s* if the new word is easy to pronounce. However, if it is hard to pronounce, you can add just an apostrophe.	the scowl of his boss ⟶ his *boss's* scowl the house of Mrs. Jenkins ⟶ Mrs. *Jenkins'* house
For plural nouns that already end in *s*, add just an apostrophe.	the pencils of the students ⟶ the *students'* pencils
For plural nouns that do not end in *s*, add an apostrophe and *s*.	the dresses of the women ⟶ the *women's* dresses
For singular or plural compound nouns that already end in *s*, add just an apostrophe to the last word.	the family crest of the Earl of Ross ⟶ the *Earl of Ross'* family crest

Identifying Correct Possessive Nouns

A. DIRECTIONS: *Circle the correct form of the noun in parentheses.*

1. (Parsons'; Parsonses) brother-in-law drove to Los Angeles.
2. He was going to see the (men's; mens') basketball team, the Lakers.
3. (Los Angeles'; Los Angeles's) traffic jams can be very bad.
4. Her (brother-in-law's; brother's-in-law) trip was a slow one.

Fixing Incorrect Possessive Nouns

B. DIRECTIONS: *On the lines provided, rewrite these sentences so that they use correct possessive nouns. If a sentence is correct as presented, write* correct.

1. Years ago, I read a childrens' book about the worlds' mysteries.

   _____

2. The books first chapter was about Loch Ness's famous monster.

   _____

3. Another chapter's pages were devoted to legends of Bigfoot.

   _____

4. The two monsters origin's are a mystery.

   _____

126

Unit 1: Fiction and Nonfiction
Benchmark Test 1

Literary Analysis: Plot *Read the selection. Then, answer the questions that follow.*

I smiled to myself as I remembered the game that made me a star ten years ago . . . The rain was pouring down as I stepped out onto the football field. It was the last game of the season, and we had yet to lose a game. Today might be different. We were playing the state champions, and they were undefeated. I took a deep breath and fastened my helmet. The game was about to begin.

1. What is the conflict in this selection?
   A. It is the last game of the season.
   B. The team has won all its games.
   C. The weather is rainy.
   D. The team is playing the state champions.

2. Which of the following details foreshadows the outcome of the game?
   A. The team is undefeated.
   B. The team is playing the state champions.
   C. It is raining.
   D. The game made the narrator a star.

3. Which of the following describes a possible resolution to the conflict in the selection?
   A. The game begins.
   B. The best player on the narrator's team injures himself.
   C. The opposing team take the lead.
   D. The narrator's team wins the game.

4. What is the most accurate description of this part of the selection?
   A. climax   B. rising action   C. falling action   D. resolution

Literary Analysis: Narrative Essay and Significant Details *Read the selection. Then, answer the questions that follow.*

I had only been out of school for two years when I was asked to teach in a small rural school. I had no experience with small children and was apprehensive about taking the job. After I arrived on that first day so many years ago, I knew I had found my calling.

5. Which detail lets the reader know that the writer enjoyed teaching?
   A. The writer was comfortable around children.
   B. The writer has no experience.
   C. The writer refers to teaching as his calling.
   D. The writer was young.

6. Which detail from the selection best demonstrates that the author is not elderly when he arrives at the school?
   A. The author was a recent graduate.
   B. The author could drive a car.
   C. The author lived in a rural area.
   D. The author was a teacher.

7. What does the detail about the writer's lack of experience suggest about the selection?
   A. The writer will describe his own education.
   B. The writer will describe the early teaching experiences that showed him he loved teaching.
   C. The writer will describe his difficulties finding a teaching job.
   D. The writer will explain how he came to be fired from his teaching job.

8. Which of the following would indicate that this selection is from a narrative essay?
   A. It reports facts about history.
   B. It offers information.
   C. It is a work of fiction.
   D. It tells a true story.

Literary Analysis: Point of View *Read the selection. Then, answer the questions that follow.*

Sam gripped the branch tighter. If he could just build up enough momentum, he should be able to pole vault over the fence. Sweat trickled down his forehead. He wondered what further obstacles Richards had planted on the other side. He crouched, planted his right foot in the dirt behind him, and was about to sprint forward when a voice rang out behind him. "Going somewhere, Mr. Smith?" Sam gasped. It was Richards.

9. From which point of view is the passage written?
   A. first person
   B. third person omniscient
   C. third person limited
   D. second person

10. As the story develops, which character's thoughts will readers learn *only* if the character reveals them to another character?
    A. Sam's   B. Richards's   C. the narrator's   D. all characters'

11. From which point of view would readers likely learn the most about Richards's thoughts and actions?
    A. first person, told from Sam's point of view
    B. third person limited, with Sam as the main character
    C. third person omniscient
    D. second person, with Sam as the main character

12. What might the point of view used in the selection add to the story?
    A. suspense about what Richards will do next
    B. interesting details about pole vaulting
    C. suspense about what Sam will do next
    D. a summary of all events in the story

Reading Skill: Make Predictions

13. Why is it important to continue to read after making a prediction?
    A. to make another prediction
    B. to check the prediction
    C. to finish the story
    D. to identify the characters

Read the selection. Then, answer the questions that follow.

One sunny afternoon, a young boy walked in the canyon near his home. As he walked, he dreamed of a time when he would be old enough to go with his father to hunt and tame the beautiful horses that roamed the canyon. He loved being with his father and very much wanted to experience the hunt. Deep in thought, the boy wandered into the canyon and farther away from his home. It was beginning to get dark when the boy realized he was lost.

14. After the boy realizes he is lost, what is he most likely to do next?
    A. continue walking into the canyons
    B. climb into a nearby cave
    C. begin to look for the horses
    D. retrace his steps out of the canyon

15. Why does the author mention the horse hunt?
    A. The hunt will probably play a part later in the story.
    B. The author enjoys writing about horses.
    C. Many readers will be interested in learning about a horse hunt.
    D. More details make selections interesting.

16. Which question could readers ask that they could answer by reading on?
    A. Why did the author write about this young boy?
    B. Will the young boy find his way home?
    C. Why was the young boy so absentminded?
    D. Will the horses escape?

17. When the boy fails to return home on time, what will most likely happen?
    A. His father will look for him.
    B. His mother will make a bed for him.
    C. His father will hunt without him.
    D. His mother will prepare a meal.

Informational Texts: Read to Perform a Task *Read the selection. Then, answer the questions that follow.*

How To Fry an Egg

First, place the skillet on the stovetop. Turn the heat on medium and place a teaspoon of butter in the skillet. Let the butter slowly melt. Be careful not to burn it. Next, take an egg from the refrigerator. Tap the egg gently on the side of the skillet. When the egg cracks, pry it apart with your thumbs and place the egg in the skillet. Throw the shells away. Then, cook the egg until it is done on one side. Flip it with a spatula. Continue to cook the egg until it is done. Finally, you have an egg for breakfast!

18. After the heat is turned on under the skillet, what should you do next?
    A. Get the egg from the refrigerator.
    B. Crack the egg on the skillet.
    C. Place butter in the skillet.
    D. Wait for the butter to melt.

19. Which of the following words from the selection signals a significant detail?
    A. let   B. medium   C. refrigerator   D. breakfast

20. How many separate steps does frying an egg require?
    A. 2   B. 6   C. 8   D. 12

21. After you crack the egg, what is your next task?
    A. Throw the shells away.
    B. Put the egg in the skillet.
    C. Turn the stove on low.
    D. Flip it with a spatula.

Vocabulary: Prefixes and Suffixes

22. The prefix *fore-* means "come before." Using this knowledge, what is the meaning of the word *forebears*?
    A. old friends   B. ancestors   C. descendants   D. offspring

23. In the following sentence, what is the meaning of the word *conceded*?

    The timer had run out before Marc could shoot the basket—he conceded the loss to Pat.

    A. acknowledged
    B. refused
    C. argued
    D. regretted

24. What is the meaning of the word formed by adding *con-* to *-current*?
    A. at odds
    B. occurring at the same location
    C. occurring at the same time
    D. in order

25. The suffix *-tion* is used to form nouns from verbs. Which of the following answer choices means "a sudden or radical change"?
    A. retribution
    B. condemnation
    C. revocation
    D. revolution

26. In the following sentence what is the meaning of the word *reciprocate*?

    Every year Jim mails holiday cards to all of his friends even though they don't always reciprocate.

    A. say "thank you"
    B. give in return
    C. read them
    D. buy him a gift

27. Which of the following answer choices **does not** indicate a position or title?
    A. magistrate
    B. consulate
    C. electorate
    D. agitate

Grammar: Nouns

28. How many common nouns are in this sentence?

    "Spring flowers are the prettiest," said Anna to Jen, her best friend. "Crocus, tulips, daffodils, hyacinths: I love them all."

    A. 3
    B. 4
    C. 5
    D. 6

29. Which of the following sentences contains two proper nouns?
    A. The boy went to the backyard to play ball.
    B. The train ran from San Francisco to Los Angeles each afternoon.
    C. The bus ran between the suburbs and Cleveland.
    D. The school was named after Mr. Washington.

30. How does a proper noun differ from a common noun?
    A. A proper noun is more formal than a common noun.
    B. A common noun may be someone's name, but a proper noun may not.
    C. A proper noun is harder to spell than a common noun is.
    D. A proper noun is the name of an individual person, place, or thing.

31. Which one of the following nouns is a concrete noun?
    A. patience
    B. pleasure
    C. pride
    D. petunia

32. Which one of the following nouns is an abstract noun?
    A. confidence
    B. confetti
    C. formula
    D. cannibal

33. Which of the following nouns is a concrete noun?
    A. cloud
    B. preference
    C. skill
    D. attitude

34. Which of the following possessive nouns is written correctly?
    A. workers
    B. worker's
    C. workeres
    D. worker'es

35. How do possessive nouns function in sentences?
    A. as nouns
    B. as verbs
    C. as adjectives
    D. as adverbs

36. Which of the following possessive nouns is written correctly?
    A. pitchers
    B. pitcher's
    C. pitcher'es
    D. pitche'rs

ESSAY

Writing

37. Write a brief anecdote in which a character causes trouble by saying the wrong thing at the wrong time—or to the wrong person. Clearly describe the conflicts that result. Narrate the events that lead to the resolution of the conflicts in a logical order.

38. Choose a work of literature that you read recently that had some weaknesses: for example, uninteresting characters or situations, a predictable plot, or dull dialogue. Write a brief critique of the work. Provide enough background information so that readers who have not read the work will be able to understand your points. Support each point you make with examples from the work.

39. Think about one skill that you learned or a task you completed in the last year. Write a brief autobiographical narrative that traces the way in which you learned the skill or mastered the task.

Name _____

Unit 1: Fiction and Nonfiction Skills Concept Map—2
Can truth change?

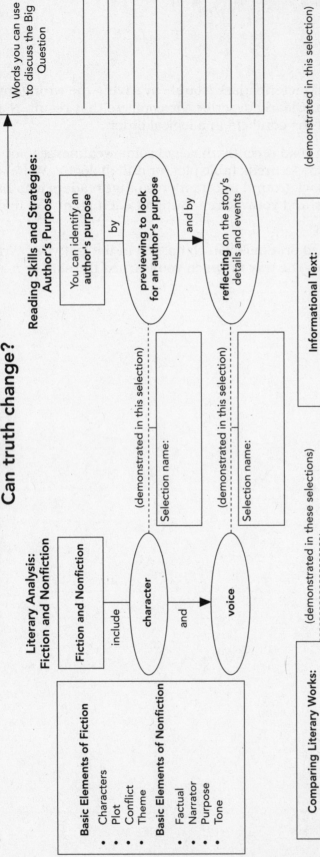

Literary Analysis:
Fiction and Nonfiction

Fiction and Nonfiction

include

character

and

voice

(demonstrated in this selection)
Selection name:

(demonstrated in this selection)
Selection name:

Basic Elements of Fiction

- Characters
- Plot
- Conflict
- Theme

Basic Elements of Nonfiction

- Factual
- Narrator
- Purpose
- Tone

Reading Skills and Strategies:
Author's Purpose

You can identify an author's purpose

by

previewing to look for an author's purpose

and by

reflecting on the story's details and events

(demonstrated in this selection)
Selection name:

Informational Text:
Train Schedule

You can examine how information is organized and presented

by

analyzing structure and format

Comparing Literary Works:
Theme

developed through

nonfiction

fiction and poetry

(demonstrated in these selections)
Selection names:

1.
2.

Words you can use to discuss the Big Question

_____
_____
_____
_____
_____

Student Log

Complete this chart to track your assignments.

Writing	Extend Your Learning	Writing Workshop	Other Assignments

Vocabulary Warm-up Word Lists

Study these words from A White House Diary. *Then, complete the activities.*

Word List A

compassion [kuhm PASH uhn] *n.* sympathy
People who give money to fight diseases are often motivated by compassion.

composed [kuhm POHZD] *adj.* calm and in control
When Carmen won first prize, she looked composed, but inside she was screaming for joy.

departure [di PAHRT cher] *n.* act of leaving or going away
Our departure from home was delayed when the car would not start.

dignified [DIG nuh fyd] *adj.* showing honorable or proper behavior
People expect the President to be dignified and not to act silly.

element [EL uh muhnt] *n.* basic part or quality of something
January always has an element of excitement that comes with the start of a new year.

enormity [i NAWR muh tee] *n.* great importance or impact
After the war, the enormity of the destruction was everywhere.

federal [FED ur uhl] *adj.* having to do with the U.S. government
The FBI is a federal agency that can hunt criminals anywhere in America.

rapid [RAP id] *adj.* very fast
After the operation, he made a rapid recovery and was back in school in no time.

Word List B

agonizing [AG uh nyz ing] *adj.* extremely painful or difficult
Mark was so shy that asking Kellie to the dance was agonizing.

aide [AYD] *n.* helper or assistant
Jasmin is an aide in a hospital, where she helps the nurses care for patients.

assassin [uh SAS uhn] *n.* killer of an important or a famous person
John Wilkes Booth was the assassin who shot President Abraham Lincoln.

desolate [DES uh luht] *adj.* deeply sad and lonely
After her mother died, a desolate Amanda needed her friends' support and help.

insulated [IN suh lay tid] *v.* protected
When I am wearing a down jacket, I am insulated against the cold.

onward [AHN werd] *adv.* moving or directed forward
Ryan was pushed onward by the fear of being lost in the forest overnight.

presidential [prez uh DEN chuhl] *adj.* having to do with the president
The presidential helicopter is the only one that lands on the White House lawn.

succession [suhk SE shuhn] *n.* persons or things that follow one after the other
Two Presidents in succession, Bill Clinton then George W. Bush, were southern governors.

Name _____ Date _____

from **A White House Diary** by Lady Bird Johnson
Vocabulary Warm-up Exercises

Exercise A *Fill in each blank in the paragraph below with an appropriate word from Word List A. Use each word only once.*

It was hard for Nate to stay [1] _____ as he thought about how he had
missed the game. He had planned his [2] _____ from home so he would
have plenty of time to get to school. Then, his neighbor's dog was hit by a U.S. mail
truck, and Nate had too much [3] _____ not to help. His neighbor,
Mrs. Tate, was usually very [4] _____, but there she was, screaming that
the [5] _____ government would hear about it if her dog was hurt. As
they drove to the animal hospital, Nate could feel the [6] _____ heartbeat of the dog. He felt an [7] _____ of frustration knowing that he would
never make the game. Yet, when they were told the dog was okay, seeing Mrs. Tate's joy
made him recognize the [8] _____ of the accident for her. The game was
not that important after all!

Exercise B *Answer the questions with complete explanations.*

Example: If someone is <u>insulated</u> from poverty, is that person more likely to be rich or
poor? Why?
   The person is more likely to be rich because insulated *means "protected." If that person is protected against being poor, he or she likely has money.*

1. What kind of work would you expect a <u>presidential aide</u> to do?
   _____

2. Would an <u>agonizing</u> problem be an easy one to solve? Why or why not?
   _____

3. If a friend told you she was <u>desolate</u>, what could you do to help?
   _____

4. What might you see in <u>succession</u> at a parade? Explain.
   _____

5. If you are asked to move <u>onward</u> to a seat, are the seats in front of you or behind
   you? Explain.
   _____

6. If you watched a news report about a hunt for an <u>assassin</u>, what would this mean?
   _____

from **A White House Diary** by Lady Bird Johnson
Reading Warm-up A

Read the following passage. Pay special attention to the underlined words. Then, read it again, and complete the activities. Use a separate sheet of paper for your written answers.

Many older adults still remember the day when President Kennedy was assassinated. This act of violence came as a great shock to the nation. The <u>rapid</u> response of Americans showed the country's quick unity in grief. People cried in their homes and on the streets. Work stopped in many office buildings. It was even hard for reporters to be calm and <u>composed</u> when they had to announce that the President was dead.

Everyone felt <u>compassion</u> for the President's wife, Jacqueline, and for their children, Caroline and John Jr. Jacqueline Kennedy was a popular First Lady, and the children, both very young, were much beloved. She had seen her husband killed, and the children would grow up without their father.

Nevertheless, Jacqueline Kennedy gave the country strength, and her <u>dignified</u> behavior inspired respect. If she could behave well at such a time, people wanted to do the same.

Mrs. Kennedy also gave the President's funeral an <u>element</u> of history by following traditions from Abraham Lincoln's funeral. In the White House, President Kennedy's casket sat on the same catafalque, or raised platform, that had been used for Lincoln's, nearly a century before.

People remember the day that President Kennedy was buried. When the President's coffin made its <u>departure</u> from the White House, it was carried on a horse-drawn wagon called a caisson. There was also a riderless horse, representing the fallen leader. Young John, just three years old, saluted the coffin as it rolled slowly by. For many people, that simple moment captured the <u>enormity</u> of the tragedy and the country's sorrow.

Each year on November 22, countless individuals remember the death of President John F. Kennedy. It is not a federal holiday on which Americans get off from school and work. Rather, they remember because John Kennedy, a young and promising leader, was one of only four U.S. Presidents ever to be killed in office.

1. Underline a synonym for <u>rapid</u>. Describe a situation that would demand a *rapid* response.

2. Circle the word that is a clue to the meaning of <u>composed</u>. Describe how someone acts when he or she is *composed*.

3. Underline two reasons why people felt <u>compassion</u> for Jacqueline Kennedy and her children. Give a synonym for *compassion*.

4. Underline the sentence that tells the impact of Mrs. Kennedy's <u>dignified</u> behavior. Write what *dignified* means.

5. How did Mrs. Kennedy bring an <u>element</u> of history to her husband's funeral? Give a synonym for *element*.

6. Circle the words that tell from where the President's coffin made its <u>departure</u>. Give an antonym for *departure*.

7. Circle the words that are clues to the meaning of <u>enormity</u>. What other event might have *enormity*?

8. Underline two aspects of a <u>federal</u> holiday. Name two *federal* holidays that your school observes.

from **A White House Diary** by Lady Bird Johnson
Reading Warm-up B

Read the following passage. Pay special attention to the underlined words. Then, read it again, and complete the activities. Use a separate sheet of paper for your written answers.

John Kennedy was the last U.S. President to die in office. Yet, over the course of <u>presidential</u> history, there had been seven instances before 1963 when America had mourned a sitting President. The first was William Henry Harrison who, in 1841, after delivering a lengthy inaugural address in inclement weather, developed pneumonia and died. The next was Zachary Taylor, who took ill after attending a dedication ceremony for the new Washington Monument in 1850. He succumbed to typhoid fever. Two other Presidents died of natural causes: Warren Harding, of a heart attack, in 1923; and Franklin Roosevelt, of a cerebral hemorrhage, or stroke, in 1945.

Naturally, the nation grieved for each fallen leader. However, it was after the assassination of Abraham Lincoln, in 1865, that Americans first experienced the <u>agonizing</u> ordeal of having a President brutally murdered. Lincoln's death only days after the surrender that ended the Civil War must have been extraordinarily painful. Just when it seemed that the nightmare of blood and sacrifice was over, more sorrow was created by the gun of Lincoln's <u>assassin</u>, southern sympathizer John Wilkes Booth.

Appallingly, two more Presidents were shot and killed in less than 40 years: James Garfield in 1881 and William McKinley in 1901. Consider how <u>desolate</u> some Americans may have felt then. In their deep sadness, people must have questioned if there was hope for America.

Fortunately, the country's Presidents have always taken office in unbroken <u>succession</u>, without a hitch. When a chief executive dies, the Vice President is immediately sworn in and the nation pushes forward, moving <u>onward</u> with a new leader who sets new goals to meet.

Nonetheless, today it strains the imagination to think of a President riding in an open car, as Kennedy was when he was shot. The President is more <u>insulated</u> now, the protective bubble harder to break. The Secret Service agents are ever watchful. The President's staff, including every <u>aide</u>, is vigilant, too.

1. Underline an example of "<u>presidential</u> history" from paragraph 1. Write what *presidential* means.

2. Underline the words that explain what <u>agonizing</u> means. What is *agonizing* about an assassination?

3. Explain what John Wilkes Booth did and why. Give a synonym for *assassin*.

4. Underline the sentence that tells the meaning of <u>desolate</u>. Give reasons from the passage telling why people were *desolate*.

5. Circle the word that gives a clue to the meaning of <u>succession</u>. Explain something you do in *succession* every day.

6. Explain how the nation moves <u>onward</u> after a President's death.

7. Underline an example that shows the opposite of a President's being <u>insulated</u>, and explain why.

8. Based on the passage, where would you find a person who was an <u>aide</u> to the President?

from **The White House Diary** by Lady Bird Johnson
Writing About the Big Question

Can truth change?

Big Question Vocabulary

assumption	belief	circumstance	context	convince
credible	distort	evidence	manipulate	perceive
perspective	skeptics	speculate	truth	verify

A. *Use one or more words from the list above to complete each sentence.*

1. Lady Bird Johnson's _____ as the vice-president's wife gave her a unique _____ into events.

2. Did her personal account of the experience _____ your understanding of events or _____ it?

3. For many people, time changes what we _____ to be true.

4. The role someone like Lady Bird Johnson has in an event can make the stories more or less _____ .

B. *Follow the directions in responding to each of the items below.*

1. Describe an experience in which you were surprised by a sudden, unexpected event.
   _____
   _____

2. In two sentences, tell how your reaction to this experience changed over time. Use at least two of the Big Question vocabulary words.
   _____
   _____

C. *Complete the sentence below. Then, write a short paragraph in which you connect this experience to the Big Question.*

In this passage from *A White House Diary*, Lady Bird Johnson recalls details about the day President John F. Kennedy was assassinated. Complete this sentence:

Abrupt changes in circumstances can _____.

_____
_____
_____

Name _____ Date _____

from **A White House Diary** by Lady Bird Johnson
Literary Analysis: Autobiographical Writing and Author's Voice

Voice is the way a writer sounds on the page. For example, the writer's voice in a work can be *smooth and sophisticated, choppy and blunt,* or *breathless and full of wonder.* Voice is a result of several elements:

- *word choice:* the kinds of words the writer uses
- *attitude:* the way the writer feels about his or her subject
- *sentence length and structure:* the arrangement of words and ideas in sentences

In **autobiographical writing,** the author tells all or part of his or her own life story. The kinds of details that are included show what the writer notices, thinks, and feels about events. The voice of autobiographical writing usually reflects the writer's own personality and way of speaking.

In the following excerpt from *A White House Diary,* notice the words that seem to reveal feeling, and think about what they say about Mrs. Johnson's attitude toward her subject.

> It's odd the little things that come to your mind at times of utmost stress, the flashes of deep compassion you feel for people who are really not at the center of the tragedy.

Words that reveal feelings: utmost stress, deep compassion, tragedy

Writer's attitude: All of these words help to show the depth of her very sad feelings.

DIRECTIONS: *Analyze the writer's voice in each passage. First, underline words that help reveal the writer's feelings. Then, tell what you think the writer's attitude is. Finally, tell what the syntax (sentence length and structure) reveals.*

1. We got in. Lyndon told the agents to stop the sirens. We drove along as fast as we could. I looked up at a building and there, already, was a flag at half-mast. I think that was when the enormity of what had happened first struck me.

   Words that reveal feelings: _____

   Writer's attitude: _____

   Syntax: _____

2. I looked at her. Mrs. Kennedy's dress was stained with blood. One leg was almost entirely covered with it and her right glove was caked, it was caked with blood—her husband's blood. Somehow that was one of the most poignant sights—that immaculate woman exquisitely dressed, and caked in blood.

   Words that reveal feelings: _____

   Writer's attitude: _____

   Syntax: _____

from **A White House Diary** by Lady Bird Johnson
Reading: Preview the Text to Identify an Author's Purpose

An **author's purpose** is his or her main reason for writing. An author writes for a general purpose, such as to inform, to entertain, or to persuade. He or she also writes for a specific purpose, such as to expose a particular problem in society. Before you read, **preview the text to look for an author's purpose.**

- Notice the focus of the title.
- Look for any organizing features, such as subheads.
- Identify the subject of photos, illustrations, or diagrams.
- Read the first sentences of the opening paragraphs.

Make educated guesses about the author's purpose based on your preview. Later, as you read the full text, confirm whether your ideas are correct.

DIRECTIONS: *Preview the following opening paragraphs from an article. Then, answer the questions below.*

First Ladies Hall of Fame

Of course, there is no such thing as the First Ladies Hall of Fame, nor is there ever likely to be one. But if there were, two Presidents' wives—Abigail Adams and Eleanor Roosevelt—would be among the first to be nominated.

A Legacy in Letters

Abigail Adams was the wife of the second President of the United States, John Adams. She was also the mother of the sixth President, John Quincy Adams. Fortunately, her letters to her husband and sister have been preserved. They are filled with details that provide an accurate, lively account of Colonial life during the Revolutionary period.

Her Childhood and Education

She was born Abigail Smith in Weymouth, Massachusetts, in 1744. Both her mother's family and her father's were leaders during the Colonial period. Like the girls of her time, even wealthy ones, Abigail had no formal education. Abigail was an avid reader, however, and extremely curious about everything. It was partly her intelligence that attracted the young lawyer, John Adams, whom she married in 1764.

Her Major Accomplishments

During long separations from her husband, she managed the family farm and taught her children. (You may remember how she was vividly portrayed in the musical *1776*.)

1. Identify the author's purpose in this article. _____

_____

2. Identify the main subject or subjects of the article. _____

_____

3. When the author finishes writing about Abigail Adams, what will the author discuss next?

_____

_____

4. What does the title reveal about the author's attitude toward his subject? _____

_____

from **A White House Diary** by Lady Bird Johnson
Vocabulary Builder

Word List

confines   desolate   immaculate   implications   poignant   tumultuous

A. DIRECTIONS: *Write the letter of the word or phrase that is the best synonym for the Word List word.*

____ 1. tumultuous
    A. in order
    B. in an uproar
    C. in a rage
    D. in surprise

____ 2. implications
    A. hints or suggestions
    B. signs or symbols
    C. important events
    D. indirect results

____ 3. poignant
    A. tense and exciting
    B. terrifying
    C. emotionally touching
    D. surprising

____ 4. confines
    A. expands
    B. limits
    C. restores
    D. begins

____ 5. desolate
    A. colorful
    B. appealing
    C. ideal
    D. wretched

____ 6. immaculate
    A. perfect
    B. sensible
    C. approximate
    D. dangerous

B. WORD STUDY The Latin root *-fin-* means "end." Answer each of the following questions using one of these words containing *-fin-*: *refine, infinity, definitely.*

1. Why do scientists use the word *infinity* when they describe space?

_____

2. Why might a writer want to *refine* his writing before submitting it to a publisher?

_____

3. When would you *definitely* want to impress your teacher?

_____

from **A White House Diary** by Lady Bird Johnson
Enrichment: An Orderly Succession

Who Succeeds the President?

What happens when a U.S. President leaves office before his or her term is completed? A President may die, become disabled, resign from office, or be impeached and removed from office. All of these situations are possible.

Early Plans for Succession

The Founding Fathers realized the need for an orderly succession in the event that something happened to the President. The transition from one President to the next was outlined in the Presidential Succession Act of 1792. Here was their plan: First, the Vice President would succeed as President, then the Senate president *pro tempore* (the senator who presides over the Senate in the absence of the Vice President), then the Speaker of the House.

In 1886, the order of succession changed. Congress passed a law saying that members of the Cabinet would succeed the Vice President in the event that this was necessary. Cabinet members, they felt, had experience running large government departments.

Further Changes in 1947 and 1967

President Harry Truman signed the Presidential Succession Act of 1947. That act changed the order of succession again to the order that is in place today. The Vice President would succeed the President, just as Lyndon B. Johnson became President when President Kennedy was assassinated. Next in order would be the Speaker of the House, then the president *pro tempore* of the Senate. In succeeding order, there would be the Secretary of State and Secretary of the Treasury. Next would come all other Cabinet members in the order in which the Cabinet office was established.

In 1967, the Twenty-fifth Amendment to the U.S. Constitution provided a procedure for filling the office of Vice President. The Vice President is nominated by the President and confirmed by Congress.

DIRECTIONS: *Use the paragraphs above to answer the following questions.*

1. Today, if a President resigns, who becomes the next President? _____

   _____

2. Suppose that the Vice President also resigns at the same time as the President. Who would succeed as President today? _____

   _____

3. According to the Twenty-fifth Amendment, if the Vice President succeeds to the office of President, how is a new Vice President chosen? _____

   _____

4. What is the advantage of having an orderly chain of succession before an emergency occurs? _____

   _____

Name _____ Date _____

from **A White House Diary** by Lady Bird Johnson
Open-Book Test

Short Answer *Write your responses to the questions in this section on the lines provided.*

1. The subheading that marks the entry from *A White House Diary* provides an important piece of information about the author's purpose for writing the entry. What does it tell you?

   _____

   _____

   _____

2. Would you describe the events of November 22, 1963, as they are revealed in the entry from *A White House Diary*, as tumultuous? Explain, basing your response on the definition for *tumultuous*.

   _____

   _____

   _____

3. How is Mrs. Johnson's relationship with Jackie Kennedy different from her relationship with Nellie Connally? Support your response with details from *A White House Diary*.

   _____

   _____

   _____

   _____

4. Reread the paragraphs near the middle of the entry from *A White House Diary* describing the Johnsons' drive to the airport. What kinds of sentences does the author mainly use here? Why do you think she uses them?

   _____

   _____

   _____

5. According to the entry from *A White House Diary*, what was the mood on *Air Force One* during the flight to Washington? Give examples from the entry to support your response.

   _____

   _____

   _____

6. While on *Air Force One*, Johnson has a second encounter with Jackie Kennedy. How would you describe Johnson's voice in this passage? What words or phrases in the passage from *A White House Diary* help create this voice?

_____

_____

_____

7. In the chart, write a short quotation from *A White House Diary* that describes something unusual Mrs. Johnson notices. Then tell what the quote reveals about her thoughts or feelings.

What She Notices	**What This Reveals**

8. Mrs. Johnson admires her husband and believes he will make a good president. Record two comments Mrs. Johnson makes in *A White House Diary* that reflect this attitude.

_____

_____

_____

9. One reason Johnson wrote this entry in *A White House Diary* was to describe historic events. What other purpose do you think she may have had? Use examples from the entry to support your opinion.

_____

_____

_____

10. In autobiographies, authors usually choose to describe striking or unusual moments rather than dull or common ones. What detail or event in the entry from *A White House Diary* made the strongest impression on you? Why do you think Johnson included it?

_____

_____

_____

Unit 1 Resources: Fiction and Nonfiction

Essay

Write an extended response to the question of your choice or to the question or questions your teacher assigns you.

11. Imagine you were one of the people who had come to see the president in Dallas on November 22, 1963. Write a diary entry recording what you observed and heard and what you learned on television later in the day. Base your entry on events described in *A White House Diary*, from the point of view of a bystander who witnessed history.

12. Lady Bird Johnson named her book *A White House Diary*. In an essay, explain why you think she chose this title and whether you consider it an appropriate one. Use details and examples from the entry to support your ideas.

13. President Lyndon Johnson once said of his wife that voters "would happily have elected her over me." Based on the November 22, 1963, entry in *A White House Diary*, do you think Mrs. Johnson would have made a good president? Answer this question in an essay. In your response, name several qualities you believe a president should possess, and then use examples from the entry to show whether Mrs. Johnson possessed them.

14. **Thinking About the Big Question: Can truth change?** In an essay, explain how "the truth" changed for Lady Bird Johnson over the course of a single day. What effects might this change have had on her life? In your view, was she prepared to accept such a radical change? Use examples from *A White House Diary* to support your opinions.

Oral Response

15. Go back to question 4, 5, 6, or 10 or to the question your teacher assigns to you. Take a few minutes to expand your answer and prepare an oral response. Find additional details in the entry from *A White House Diary* that will support your points. If necessary, make notes to guide your response.

Name _____ Date _____

from **A White House Diary** by Lady Bird Johnson
Selection Test A

Critical Reading *Identify the letter of the choice that best answers the question.*

____ 1. How is an autobiography, such as *A White House Diary*, different from a biography?
   A. It tells about the writer's life.
   B. It tells about the life of a real person.
   C. It tells about a fictional character.
   D. There is no difference.

____ 2. Where was Lyndon B. Johnson sworn in as president?
   A. in the hospital
   B. in the White House
   C. on the plane
   D. in the Senate

____ 3. What is Mrs. Johnson's main purpose in this excerpt from *A White House Diary*?
   A. to describe her husband
   B. to persuade
   C. to make up a story
   D. to give information

____ 4. Which of the following could Mrs. Johnson have added to the excerpt to help fulfill her purpose?
   A. a persuasive argument about gun control
   B. a poem expressing the nation's sorrow
   C. an amusing joke her husband once told her
   D. an explanation of why the president was in Dallas

____ 5. Suppose you already know that Mrs. Johnson is the wife of the thirty-sixth U.S. president. What can you predict from the title of her book—*A White House Diary*?
   A. It is a made-up story.
   B. It is about her own life as First Lady.
   C. It is about the life of Abigail Adams.
   D. It is about the lives of many First Ladies.

____ 6. Which word best describes Mrs. Johnson's attitude, or feelings, about Mrs. Kennedy?
   A. unfriendly
   B. cheerful
   C. sympathetic
   D. angry

____ 7. In describing what happened, Lady Bird Johnson uses many very short sentences. What feeling do these short sentences convey?
   A. surprise   C. anger
   B. happiness   D. shock

____ 8. Which word best describes the author's voice in *A White House Diary*?
   A. cool   C. serious
   B. funny   D. chatty

____ 9. What does Mrs. Johnson mean when she says that her husband "is a good man in a tight spot"?
   A. He is a good mountain climber.
   B. He is an honest man.
   C. He is a good husband.
   D. He is calm in an emergency.

____ 10. What feeling is Mrs. Johnson expressing in this passage from *A White House Diary*?

   I would have done anything to help her, but there was nothing I could do, so rather quickly I left and went back to the main part of the airplane where everyone was seated.

   A. anger
   B. helplessness
   C. sadness
   D. disappointment

Vocabulary and Grammar

____ 11. What is the best synonym for *tumultuous* in this sentence?

   . . . my feelings for her were too tumultuous to put into words.

   A. unclear
   B. loving
   C. disturbed
   D. friendly

____ **12.** What is the best synonym for *poignant* in this sentence?

Somehow that was one of the most poignant sights—that immaculate woman exquisitely dressed, and caked in blood.

A. touching

B. beautiful

C. ugly

D. unbelievable

____ **13.** In the following sentence, which word is a personal pronoun?

There had been such a gala air about the day that I thought the noise must come from firecrackers—part of the celebration.

A. There

B. gala

C. day

D. I

____ **14.** How many personal pronouns can you find in this sentence?

I asked the Secret Service if I could be taken to them.

A. one

B. two

C. three

D. four

Essay

15. How would you describe Lady Bird Johnson's character, given what you have read in this excerpt from *A White House Diary*? Identify two character traits that you think Mrs. Johnson has. Then, give examples from what she says and does that illustrate each trait.

16. Write a brief television news report of the events that Mrs. Johnson describes in her diary. The events occurred in Dallas, Texas, on November 22, 1963. Before you write your news report, jot down the key events you will cover.

17. **Thinking About the Big Question: Can truth change?** On the morning of November 22, 1963, Lady Bird Johnson was the vice president's wife. Later that day, she became the First Lady, wife of the president of the United States. In a brief essay, tell how this change affected the truth of her life. Do you think Mrs. Johnson was prepared to accept this change? Use examples from *A White House Diary* to support your opinions.

from **A White House Diary** by Lady Bird Johnson
Selection Test B

Critical Reading *Identify the letter of the choice that best completes the statement or answers the question.*

____ 1. Why is the selection from *A White House Diary* considered an example of autobiographical writing?
   A. It tells about important historical events.
   B. It contains details about real people.
   C. It contains vivid details and direct quotations.
   D. It relates the writer's thoughts and feelings about her life.

____ 2. Which of the following is *not* one of Lady Bird Johnson's purposes in this excerpt from *A White House Diary*?
   A. to pay tribute to various people
   B. to describe her husband
   C. to narrate important historical events
   D. to persuade others that her husband deserved to be president

____ 3. In the excerpt from *A White House Diary*, what does the use of short sentences convey?
   A. the author's feeling of shock
   B. the author's inability to write well
   C. the author's inability to remember details
   D. the author's poetic writing style

____ 4. In the excerpt from *A White House Diary*, which word or phrase best describes the author's attitude, or feelings, about the events she describes?
   A. worried
   B. proud
   C. hopeful
   D. saddened

____ 5. Which phrase best describes the author's voice in the excerpt from *A White House Diary*?
   A. chatty and intimate
   B. serious and shocked
   C. smooth and sophisticated
   D. informal and humorous

____ 6. According to Mrs. Johnson, why did Jackie Kennedy continue to wear her blood-stained clothes when Lyndon B. Johnson was sworn in as president?
   A. She did not have any other clothes to change into.
   B. She wanted people to see what had been done to the president.
   C. It was too dangerous for her to change her clothes.
   D. The Secret Service asked her not to change her clothes.

____ 7. What does the author mean by "the answer" in the following passage, which describes the wait in the hospital?

> Every face that came in, you searched for the answer. I think the face I kept seeing the answer on was the face of Kenny O'Donnell, who loved President Kennedy so much.

A. who was responsible for the shooting
B. why President Kennedy was shot
C. whether President Kennedy would live
D. whether Lyndon Johnson would live

____ 8. What is Mrs. Johnson's purpose in including the description of Mrs. Kennedy covered in blood?
A. to present a key fact
B. to emphasize the brutality of the event
C. to persuade readers that President Kennedy was a hero
D. to persuade readers that Mrs. Kennedy was a hero

____ 9. What feeling is Mrs. Johnson expressing in this passage from *A White House Diary*?

> I would have done anything to help her, but there was nothing I could do, so rather quickly I left and went back to the main part of the airplane where everyone was seated.

A. anger
B. shock
C. disbelief
D. helplessness

____ 10. What does Lady Bird Johnson mean when she says that her husband "is a good man in a tight spot"?
A. He is calm in an emergency.
B. He is a skillful mountain climber.
C. He is an honest government official.
D. He is a good husband.

____ 11. What is Mrs. Johnson's purpose in writing the following passage?

> The streets were lined with people—lots and lots of people—the children all smiling, placards, confetti, people waving from windows. One last happy moment I had was looking up and seeing Mary Griffith leaning out of a window waving at me.

A. She is writing a screenplay for a movie based on the events.
B. She is describing downtown Dallas on a typical November morning.
C. She is protesting the lack of security given to the president.
D. She is describing the scene moments before the president was shot.

____ 12. What is Mrs. Johnson's purpose in including details about her feelings toward others?
A. to present a complete account of history
B. to present a complete account of her own experience
C. to flatter the people she describes
D. to persuade others to share her feelings about people

Vocabulary and Grammar

____ **13.** What does the word *poignant* mean in this sentence from *A White House Diary*?

Somehow that was one of the most poignant sights—that immaculate woman exquisitely dressed, and caked in blood.

    A. frightening   **C.** contradictory

    B. maddening   **D.** touching

____ **14.** How many personal pronouns can you find in this passage from *A White House Diary*?

I asked the Secret Service if I could be taken to them. They began to lead me up one corridor and down another.

    A. four   **C.** six

    B. five   **D.** seven

____ **15.** Identify the reflexive pronoun in this passage from *A White House Diary*.

Suddenly I found myself face to face with Jackie in a small hallway. I believe it was right outside the operating room.

    A. I   **C.** Jackie

    B. myself   **D.** it

____ **16.** In which sentence is the word *implications* used correctly?

    A. November 22, 1963, began as a day of beautiful implications.

    B. Jackie Kennedy is someone whose implications the author greatly admired.

    C. There are national and worldwide implications to a president's assassination.

    D. A suspect was arrested, but his implications were not known.

Essay

17. Using the information in the excerpt from *A White House Diary*, write a brief television news report of the events Mrs. Johnson describes, which occurred in Dallas, Texas, on November 22, 1963. Remember that a news report (in contrast to Mrs. Johnson's diary) is objective; it states the facts but does not reveal the writer's feelings or opinions. Before you begin writing your news report, jot down the key events you will cover. Write them in chronological order—the order in which the events occurred.

18. You are writing a research paper on President Kennedy's assassination. In a brief essay, evaluate how reliable you think *A White House Diary* is as a source of information for your report. Tell how you use Mrs. Johnson's book as you write your report. Would you trust *A White House Diary* more than an encyclopedia article or a nonfiction book about the assassination by a noted historian? Would you trust Mrs. Johnson's book more than a TV documentary about the events?

19. **Thinking About the Big Question: Can truth change?** In an essay, explain how "the truth" changed for Lady Bird Johnson over the course of a single day. What effects might this change have had on her life? In your view, was she prepared to accept such a radical change? Use examples from the text to support your opinions.

Vocabulary Warm-up Word Lists

Study these words from "My English." Then, complete the activities.

Word List A

acquired [uh KWYRD] *adj.* gained through experience
 During her visit to France, she developed an <u>acquired</u> taste for cheese.

anxiety [ang ZY uh tee] *n.* uneasiness
 My <u>anxiety</u> increased as we approached the edge of the cliff.

childhood [CHYLD hood] *n.* time of being a child
 She spent her <u>childhood</u> in the city, but she moved away when she was a teen.

enlisted [en LIS tid] *v.* got help or support from
 Sam <u>enlisted</u> the services of a tutor to help him prepare for the exam.

necessarily [nes uh SER uh lee] *adv.* unavoidably; definitely
 People who argue loudly are not <u>necessarily</u> correct in their opinions.

particularly [pahr TIK yuh ler lee] *adv.* especially; specifically
 His parents were <u>particularly</u> concerned about his safety when he drove.

referring [ri FER ing] *v.* directing attention to
 When I mentioned "the Scottish play," I was <u>referring</u> to *Macbeth*.

superior [soo PEER ee er] *adj.* in a higher position
 His accent in Chinese was far <u>superior</u> to his writing in that language.

Word List B

animated [AN i may tid] *adj.* lively; energetic
 It was fascinating to listen to their <u>animated</u> discussion.

bland [BLAND] *adj.* dull; without flavor
 I find popcorn too <u>bland</u> without salt.

demonstration [dem uhn STRAY shun] *n.* explanation by example
 We understood the experiment better after the teacher's <u>demonstration</u>.

drastically [DRAS tik lee] *adv.* extremely; harshly
 Heating costs increased <u>drastically</u> during the recent oil shortage.

expressive [ek SPRES iv] *adj.* full of meaning or feeling
 Her <u>expressive</u> face reveals exactly what she is thinking.

fluent [FLOO uhnt] *adj.* speaking smoothly and easily
 Thanks to his <u>fluent</u> command of the language, he could even tell jokes in Thai.

tradition [truh DISH uhn] *n.* custom; established practice
 It is a Japanese <u>tradition</u> to remove one's shoes before entering a room.

version [VER zhuhn] *n.* form or variation
 I saw an earlier <u>version</u> of her report before she revised it.

Name _____ Date _____

"My English" by Julia Alvarez
Vocabulary Warm-up Exercises

Exercise A *Fill in each blank in the paragraph below with an appropriate word from Word List A. Use each word only once.*

Rafe had a happy [1] _____ and did very well in school as a young boy.
He learned to read at an early age and soon had an [2] _____ love of
books. He was [3] _____ interested in books about history and science,
but he did not [4] _____ enjoy answering questions about the books he
read. Although he was an excellent student who always did [5] _____
work in class, Rafe sometimes felt [6] _____ when it came to taking
exams. To help him overcome his fear, his parents [7] _____ the help of
a tutor. "She really taught me a lot," said Rafe, [8] _____ to his tutor.
"Now exams do not worry me at all!"

Exercise B *Answer each question in a complete sentence. Use a word from Word List B to replace each underlined word or group of words without changing the meaning.*

Example: How many languages can you speak in a smooth and flowing manner?
I am fluent in English and Spanish.

1. How could you make flavorless food tastier?

    _____

2. Giving someone flowers would be a showing of what kind of feeling?

    _____

3. What holiday custom do you observe in your family?

    _____

4. Which member of your family has the most revealing face?

    _____

5. What event can you think of that greatly changed world history?

    _____

6. What topic would you enjoy hearing a lively debate about?

    _____

7. Can there be more than one variation of a story?

    _____

Name _____ Date _____

"**My English**" by Julia Alvarez
Reading Warm-up A

Read the following passage. Pay special attention to the underlined words. Then, read it again, and complete the activities. Use a separate sheet of paper for your written answers.

My love of language began early in my <u>childhood</u>. Long before I could read, I developed an <u>acquired</u> love of picture books that my parents read to me over and over. I can still recall the <u>anxiety</u> I felt when our dog chewed up one of my favorite books. It was not <u>necessarily</u> the best story in my collection. I think it may have had only one or two words on each page. Yet I loved gazing at those brightly colored images while my mother or father made up marvelous stories to go with them. As a child, I refused to fall asleep until someone read me one of my favorite books. When my parents went out for the evening, I invariably <u>enlisted</u> the babysitter as my evening reader. To get me into my pajamas, all my sitter had to do was promise a bedtime story.

As I grew older, my love of language grew even stronger. I suppose it was my early fascination with words that helped me to become a <u>superior</u> writer. I won many contests and awards as I was growing up. I <u>particularly</u> enjoyed writing poetry. In a poem, every syllable counts. Every word must be chosen with the utmost care. Whether you are <u>referring</u> to something as sublime as an autumn sunrise or as ordinary as a pack of chewing gum, you must pay attention to the sound and rhythm of every word in every line.

When you come right down to it, words are really nothing more than the tools we use to paint vivid pictures in the minds of our readers or listeners. Language is the instrument through which we express our innermost thoughts and feelings. The more we practice that instrument, the more successful we become at communicating our thoughts to others.

If that is not magic, I do not know what is.

1. Underline the words that help you know when <u>childhood</u> is. What began in the author's *childhood*?

2. Circle the words that tell what the author <u>acquired</u>. Explain how she developed this *acquired* love.

3. Underline the words that explain the cause of the author's <u>anxiety</u>. What might cause you *anxiety*?

4. Which book was not <u>necessarily</u> the best in the narrator's collection? Tell what *necessarily* means.

5. Circle the words that tell what job the babysitter was <u>enlisted</u> to do. For what other tasks might a babysitter be *enlisted*?

6. Underline the words that tell what helped the author become a <u>superior</u> writer. What proof does the author give for this claim?

7. Circle the words that tell what the author <u>particularly</u> enjoyed. What do you *particularly* enjoy doing?

8. Underline examples of images or actions that a writer might be <u>referring</u> to. Then, write what *referring* means.

"My English" by Julia Alvarez
Reading Warm-up B

Read the following passage. Pay special attention to the underlined words. Then, read it again, and complete the activities. Use a separate sheet of paper for your written answers.

Maya Angelou is one of the most popular poets of recent times. She has enjoyed great success, though not just as a poet. She is also known as an author, a playwright, an actress, a dancer, a director, a producer, and an educator. Angelou is a <u>fluent</u> speaker of half a dozen languages and uses them as she travels the world spreading her message of love and social equality. Millions of people have been touched by Angelou's <u>expressive</u> readings of her work on television and at live performances. Her powerful and <u>animated</u> reading of her poem "On the Pulse of Morning" was a high-light of President Clinton's 1993 inauguration. The poem asks the people of America to work together to build a more loving nation. The work is a clear <u>demonstration</u> of the poet's devotion to making the world a better place for us all.

Maya Angelou has always believed in the power of words to bring about social change. The southern <u>tradition</u> of storytelling played a big part in her life growing up as an African American child in rural Arkansas. Then, when she was eight years old, Angelou's life was <u>drastically</u> altered by an assault. For the next five years, Angelou refused to speak at all! Even then, she never stopped paying attention to the col-orful language she heard all around her at home, at church, and in her grandmother's general store. You can read Angelou's own <u>version</u> of her remarkable childhood in her autobiography, *I Know Why the Caged Bird Sings.*

In her poetry, Maya Angelou uses short lines and everyday vocabulary to describe the great joy and terrible sadness she has known in her life. The words she prefers to use may not be very fancy. Still, the feelings and ideas she expresses through her poetry are anything but <u>bland</u>. Her poems are filled to overflowing with strong emotions and powerful images. Despite her long child-hood silence—or perhaps because of it—Maya Angelou clearly understands that language is a gift to be cher-ished and used wisely. Words have the power to hurt or heal. Properly handled by a great poet, they can even change the world.

1. Underline the words that tell what Angelou is <u>fluent</u> in. Tell how she uses this skill.

2. Underline the words that tell where people might see Angelou's <u>expressive</u> readings. Why might an *expressive* reading touch them?

3. How could you make a reading <u>animated</u>? Why do people call cartoons *animated* films?

4. Of what does Angelou's inau-gural poem provide a clear <u>demonstration</u>? Explain.

5. Circle the word that identifies a <u>tradition</u> from Angelou's childhood. What childhood *tradition* was important to you?

6. In what way was Angelou's life <u>drastically</u> altered by the assault? Write an antonym of *drastically*.

7. Whose <u>version</u> of a person's life would you find in an auto-biography? How might her mother's *version* of Angelou's life be different from her own?

8. Underline the sentence that says why Angelou's poems are not <u>bland</u>. What makes a poem *bland*?

Name _____ Date _____

"My English" by Julia Alvarez
Writing About the Big Question

Can truth change?

Big Question Vocabulary

assumption	belief	circumstance	context	convince
credible	distort	evidence	manipulate	perceive
perspective	skeptics	speculate	truth	verify

A. *Use one or more words from the list above to complete each sentence.*

1. Juan thought there was one _____ in life until his experience forced him to see that everything changes.

2. To _____ the truth, Keiko began looking for more _____ .

3. What _____ in Alvarez's life changed her perception of the truth?

4. From Mia's _____ , life would never be the same after they moved.

B. *Follow the directions in responding to each of the items below.*

1. Everyone occasionally misunderstands what someone says. Give an example of a time when you misunderstood someone.

   _____

   _____

2. How did the misunderstanding you listed above change what you thought or how you acted? Use at least two of the Big Question vocabulary words.

   _____

   _____

C. *Complete the sentence below. Then, write a short paragraph in which you connect this experience to the Big Question.*

In "My English," Alvarez describes how her view of her place in the world changes as she learns English. Complete this sentence:

Learning a language can affect our _____ .

_____

_____

_____

Name _____ Date _____

"My English" by Julia Alvarez
Literary Analysis: Autobiographical Writing and Author's Voice

Voice is the way a writer sounds on the page. For example, the writer's voice in a work can be *smooth and sophisticated, choppy and blunt,* or *breathless and full of wonder.* Voice is a result of several elements:

- *word choice*: the kinds of words the writer uses
- *attitude*: the way the writer feels about his or her subject
- *sentence length and structure, or syntax*: the arrangement of words and ideas in sentences

In **autobiographical writing,** the author tells all or part of his or her own life story. The kinds of details that are included show what the writer notices, thinks, and feels about events. The voice of autobiographical writing usually reflects the writer's own personality and way of speaking.

As you read an autobiography, notice the words that seem to reveal feeling. Think about what they say about Julia Alvarez's attitude toward her subject.

In sixth grade, I had one of the first in a lucky line of great English teachers who began to nurture in me a love of language, a love that had been there since my childhood of listening closely to words.

Words that reveal feelings:	lucky, great, nurture, love
Writer's attitude:	All of these words have positive connotations and help to show the writer's great joy in using words.

DIRECTIONS: *Analyze the writer's voice in each passage. First, underline words that you think reveal something about the writer's voice. Then, tell what you think the writer's attitude is. Finally, tell what the syntax (sentence length and structure) reveals.*

1. Those women yakked as they cooked, they storytold, they gossiped, they sang—boleros, merengues, canciones, salves. Theirs were the voices that belonged to the rain and the wind and the teeny, teeny stars even a small child could blot out with her thumb.

   Word choice: _____

   Writer's attitude: _____

   Syntax: _____

2. *Butter, butter, butter, butter.* All day, one English word that had particularly struck me would go round and round in my mouth and weave through all the Spanish in my head until by the end of the day, the word did sound like just another Spanish word. And so I would say, "Mami, please pass la mantequilla." She would scowl and say in English, "I'm sorry, I don't understand. But would you be needing some butter on your bread?"

   Word choice: _____

   Writer's attitude: _____

   Syntax: _____

"My English" by Julia Alvarez

Reading: Preview the Text to Identify an Author's Purpose

An **author's purpose** is his or her main reason for writing. An author writes for a general purpose, such as to inform, to entertain, or to persuade. He or she also writes for a specific purpose, such as to expose a particular problem in society. Before you read, **preview the text to look for an author's purpose.**

- Notice the focus of the title.
- Look for any organizing features, like subheads.
- Identify the subject of photos, illustrations, or diagrams.
- Read the first sentences of the first few paragraphs.

Make educated guesses about the author's purpose based on your preview. Later, as you read the full text, confirm whether your ideas are correct.

DIRECTIONS: *Preview the following opening paragraphs from an article. Then, answer the questions below.*

Evolving English

The one thing you can count on with a living language (one that is still in use) is that it changes. English has been changing since it first appeared as Old English about A.D. 500. Here are four ways in which English changes: new words, old words with new meanings, out-of-fashion words, and borrowed words.

New Words

Once these words did not exist: *cell phone, laptop, DVD player.* New words enter the English language when manufacturers invent names for their new products. Some people send new words they have made up to dictionary editors and try to sell them, but that is not how words are added to a language. They enter the language by being in common use.

Old Words With New Meanings

Another way language changes is by words taking on new meanings. *Memory,* for example, added a computer meaning when computers became common. Slang is another way that old words acquire new meanings. Long ago, *cool* simply meant the opposite of *warm*, but the slang meaning of *cool* has been around for a long time.

Out-of-Fashion Words

Dictionaries label some words as archaic or obsolete, which means they are no longer in common use. *Thee, prithee, whilst,* and *ere* are some examples of words that have disappeared.

1. Identify the author's purpose in this article. _____

_____

2. Identify the main subject or subjects of the article. _____

_____

3. When the author finishes writing about out-of-fashion words, what will the author discuss next? _____

_____

Name _____ Date _____

"My English" by Julia Alvarez
Vocabulary Builder

Word List

accentuated   bilingual   countenance   enumerated   interminably   ponderously

A. DIRECTIONS: *Write the letter of the word or phrase that is the best synonym for the Word List word.*

____ 1. bilingual
     A. being confused   C. using two languages
     B. having three languages   D. learning new languages

____ 2. countenance
     A. face   C. reaction
     B. thoughts   D. feelings

____ 3. interminably
     A. excitedly   C. emotionally
     B. terrifyingly   D. endlessly

____ 4. ponderously
     A. in a hesitant manner   C. in a quick way
     B. in a dull way   D. in a reluctant manner

____ 5. enumerated
     A. listed   C. required
     B. created   D. forgot

____ 6. accentuated
     A. estimated   C. emphasized
     B. excited   D. abbreviated

B. WORD STUDY The Latin root *-term-* means "limit, end, boundary." Answer each of the following questions using one of these words containing *-term-*: *determined, exterminator, interminable.*

1. Why might a football player be very *determined* in the final minutes of a game?

_____

2. Why might you call an *exterminator* if your house had roaches?

_____

3. On what occasion have you felt that every minute seemed *interminable*?

_____

Unit 1 Resources: Fiction and Nonfiction
160

Name _____ Date _____

"My English" by Julia Alvarez
Enrichment: Take a Survey

With a small group of students, plan a survey about the languages that people in your community speak and understand. Interview three students in your school. You may ask them questions like the ones below or plan your own questions.

SURVEY
• **Where were you born?** _____ _____
• **What was the first language that you learned to speak?** _____ _____
• **What languages does your family speak at home?** _____ _____
• **What languages can you speak and understand?** _____ _____
• **What languages can you read?** _____ _____
• **What languages can you write?** _____ _____
• **Do you think a foreign language should be required for high school graduation?** ❑ **Yes** ❑ **No** **Please explain why you feel that way.** _____ _____
• **If you think a foreign language should be required, please tell for how many years it should be studied.** _____ _____
• **What language or languages would you like to study?** _____ _____

Now, work with your small group to tally the responses you received during your interviews. Share your results with your classmates in a brief oral or written report.

from **A White House Diary** by Lady Bird Johnson
"My English" by Julia Alvarez

Integrated Language Skills: Personal Pronouns

The most common pronouns are those that you use to refer to yourself and the people and things around you. These pronouns are called **personal pronouns.** Personal pronouns refer to the person speaking (first person), the person spoken to (second person), or the person, place, or thing spoken about (third person). Here is a chart of the personal pronouns.

	Singular	Plural
First Person	I, me, my, mine	we, us, our, ours
Second Person	you, your, yours	you, your, yours
Third Person	he, him, his; she, her, hers; it, its	they, them, their, theirs

The ending *-self* or *-selves* can be added to some personal pronouns to form reflexive pronouns. A **reflexive pronoun** indicates that someone or something performs an action to, for, or upon itself. Reflexive pronouns point back to a noun or pronoun earlier in the sentence. The eight reflexive pronouns are *myself, ourselves, yourself, yourselves, himself, herself, itself,* and *themselves.*

Reflexive Pronoun   She asked *herself* why everyone spoke English in New York.

A. DIRECTIONS: *Underline all of the personal pronouns in these passages from "My English."*

1. Why my parents didn't first educate us in our native language by enrolling us in a Dominican school, I don't know. Part of it was that Mami's family had a tradition of sending the boys to the States to boarding school and college, and she had been one of the first girls to be allowed to join her brothers. [You should find eight personal pronouns.]

2. There was also a neat little trick I wanted to try on an English-speaking adult at home. I had learned it from Elizabeth, my smart-alecky friend in fourth grade, whom I alternately worshiped and resented. [You should find five personal pronouns.]

B. DIRECTIONS: *You are planning to meet a pen pal, whom you have never seen before, in the train station. Write a short description of yourself so that your pen pal will recognize you. Use several personal pronouns and at least one example of reflexive pronouns in your description. Then, underline the pronouns.*

_____

_____

_____

_____

_____

_____

Unit 1 Resources: Fiction and Nonfiction

Name _____ Date _____

from **A White House Diary** by Lady Bird Johnson
"My English" by Julia Alvarez

Integrated Language Skills: Support for Writing a Journal Entry

Use the chart below to gather information for your **journal entry.** Write your ideas in complete sentences.

1. My subject:
2. Why my subject is important to me:
3. Who else was affected by the event:
4. How they were affected:
5. How I felt during/about the event:
6. Specific words I associate with my subject:
7. Specific images I associate with my subject:

Now, write your journal entry about a subject that is important to you. As you describe your subject, try to use the specific words and images you thought of, but feel free to add others.

from **A White House Diary** by Lady Bird Johnson
"My English" by Julia Alvarez

Integrated Language Skills: Support for Extend Your Learning

Research and Technology: *from* **A White House Diary**

Before you begin writing your script, jot down some ideas to plan your multimedia presentation.

Topic: _____

Purpose: _____

Ideas for introduction: _____
_____

Main point #1: _____
_____

Main point #2: _____
_____

Main point #3: _____
_____

Visual elements and where to put them: _____
_____
_____

Research and Technology: "My English"

As you gather information for your multimedia report on immigration since 1800, use the lines below to record your information. Put a check mark next to information that will be one of your three key points.

Some important immigration laws: _____
_____

Periods of greatest immigration: _____
_____

Immigrants' countries of origin: _____
_____

Reasons why they left: _____
_____

Ideas for visuals: _____
_____

Name _____ Date _____

"My English" by Julia Alvarez
Open-Book Test

Short Answer *Write your responses to the questions in this section on the lines provided.*

1. Based on the title and first sentence of the essay "My English," what predictions can a reader make? Explain.

   _____

   _____

2. Based on the first four paragraphs of "My English," what would you say was the author's purpose for writing this essay? Cite one or two details from the essay to support your answer.

   _____

   _____

   _____

3. In "My English," what kinds of things can Julia learn from looking at her mother's countenance? Base your answer on the meaning of *countenance,* and provide an example from the essay.

   _____

   _____

   _____

4. Reread the paragraphs in the middle of "My English" about speaking English at the Carol Morgan School. To what does Alvarez compare the Spanish words that slip into her sentences? What is the author's attitude toward Spanish in this part of the essay?

   _____

   _____

   _____

5. In the chart, write a detail from "My English" that the author uses to tell about her teacher at the Carol Morgan School. Then, below the graphic organizer, tell what the detail shows about Julia's thoughts or feelings.

Detail	Writer Notices

   _____

6. Idioms include slang, clichés, and sayings. Once Julia begins speaking English, she encounters English idioms. Provide an example of an English idiom from "My English," and tell what it means.

_____

_____

7. In the middle section of "My English," the author describes a Sunday dinner with her grandfather at the Alvarez home. Does the voice in this section have a respectful or disrespectful attitude toward the grandfather? Explain, using an example from the essay.

_____

_____

_____

8. Near the end of "My English," Alvarez compares English to the skyscrapers of New York City. Look back at this part of the essay. Then look at the photos that go with it. In your opinion, does the author make a good comparison? Explain.

_____

_____

_____

9. Alvarez's voice, or the way her writing sounds on the page, has a poetic quality in the last paragraph of "My English." According to the author, in what two ways is Sister Maria's writing like snow?

_____

_____

_____

10. What detail or event in "My English" made the strongest impression on you? Why do you think Alvarez included it?

_____

_____

_____

Essay

Write an extended response to the question of your choice or to the question or questions your teacher assigns you.

11. An author's purpose is his or her main reason for writing. Choose one of the following purposes for writing "My English": *to entertain, to inspire, to show gratitude.* Then, in an essay, describe how Julia Alvarez accomplishes the purpose you've chosen. Use examples from "My English" to support your ideas.

12. In one sense, "My English" is a love story: It describes how the author fell in love with English. In an essay, explain how each of the following stages of a love story are present in "My English": (1) meeting for the first time; (2) getting to know each other; (3) falling in love; (4) living happily ever after.

13. What makes "My English" autobiographical? In an essay, identify several elements of an autobiographical work, and tell how these elements are present in Alvarez's essay.

14. **Thinking About the Big Question: Can truth change?** What did Alvarez believe about English—and English-speakers—when she first arrived in New York City? How did this belief change over time? Answer these questions in a brief essay, citing examples from "My English" to support your response.

Oral Response

15. Go back to question 4, 5, 7, or 8 or to the question your teacher assigns to you. Take a few minutes to expand your answer and prepare an oral response. Find additional details in "My English" that support your points. If necessary, make notes to guide your response.

"My English" by Julia Alvarez
Selection Test A

Critical Reading *Identify the letter of the choice that best answers the question.*

____ 1. When she was a child, why did Julia Alvarez think English was a "harder Spanish"?
A. Her parents tried unsuccessfully to teach her English.
B. Her parents spoke English when they did not want the children to understand.
C. Her grandfather spoke English in his job with the United Nations.
D. Her teachers did not allow her to speak English.

____ 2. What is Julia Alvarez's main purpose in "My English"?
A. to persuade
B. to teach
C. to entertain
D. to criticize

____ 3. What can you predict about Julia Alvarez's purpose from the title "My English"?
A. She will tell about living in America.
B. She will tell about learning English.
C. She will tell about an American friend.
D. She will tell about her family.

____ 4. In this sentence, what type of voice does the word *yakked* help create?
Those women yakked as they cooked, they storytold, they gossiped, they sang. . . .
A. serious or formal
B. angry or irritated
C. casual or chatty
D. upset or sorrowful

____ 5. What is Spanglish, according to Julia Alvarez?
A. a mixture of many languages
B. a mixture of Spanish and English
C. the incorrect use of English
D. the Spanish spoken in Spain

____ 6. Which word best describes Julia Alvarez's voice in "My English"?
A. serious
B. angry
C. formal
D. informal

_____ 7. What is the main idea of this passage from "My English"?

> Soon it wasn't so strange that everyone was speaking in English instead of Spanish. I learned not to hear it as English, but as sense.

A. The author is having a difficult time understanding English.

B. The author thinks that English makes no sense.

C. The author prefers to speak in Spanish, not English.

D. The author feels comfortable understanding English.

_____ 8. What is special about Alvarez's sixth-grade teacher, Sister Maria Generosa?

A. She encourages students' imaginations.

B. She teaches grammar rules.

C. She makes students memorize poems.

D. She speaks six languages.

_____ 9. What is the best interpretation of these last two sentences from "My English"?

> I was no longer a foreigner with no ground to stand on. I had landed in the English language.

A. The author is having a very hard time learning English in America.

B. The author is homesick for the Dominican Republic.

C. The author is determined to become a writer.

D. The author feels at home reading, writing, and speaking English.

_____ 10. What is Julia Alvarez's purpose in including Sister Maria Generosa's sentence about snow?

A. to help readers see exactly what Alvarez loves about language

B. to prove how difficult it is to learn English

C. to persuade readers that English is easy to learn

D. to explain how to write a good sentence

_____ 11. Which sentence from "My English" contains a simile, a comparison of two unlike things using the words *like* or *as*?

A. When the little lines on the corners of her eyes crinkled, she was amused.

B. Imagine this whole table is the human brain.

C. Sister Maria filled the chalkboard with snowy print. . . .

D. . . . a Spanish word would suddenly slide into my English like someone butting into line.

Vocabulary and Grammar

____ **12.** Julia Alvarez is *bilingual.* What does that mean?

A. She can use two languages.

B. She speaks only English.

C. She learns new languages easily.

D. She writes only in Spanish.

____ **13.** Which word is a synonym of *interminably* in this sentence from "My English"?

Sister Maria Generosa did not make our class interminably diagram sentences from a workbook. . . .

A. quickly   C. uselessly

B. cleverly   D. endlessly

____ **14.** In this sentence from "My English," which word is a personal pronoun?

Soon, I began to learn more English, at the Carol Morgan School.

A. Soon   C. English

B. I   D. School

____ **15.** How many personal pronouns are in this sentence from "My English"?

When we arrived in New York, I was shocked.

A. none   C. two

B. one   D. three

Essay

16. In a brief essay, tell what you think Julia Alvarez's purpose is in writing "My English." How well do you think she accomplishes her purpose? Use examples from the text to support your statements.

17. Julia Alvarez's sixth-grade teacher was important in her life. In an essay, describe what qualities made Sister Maria Generosa important to Alvarez. Then, think of a special teacher you have had, one who has made a difference in your life. Explain why that teacher's class was special, and give some examples. Then, tell whether this teacher and Alvarez's teacher share any of the same characteristics.

18. **Thinking About the Big Question: Can truth change?** When author Julia Alvarez arrived in New York, she heard many people speaking English with ease. She thought these English-speakers were smarter than non-English-speakers because they could speak this difficult language. How did Alvarez's belief change over time? In a brief essay, use examples from "My English" to support your response.

"**My English**" by Julia Alvarez
Selection Test B

Critical Reading *Identify the letter of the choice that best completes the statement or answers the question.*

____ 1. From this opening sentence and from the title, what can you predict about Julia Alvarez's purpose in "My English"?

   Mami and Papi used to speak it when they had a secret they wanted to keep from us children.

   A. She will describe the best way to learn English.
   B. She will discuss her personal experience learning English.
   C. She will explain her family history.
   D. She will argue that keeping secrets is not a good idea.

____ 2. Which of the following purposes does Julia Alvarez *not* have in "My English"?
   A. to persuade readers to learn Spanish
   B. to share her love of language
   C. to entertain the reader with tales from her childhood
   D. to pay tribute to Sister Maria Generosa

____ 3. Which of the following quotations from "My English" best shows Julia Alvarez's informal voice?
   A. Spanish had its many tongues as well.
   B. Soon, I began to learn more English, at the Carol Morgan School.
   C. . . . a Spanish word would suddenly slide into my English like someone butting into line.
   D. . . . my grandfather sat down at the children's table to chat with us.

____ 4. What is the main idea of the following sentence from "My English"?

   Whenever she spoke that gibberish English, I translated the general content by watching the Spanish expressions on her face.

   A. She could never understand what her mother was saying.
   B. She had trouble understanding her mother's native speech—campuno Spanish.
   C. She did not understand the English words, but could read her mother's facial expressions.
   D. Because she could not hear what her mother was saying, she read her mother's lips.

____ 5. What does Julia Alvarez mean by the language she calls "mix-up" or Spanglish?
   A. the ungrammatical use of English
   B. the ungrammatical use of Spanish
   C. a mixture of many languages
   D. a mixture of Spanish and English

____ 6. Why does Julia Alvarez mention "*Cat got your tongue? No big deal! So there! Take that!*"?
   A. She is terrified by English idioms.
   B. She loves learning English idioms.
   C. She cannot speak in long sentences.
   D. She prefers to speak Spanish.

____ 7. Which of the following sentences from "My English" contains a metaphor, a comparison of two unlike things that does not use the words *like* or *as?*
   A. Those women yakked as they cooked, they storytold, they gossiped, they sang. . . .
   B. At school, a Spanish word would suddenly slide into my English like someone butting into line.
   C. There wasn't a sentence that wasn't colonized by an English word.
   D. He was a Cornell man, a United Nations representative from our country.

____ 8. What does Julia Alvarez mean by the phrase "a beginning wordsmith" in this sentence?
   A beginning wordsmith, I had so much left to learn; sometimes it was disheartening.
   A. She is just learning to speak Spanish.
   B. She is just starting to become a writer.
   C. She is homesick for her friends in the Dominican Republic.
   D. She is studying hard for a weekly vocabulary test.

____ 9. Why was Julia Alvarez shocked when she and her family arrived in New York?
   A. The city had many skyscrapers.
   B. She saw snow for the first time.
   C. Everyone spoke English.
   D. She saw a subway for the first time.

____ 10. What special thing did Sister Maria Generosa, Alvarez's teacher, ask her students to do in "My English"?
   A. diagram sentences
   B. write little stories
   C. memorize poems
   D. study spelling words

____ 11. How would you describe the writer's voice in this passage from "My English"?
   Sister Maria filled the chalkboard with snowy print, on and on, handling and shaping and moving the language, scribbling all over the board until English, those verbal gadgets, those tricks and turns of phrases, those little fixed units and counters, became a charged, fluid mass. . . .
   A. careless
   B. solemn
   C. uncertain
   D. poetic

____ 12. What is Julia Alvarez's purpose in the following quotation from "My English"?
   Theirs were the voices that belonged to the rain and the wind and the teeny, teeny stars even a small child could blot out with her thumb.
   A. to explain why she had difficulty learning English
   B. to persuade readers that poetic writing is fun
   C. to explain a trick of vision
   D. to capture the feeling of being a child

Unit 1 Resources: Fiction and Nonfiction

_____ 13. Which of the following phrases best describes Alvarez's voice in "My English"?
   A. poetic and formal
   B. conversational and poetic
   C. humorously disrespectful
   D. informal and relaxed

Vocabulary and Grammar

_____ 14. Which word means the opposite of *interminably* in this sentence from "My English"?
   Sister Maria Generosa did not make our class interminably diagram sentences from a workbook or learn a catechism of grammar rules.

   A. endlessly   C. uselessly
   B. briefly   D. cleverly

_____ 15. In which sentence is the word *countenance* used correctly?
   A. The busy countenance of New York City was something of a shock.
   B. Sister Maria Generosa gave writing assignments that stimulated students' countenance.
   C. She could read every expression on her mother's countenance.
   D. Without a countenance, it is difficult to learn a new language.

_____ 16. How many personal pronouns are there in this sentence from "My English"?
   She always used the possessive pronoun: *your* English, an inheritance we had come into and must wisely use.

   A. two   C. four
   B. three   D. five

_____ 17. What is the reflexive pronoun in the following sentence?
   In "My English," Alvarez writes of her amazement when she finds herself in a country where everybody is able to speak and understand English.

   A. My   C. she
   B. Alvarez   D. herself

Essay

18. Write an essay comparing one of your own experiences with language with Alvarez's. You might write about a word you were proud to learn, a phrase that puzzles you, or a writer whose style you appreciate. In your essay, mention specific experiences of Alvarez's and explain how they resemble or differ from your own experience.

19. In a brief essay, describe Julia Alvarez's voice in "My English." Then, tell how you think she creates that voice. Consider her word choice, her attitude toward her subject, and her sentence lengths and structure.

20. **Thinking About the Big Question: Can truth change?** What did Alvarez believe about English—and English-speakers—when she first arrived in New York City? How did this belief change over time? Answer these questions in a brief essay, citing examples from "My English" to support your response.

Vocabulary Warm-up Word Lists

Study these words from "The Secret Life of Walter Mitty." Then, complete the activities.

Word List A

complicated [KAHM pli kay tid] *adj.* hard to understand or solve
   We got mixed up trying to follow the <u>complicated</u> directions.

delicately [DEL uh kuht lee] *adv.* gently; sensitively
   We <u>delicately</u> wrapped each fragile dish in bubble wrap.

menacing [MEN is ing] *adj.* threatening
   The <u>menacing</u> wolves circled the trapped elk.

misty [MIS tee] *adj.* hidden by mist; hazy; vague
   I could barely see the house through the <u>misty</u> morning light.

objection [uhb JEK shuhn] *n.* expression of disapproval
   My <u>objection</u> to your plan is that it will cost too much.

occur [uh KUR] *v.* come to mind
   Did it ever <u>occur</u> to you that Liz might be busy that night?

performance [per FOR muhns] *n.* something that is accomplished
   The boss praised him for his excellent <u>performance</u> on the job.

specialists [SPESH uh lists] *n.* those who know a great deal about something
   Pediatricians are <u>specialists</u> in childhood illnesses.

Word List B

aimlessly [AYM luhs lee] *adv.* without direction or purpose
   He wandered <u>aimlessly</u> along the seashore.

bickering [BIK er ing] *v.* quarreling noisily
   My mother separated me from my brother so we would stop <u>bickering</u>.

carelessly [KAIR luhs lee] *adv.* without paying close attention
   He almost walked into a cyclist when he stepped <u>carelessly</u> off the curb.

fleeting [FLEET ing] *adj.* passing swiftly; not lasting
   The shooting star was little more than a <u>fleeting</u> glimmer in the sky.

initiative [i NISH ee uh tiv] *n.* right of citizens to introduce ideas for laws
   The voters approved the <u>initiative</u> to build a new stadium downtown.

inserted [in SERT id] *v.* put into
   He <u>inserted</u> the key into the lock.

scornfully [SKAWRN fuhl lee] *adv.* with disgust or distaste
   Only a heartless person would look <u>scornfully</u> at a homeless family.

squad [SKWAHD] *n.* small group of people working together
   The clean-up <u>squad</u> showed up with mops and pails.

Name _____ Date _____

"The Secret Life of Walter Mitty" by James Thurber
Vocabulary Warm-up Exercises

Exercise A *Fill in each blank in the paragraph below with an appropriate word from Word List A. Use each word only once.*

Dr. Diaz is one of the clinic's heart surgery [1] _____. People's

lives depend on her [2] _____ in the operating room. It may

[3] _____ to some patients that heart surgery is a very long and

[4] _____ procedure, but Dr. Diaz always puts their minds at ease. She

has a very pleasant manner and is not at all [5] _____. If a patient raises

an [6] _____ to her plan, she calmly and [7] _____

explains why the procedure is necessary. Her explanations are never vague or

[8] _____. Dr. Diaz always speaks from the heart!

Exercise B *Answer the questions with complete explanations.*

Example: If you <u>inserted</u> a sentence into a paragraph, would the paragraph be shorter or longer?
   It would be longer because something that is inserted *is put in, not taken out.*

1. If a person wandered <u>aimlessly</u>, would he or she have a specific destination in mind?
   _____

2. What might you think about the relationship between two people who are always <u>bickering</u>?
   _____

3. If you want to avoid an accident, should you drive <u>carelessly</u>?
   _____

4. Could you memorize a poem if you gave the text a <u>fleeting</u> glance?
   _____

5. If people want to make a new law, could they present an <u>initiative</u>?
   _____

6. If your friend regards your hat <u>scornfully</u>, does she like it?
   _____

7. Could a <u>squad</u> consist of just one person?
   _____

Unit 1 Resources: Fiction and Nonfiction

"The Secret Life of Walter Mitty" by James Thurber
Reading Warm-up A

Read the following passage. Pay special attention to the underlined words. Then, read it again, and complete the activities. Use a separate sheet of paper for your written answers.

You may not remember your dreams. Even so, you could have more than half a dozen of them every night.

We have most of our dreams during the Rapid Eye Movement (REM) stage of sleep. During that time our eyes dart back and forth beneath our eyelids. If you remember a dream at all, you probably had it an hour or two before you woke up.

The study of dreams may seem simple, but it is actually an extremely <u>complicated</u> subject. A <u>specialist</u> in the study of dreams must be an expert in biology, psychology, and several other fields of science. Dream researchers observe people while they sleep. They wake them periodically to ask about their dreams. Although researchers awaken their subjects as <u>delicately</u> as possible, most people forget their dreams almost as soon as they are awake. Once we are awake, our dreams are usually no more than <u>misty</u> memories of vague events. We usually cannot quite bring them back into focus.

People often report similar types of dreams. Many people dream about a <u>menacing</u> figure—a person, an animal, or a monster of some type—that threatens their safety. Other common dreams feature some kind of <u>performance</u> that goes horribly wrong. For example, you are in a play and you forget all your lines. Of course, not all dreams arise from stress. If you spend a lot of your waking hours thinking about your favorite sport or someone you have a crush on, chances are that those things will show up in your dreams as well.

Did it ever <u>occur</u> to you that your dreams might have hidden meanings? Some experts believe that dreams reveal secret feelings that we cannot express in our waking hours. Others have voiced their <u>objection</u> to this idea. They suggest that dreams are just meaningless stories that our brains make up while we sleep.

May all your dreams be happy ones—whether you remember them or not!

1. Underline the word that means the opposite of <u>complicated</u>. Write a sentence about something you think is **complicated**.

2. Circle the word that means almost the same as <u>specialist</u>. Write a sentence about another kind of **specialist**.

3. Underline the words that tell what the researchers do <u>delicately</u>. Write a sentence about something you might do **delicately**.

4. Circle the word that has the same meaning as <u>misty</u>. Explain in your own words why the author compares dreams to **misty** memories.

5. Underline the words that tell what a <u>menacing</u> figure might do to people. Explain how a person or an animal could be **menacing**.

6. Circle an example of a <u>performance</u>. Write a sentence about how some other **performance** might go wrong.

7. Write a question that might <u>occur</u> to a dream researcher. Then, write a question that **occurs** to you about dreams.

8. Underline the idea that researchers raise an <u>objection</u> to. What is your opinion on this subject?

"The Secret Life of Walter Mitty" by James Thurber
Reading Warm-up B

Read the following passage. Pay special attention to the underlined words. Then, read it again, and complete the activities. Use a separate sheet of paper for your written answers.

Billy was a daydreamer.

It started when he was in preschool. Billy would start doing a jigsaw puzzle, but his mind would begin to wander even before he <u>inserted</u> the first puzzle piece into the rectangular frame. At first, his thoughts would drift <u>aimlessly</u>, with no apparent direction. Then, his eyes would close, and a story would start to take shape in his mind. Soon, Billy would be off on a great adventure in some distant land that was far more exciting than Miss Hannah's Preschool.

That is when Miss Hannah would tap him on the shoulder and ask why he was not working on his puzzle like the other kids.

When he got older, Billy learned to daydream with his eyes open. He would be sitting in class, <u>carelessly</u> doodling in his notebook, when suddenly his mind would be elsewhere. For a few <u>fleeting</u> moments that never lasted long enough, Billy would know what it felt like to lead a <u>squad</u> of fearless soldiers into battle or pilot a space shuttle through the treacherous rings of Saturn.

Then he would feel the teacher's fingers tapping sharply on his shoulder.

"Time to rejoin the real world," she would remark <u>scornfully</u>, and the whole class would start to laugh.

Billy did not care, though. Sometimes, when his parents were <u>bickering</u>, Billy would escape into a private world where people never argued or raised their voices.

When he reached high school, Billy began to write down some of his daydreams as stories. His teachers had to admit that the stories were good, even if Billy did have trouble paying attention in class.

By his sophomore year, Billy suggested that he and other student authors begin a school literary magazine. The faculty decided it could be funded with money from the school enrichment <u>initiative</u> passed by local voters. Before long, this particular dream of Billy's had become a reality!

1. Underline the words that tell what Billy <u>inserted</u>. Then, tell what *inserted* means.

2. Underline the words that explain what <u>aimlessly</u> means. Write a sentence about something that might be done *aimlessly*.

3. Circle the word that tells what Billy did <u>carelessly</u>. What does his *carelessness* suggest about him?

4. Underline the words that suggest what <u>fleeting</u> means. Write a sentence about something else that is *fleeting*.

5. Underline the words that identify the members of Billy's <u>squad</u>. What kind of *squad* would you enjoy leading?

6. Why does the teacher make her remark <u>scornfully</u>? What could she have said if she did not want to speak *scornfully*?

7. Circle the words that tell what Billy's parents did when they were <u>bickering</u>. How does Billy respond to his parents' *bickering*?

8. Underline the words that tell what the voters decided to pay for when they passed the <u>initiative</u> in the local election. How did the *initiative* help Billy?

Name _____ Date _____

"The Secret Life of Walter Mitty" by James Thurber
Writing About the Big Question

Can truth change?

Big Question Vocabulary

assumption	belief	circumstance	context	convince
credible	distort	evidence	manipulate	perceive
perspective	skeptics	speculate	truth	verify

A. *Use one or more words from the list above to complete each sentence.*

1. Although a story is fiction, an author can still tell the _____ .

2. A narrator's _____ determines what we know and believe.

3. Writers deliberately _____ the truth to make stories interesting.

4. The reality Mitty _____ as true differs from the one his wife sees.

B. *Follow the directions in responding to each of the items below.*

1. Do you sometimes daydream? Give an example.

   _____

   _____

2. How does the daydream you listed above change how you see your life? Use at least two of the Big Question vocabulary words.

   _____

   _____

C. *Complete the sentence below. Then, write a short paragraph in which you connect this experience to the Big Question.*

In "The Secret Life of Walter Mitty," Mitty lives two lives: the life dominated by his wife and the life of his imagination. Complete this sentence:

Compared to our everyday lives, the life of our imagination is _____ .

_____

_____

_____

178

Name _____ Date _____

"The Secret Life of Walter Mitty" by James Thurber
Literary Analysis: Character

A **character** is a person or an animal who takes part in the action of a literary work.

- A **round character** is complex, showing many different qualities—revealing faults as well as virtues. For example, a character might be honest but foolish or dishonest but intelligent. A **flat character** is one-dimensional, showing only a single trait.
- A **dynamic character** develops, changes, and learns something during the course of a story, unlike a **static character,** who remains the same.

The main character of a story is almost always a round character and is usually dynamic. The main character's development and growth are often central to a story's plot and theme. As you read, consider the traits that make characters seem round or flat, dynamic or static.

DIRECTIONS: *For each numbered item, write a sentence telling what character trait or traits the passage reveals.*

1. **Mrs. Mitty:** "We've been all through that," she said, getting out of the car. "You're not a young man any longer." He raced the engine a little. "Why don't you wear your gloves? Have you lost your gloves?"

   Character traits of Mrs. Mitty: _____

   _____

2. **Walter Mitty:** Once he had tried to take his chains off [the tires], outside New Milford, and he had got them wound around the axles. A man had had to come out in a wrecking car and unwind them, a young, grinning garageman. Since then Mrs. Mitty always made him drive to a garage to have the chains taken off. The next time, he thought, I'll wear my right arm in a sling; they won't grin at me then.

   Character traits of Walter Mitty: _____

   _____

3. **Walter Mitty:** A woman's scream rose above the bedlam and suddenly a lovely, dark-haired girl was in Walter Mitty's arms. The District Attorney struck at her savagely. Without rising from his chair, Mitty let the man have it on the point of the chin. "You miserable cur!" . . .

   Character traits of Walter Mitty: _____

   _____

4. **Mrs. Mitty and Walter Mitty:** "Did you get the what's-its-name? The puppy biscuit? What's in that box?" "Overshoes," said Mitty. "Couldn't you have put them on in the store?" "I was thinking," said Walter Mitty. "Does it ever occur to you that I am sometimes thinking?" She looked at him. "I'm going to take your temperature when I get you home," she said.

   Character traits of Mrs. Mitty and Walter Mitty: _____

   _____

"The Secret Life of Walter Mitty" by James Thurber
Reading: Reflect on Details and Events to Determine an Author's Purpose

An **author's purpose** is his or her main reason for writing. In fiction, the specific purpose is often to convey the story's theme, message, or insight. Pause periodically while reading and **reflect** on the story's details and events to determine the author's purpose. Ask questions such as, *What significance might this event have?* or *Why does the author include this detail?* Based on your reflections, formulate ideas about what the author's purpose might be.

DIRECTIONS: *Write one or two sentences telling why, in your opinion, James Thurber might have included each of the following details or events in "The Secret Life of Walter Mitty."*

1. Mrs. Mitty scolds her husband for driving too fast and for not wearing his gloves. He does what she tells him to do.

   _____

   _____

2. Walter Mitty daydreams, imagining that he is an important surgeon who repairs a piece of medical equipment and saves a patient's life.

   _____

   _____

3. Walter Mitty tells his wife that he does not need overshoes, but his wife insists that he does. He buys the overshoes.

   _____

   _____

4. Walter Mitty daydreams, imagining that he is a heroic air force captain about to fly a two-man bomber into heavy combat by himself.

   _____

   _____

5. Walter Mitty daydreams, imagining himself heroically facing a firing squad—"proud and disdainful, Walter Mitty the Undefeated, inscrutable to the last."

   _____

   _____

   _____

Name _____ Date _____

"The Secret Life of Walter Mitty" by James Thurber
Vocabulary Builder

Word List

derisive   distraught   inscrutable   insinuatingly
insolent   pandemonium

A. DIRECTIONS: *Each item consists of a related pair of words in CAPITAL LETTERS followed by four pairs of words. Write the letter of the pair that best expresses a relationship similar to the one expressed by the pair of words in capital letters.*

____ 1. INSOLENT : RESPECTFUL ::
   A. ancient : old
   B. backward : forward
   C. curious : eager
   D. incredible : unbelievable

____ 2. INSCRUTABLE : PUZZLING ::
   A. tardy : early
   B. precise : careless
   C. circular : round
   D. energetic : exhausted

____ 3. DISTRAUGHT : CAREFREE ::
   A. dangerous : treacherous
   B. alien : stranger
   C. mammoth : enormous
   D. casual : formal

____ 4. INSINUATINGLY : DIRECTLY ::
   A. surprisingly : predictably
   B. quickly : rapidly
   C. enormously : hopefully
   D. judiciously : cautiously

____ 5. DERISIVE : RESPECTFUL ::
   A. thoughtful : philosophical
   B. anxious : nervous
   C. courageous : cowardly
   D. practical : obvious

____ 6. PANDEMONIUM : NOISE ::
   A. silence : confusion
   B. affection : resentment
   C. boredom : freedom
   D. appreciation : gratitude

B. WORD STUDY The Latin suffix *-able* means "can or will" or "capable of being." Rewrite each sentence. Use the underlined word plus the suffix *-able* in the new sentence.

1. The runner was running too fast and would not be able to <u>sustain</u> the pace.

   _____

2. I cannot <u>predict</u> how this story is going to end.

   _____

3. He can <u>attain</u> his goal of getting a college degree and then starting his own business.

   _____

"The Secret Life of Walter Mitty" by James Thurber
Enrichment: Fine Arts

To reach a better understanding of a piece of fine art, you must consider its basic elements, its content, and your response to it.

DIRECTIONS: *Consider the paintings* The Man With Three Masks *and* New Orleans Fantasy, *which illustrate "The Secret Life of Walter Mitty" in your textbook. Then, follow the instructions to compare the two paintings and assess how they relate to the theme, or central message, of "The Secret Life of Walter Mitty."*

1. The *mood* and *tone* of a painting—how the artist feels about the subject—are expressed in a number of ways. Consider choice of color, emphasis of parts of the subject, and use of distortion. What is the overall emotional impact of the paintings? Which aspects of each painting create the mood and tone?

   The Man With Three Masks: _____

   _____

   _____

   New Orleans Fantasy: _____

   _____

   _____

2. Your own reaction is the final aspect of understanding a work of art. Ask yourself: Do I like it? Is the portrayal of the subject appealing to me? Is it pleasant? Boring? How does it make me feel? Write your personal responses to the paintings.

   The Man With Three Masks: _____

   _____

   New Orleans Fantasy: _____

   _____

3. Now, compare your response to the paintings with your response to Thurber's story. Do any details in the story evoke ideas or feelings similar to those evoked by the painting? Explain.

   The Man With Three Masks: _____

   _____

   _____

   _____

   New Orleans Fantasy: _____

   _____

   _____

   _____

Name _____ Date _____

"The Secret Life of Walter Mitty" by James Thurber
Open-Book Test

Short Answer *Write your responses to the questions in this section on the lines provided.*

1. Reread the conversation between Mitty and his wife in the third paragraph of "The Secret Life of Walter Mitty." Based on this conversation, how does Mrs. Mitty view her husband? Explain.

   _____

   _____

   _____

2. Fill in the diagram with one of Walter Mitty's faults and one of his strengths. Give an example of each.

   Fault: _____   **Strength:** _____

   _____   _____

   Example: **Walter Mitty**   **Example:**

3. In "The Secret Life of Walter Mitty," how do the characters in Mitty's dreams treat him? Give two examples from the story.

   _____

   _____

   _____

4. In "The Secret Life of Walter Mitty," Mrs. Mitty is irritated by her husband's absentmindedness. Cite two pieces of evidence from the story that show this.

   _____

   _____

   _____

5. A round character shows many different traits, while a flat character shows a single trait. Would you describe Mrs. Mitty as a round or a flat character? Support your response with an example from "The Secret Life of Walter Mitty."

   _____

   _____

   _____

6. Reread the paragraph in which Walter Mitty remembers taking the chains off his tires. In your opinion, what is the author's purpose for including this memory?

_____

_____

_____

7. Cite a moment in "The Secret Life of Walter Mitty" when Mitty feels distraught. Base your answer on the definition of *distraught*.

_____

_____

_____

8. What kind of man is Walter Mitty? Use evidence from the story to support your answer.

_____

_____

_____

9. In your view, does "The Secret Life of Walter Mitty" end on a comic or a tragic note? Explain, using examples from the story.

_____

_____

_____

_____

10. In your view, is Walter Mitty inscrutable? Explain your answer on the basis of the meaning of *inscrutable*.

_____

_____

_____

Essay

Write an extended response to the question of your choice or to the question or questions your teacher assigns you.

11. Walter Mitty is treated very differently in his real life than in his imaginary life. In an essay, describe this difference, and explain why you think it exists. Are Mitty's two lives totally separate, or are they related in some way?

12. What triggers the details in each of Walter Mitty's daydreams? To answer this question, review what Mitty is doing when each daydream begins. Where is he? What is going on around him in real life? How do these events and details affect his daydreams? Answer these questions in a brief essay, using evidence from the story as support.

13. In limited third-person point of view, an author reveals the thoughts of only one character, and it is through this character's eyes that all other characters and events are viewed. In an essay, explain why you think Thurber chose to use limited third-person point of view in "The Secret Life of Walter Mitty." How does Thurber use it? What effect does it have on the story?

14. **Thinking About the Big Question: Can truth change?** Near the end of "The Secret Life of Walter Mitty," Walter tries, for the first time, to change the way his wife views him. How does he do this? Does he succeed? Does Mrs. Mitty grasp a new truth about her husband? What effect does this have on Walter? Answer these questions in an essay, using examples from the story to support your response.

Oral Response

15. Go back to question 3, 6, or 9 or to the question your teacher assigns to you. Take a few minutes to expand your answer and prepare an oral response. Find additional details in "The Secret Life of Walter Mitty" that will support your points. If necessary, make notes to guide your response.

Name _____ Date _____

"The Secret Life of Walter Mitty" by James Thurber
Selection Test A

Critical Reading *Identify the letter of the choice that best answers the question.*

____ 1. In Walter Mitty's daydreams, how do the other characters treat him?
  A. respectfully
  B. sympathetically
  C. scornfully
  D. impatiently

____ 2. Judging from what she says and does, how does Mrs. Mitty feel about her husband?
  A. She loves and respects him.
  B. She is proud of him.
  C. She is irritated and annoyed with him.
  D. She is frightened of him.

____ 3. Why might you consider Mrs. Mitty a flat character?
  A. She changes at the end of the story.
  B. She does not change.
  C. She has many character traits.
  D. She has only one main character trait.

____ 4. In his daydreams, which of the following character traits does Walter Mitty imagine that he has?
  A. humor
  B. strength
  C. courage
  D. patience

____ 5. Why might you consider Walter Mitty a round character?
  A. He needs to lose twenty-five pounds.
  B. He is meek on the outside but bold in his daydreams.
  C. He is athletic.
  D. He never says what he thinks.

____ 6. Why does Thurber include Walter Mitty's daydreams in his story?
  A. They are funny.
  B. They create suspense.
  C. They reveal Mitty's character.
  D. They reveal Mrs. Mitty's character.

_____ 7. Why do you think Thurber begins his story with the daydream of Mitty commanding a navy seaplane in a storm?

A. He introduces Mr. and Mrs. Mitty.

B. Walter Mitty is a pilot in real life.

C. He wants to grab the reader's interest.

D. The entire story takes place in a storm.

_____ 8. In "The Secret Life of Walter Mitty," what does "spoiling for a hurricane" mean in this sentence?

It's spoiling for a hurricane, if you ask me.

A. We have just been through a hurricane.

B. It looks as if a hurricane is coming.

C. Being in a hurricane is scary.

D. There is no rain or wind in sight.

_____ 9. What is the author's purpose in including this passage in "The Secret Life of Walter Mitty"?

"Not so fast! You're driving too fast!" said Mrs. Mitty. "What are you driving so fast for?"

A. to show that Walter Mitty is a skillful driver

B. to entertain the reader with Mrs. Mitty's joke

C. to create sympathy for Mrs. Mitty

D. to show that Mrs. Mitty orders her husband around

_____ 10. In this passage from Thurber's story, why is the garageman grinning when he comes to help Walter Mitty unwind the chains from his tires?

Once he had tried to take his chains off, outside New Milford, and he had got them wound around the axles. A man had had to come out in a wrecking car and unwind them, a young, grinning garageman.

A. Mitty has just told him a joke.

B. The garageman is being friendly.

C. The garageman is laughing at Mitty.

D. The garageman always grins.

_____ 11. Why is Walter Mitty a static character, not a dynamic one?

A. He has not changed or learned anything by the end of the story.

B. At the end of the story, he decides to give up daydreaming.

C. He is weak and timid.

D. He does not communicate well with Mrs. Mitty.

Vocabulary and Grammar

____ 12. In which sentence is the word *distraught* used correctly?

A. He is distraught about his missing keys.

B. The distraught bowl fell and broke.

C. Those trees are very distraught.

D. The cake is too distraught to cut.

____ 13. In Thurber's story, who is likely to be most *insolent* to Walter Mitty?

A. Walter Mitty himself

B. the characters in his daydreams

C. Mrs. Mitty

D. the friends he plays golf with

____ 14. Identify the relative pronoun in this sentence from Thurber's story.

A woman who was passing laughed.

A. woman   C. passing

B. who   D. laughed

____ 15. Which of the following relative pronouns best completes this sentence?

James Thurber, _____ wrote "The Secret Life of Walter Mitty," grew up in Ohio.

A. which   C. whose

B. that   D. who

Essay

16. In a brief essay, describe Walter Mitty's personality. Think of how he behaves with his wife and with other real-life characters in the story. Mention two of Mitty's character traits, and support each one with an example from the story.

17. In an essay, compare and contrast the way Walter Mitty is treated in his real life with the way he is treated in his fantasy life. Why does the author show us both lives? Give examples from the story to support your statements.

18. **Thinking About the Big Question: Can truth change?** Near the end of "The Secret Life of Walter Mitty," Walter tries, for the first time, to change the way his wife views him. He says, "I was thinking. . . . Does it ever occur to you that I am sometimes thinking?" How did Mrs. Mitty view her husband before he says this? Does she grasp a new truth about her husband after he says this? Explain your answer in an essay. Use examples from the story to support your response.

"The Secret Life of Walter Mitty" by James Thurber
Selection Test B

Critical Reading *Identify the letter of the choice that best completes the statement or answers the question.*

_____ 1. What is the difference between how others treat Walter Mitty in real life and how they treat him in his daydreams?
A. In real life, others treat him with more respect than they do in his daydreams.
B. In his daydreams, others see him as more dangerous than he is.
C. In his daydreams, others treat him with more respect or fear than they do in real life.
D. In his real life, others treat him with more kindness than they show in his daydreams.

_____ 2. What is one of the author's purposes in contrasting Walter Mitty's daydreams and his real life?
A. to persuade readers that they should respect others
B. to entertain readers with the humor of the contrast
C. to entertain readers with Mr. Mitty's exciting adventures
D. to pay tribute to Mrs. Mitty's patience

_____ 3. What is the author's main purpose in the following passage from "The Secret Life of Walter Mitty"?

She didn't like to get to the hotel first; she would want him to be there waiting for her as usual. He found a big leather chair in the lobby. . . .

A. to show Walter Mitty's independence
B. to show Mrs. Mitty's bossiness
C. to show how obedient Walter Mitty is to his wife
D. to help readers picture the hotel lobby

_____ 4. In "The Secret Life of Walter Mitty," which of the following describes Mrs. Mitty's character?
I. round
II. flat
III. static
IV. dynamic
A. I and IV   B. II and IV   C. I and III   D. II and III

_____ 5. In "The Secret Life of Walter Mitty," which of the following describes Walter Mitty's character?
I. round
II. flat
III. static
IV. dynamic
A. I and IV   B. II and IV   C. II and III   D. I and III

_____ 6. While reading "The Secret Life of Walter Mitty," why is it important to follow events carefully?
A. The events are based on a real person's life story.
B. The events jump back and forth between fantasy and reality.
C. The narrator does not tell the truth to the reader.
D. Walter Mitty deliberately tries to deceive his wife.

____ 7. In Thurber's story, what is the connection between Mitty's daydreams and his real life?
   A. Something in his real life triggers each daydream.
   B. Something in his daydream triggers his real life.
   C. His real life and his daydreams are the same.
   D. There is no connection between his daydreams and his real life.

____ 8. What does "Pick it up, brother," mean in this passage from "The Secret Life of Walter Mitty"?

   He put them [the gloves] on, but after she had turned and gone into the building and he had driven on to a red light, he took them off again. "Pick it up, brother!" snapped a cop as the light changed, and Mitty hastily pulled on his gloves and lurched ahead.

   A. Put your gloves back on.
   B. Pick up the glove you dropped.
   C. Put on your overshoes.
   D. Move your car.

____ 9. A limited third-person narrator reveals the thoughts of only one character, through whose eyes we see the other characters. What is the effect of Thurber's use of the third-person limited point of view in "The Secret Life of Walter Mitty"?
   A. Readers are led to sympathize with Walter Mitty.
   B. Readers are led to sympathize with Mrs. Mitty.
   C. Readers get a biased version of the real story.
   D. Readers get to know all of the characters equally well.

____ 10. Which trait of Walter Mitty's is shown in this passage from Thurber's story?

   Once he had tried to take his chains off, outside New Milford, and he had got them wound around the axles. A man had had to come out in a wrecking car and unwind them, a young, grinning garageman.

   A. his self-confidence
   B. his mechanical skills
   C. his sense of humor
   D. his inability to act effectively

____ 11. What is Thurber's purpose for including Walter Mitty's daydreams in his story?
   A. They foreshadow events to come.
   B. They create suspense.
   C. They help reveal Mrs. Mitty's character.
   D. They help reveal Walter Mitty's character.

____ 12. What feeling, or attitude, does Thurber want the reader to have toward Walter Mitty?
   A. admiration for his inventiveness
   B. sympathy for his unhappiness
   C. scorn for his cowardice
   D. respect for his intelligence

Vocabulary and Grammar

_____ 13. In which sentence is the word *distraught* used correctly?
   A. I am too distraught to concentrate.
   B. His health is distraught.
   C. She won an award for being distraught.
   D. She is only distraught when she sleeps.

_____ 14. At the end of Thurber's story, why does Mitty think of himself as *inscrutable*?
   A. No one truly knows him.
   B. No one has ever defeated him.
   C. No one has been happier with his life.
   D. No one except his wife knows his name.

_____ 15. In Thurber's story, who is most likely to be *insolent* to Walter Mitty?
   A. the characters he meets in his real life
   B. the characters in his daydreams
   C. Walter Mitty himself
   D. his friends in the retirement community

_____ 16. In the following sentence from Thurber's story, identify the relative pronoun.
   She seemed grossly unfamiliar, like a strange woman who had yelled at him in a crowd.
   A. She   C. who
   B. woman   D. him

_____ 17. Which of the following quotations from Thurber's story contains a relative pronoun?
   A. "Remember to get those overshoes while I'm having my hair done," she said.
   B. "Back it up, Mac! Look out for that Buick!"
   C. "There is no one in the East who knows how to fix it!"
   D. "I'm going to take your temperature when I get you home," she said.

Essay

18. In a brief essay, explain the connections between Walter Mitty's real life and his vivid fantasy life. Which elements of real life reappear in his fantasies? Which aspects of his real life does he ignore in his fantasies? In your essay, discuss ways in which Mitty's fantasies may help him endure certain aspects of his real life.

19. At the end of "The Secret Life of Walter Mitty," Walter Mitty seems to stand up to his wife for the first time. When she scolds him for not being easy to find in the hotel and for not putting on his overshoes, he says:

   "I was thinking," said Walter Mitty. "Does it ever occur to you that I am sometimes thinking?" She looked at him. "I'm going to take your temperature when I get you home," she said.

   In an essay, comment on this passage and on the firing-squad daydream that ends the story. Why do you think Thurber chose to end his story with these passages?

20. **Thinking About the Big Question: Can truth change?** Near the end of "The Secret Life of Walter Mitty," Walter tries, for the first time, to change the way his wife views him. How does he do this? Does he succeed? Does Mrs. Mitty grasp a new truth about her husband? What effect does this have on Walter? Answer these questions in an essay, using examples from the story to support your response.

Vocabulary Warm-up Word Lists

Study these words from "Uncle Marcos." Then, complete the activities.

Word List A

acquainted [uh KWAYN tid] *v.* aware of; familiar with
He would have played better if he had been <u>acquainted</u> with the rules.

attraction [uh TRAK shuhn] *n.* something that draws attention
The lions' den at feeding time is a major <u>attraction</u> at the zoo.

authorities [uh THAWR uh tees] *n.* people with power or knowledge
<u>Authorities</u> on handwriting and fingerprints testified during the trial.

confirmed [kuhn FERMD] *v.* proved true or valid
The scientist found that the experiment's results <u>confirmed</u> her theory.

contraption [kuhn TRAP shun] *n.* gadget; thrown-together device
The homemade ramp was a shaky <u>contraption</u> used by the skaters.

improvisations [im prah vi ZAY shuhnz] *n.* things done or made up on the spot
When the actor forgot his lines, his <u>improvisations</u> won lots of laughs.

strictly [STRIKT lee] *adv.* exactly and correctly; only
These bowls are <u>strictly</u> for decoration.

technical [TEK nuh kuhl] *adj.* used in a specific profession or craft
I lack the <u>technical</u> know-how to work on an engineering project.

Word List B

accessible [ak SES uh buhl] *adj.* reachable; able to be obtained
The statistical information was easily <u>accessible</u> on the Internet.

adventurous [ad VEN chur uhs] *adj.* daring
The <u>adventurous</u> explorers used only a compass to find their way.

aerial [AYR ee uhl] *adj.* of, by, or in the air
The pilot checked her <u>aerial</u> maps.

commercial [kuh MER shul] *adj.* done mainly for profit
Though it began as a hobby, her gardening was a <u>commercial</u> success.

farthest [FAHR thist] *adj.* most distant
The <u>farthest</u> place from home that I have visited is Acapulco, Mexico.

impassive [im PAS iv] *adj.* showing no emotion
Despite his disappointment, his face remained <u>impassive</u>.

speculate [SPEK yuh layt] *v.* think about; ponder
We tried to <u>speculate</u> on the reasons for the unusual heat wave.

withstand [with STAND] *v.* endure; put up with
I do not think I can <u>withstand</u> any more of my brother's teasing.

Name _____ Date _____

"Uncle Marcos" by Isabel Allende
Vocabulary Warm-up Exercises

Exercise A *Fill in each blank in the paragraph below with an appropriate word from Word List A. Use each word only once.*

I have always felt an [1] _____ to people who know how to create things.

My interest in becoming an inventor was [2] _____ when I began enter-

ing science fairs in high school. The first [3] _____ I built was just a pile

of nuts and bolts, but my [4] _____ skills improved when I started tak-

ing special classes after school. A good way to learn what it is like to be an inventor is to

become [5] _____ with actual inventors and talk to them about their

work. Also, be prepared to make [6] _____ when things do not work out

[7] _____ as planned. If you cannot solve a problem alone, find knowl-

edgeable [8] _____ to help you. That is what being inventive is all about!

Exercise B *Write two sentences of your own using each word on Word List B. You may use a different form of the vocabulary word in your second sentence.*

Example: aerial
    A. *The pilot performed such <u>aerial</u> stunts as flying his plane upside down.*
    B. *The circus <u>aerialist</u> swung overhead on his trapeze.*

1. **accessible** A. _____
    B. _____

2. **adventurous** A. _____
    B. _____

3. **commercial** A. _____
    B. _____

4. **farthest** A. _____
    B. _____

5. **impassive** A. _____
    B. _____

6. **speculate** A. _____
    B. _____

7. **withstand** A. _____
    B. _____

"Uncle Marcos" by Isabel Allende
Reading Warm-up A

Read the following passage. Pay special attention to the underlined words. Then, read it again, and complete the activities. Use a separate sheet of paper for your written answers.

You are probably <u>acquainted</u> with Leonardo da Vinci as the artist who painted the *Mona Lisa*. The painting is a major <u>attraction</u> that draws thousands of museum visitors every year. If your impression of Leonardo is based <u>strictly</u> on his paintings, however, you may not know that he was also one of the greatest scientific thinkers of all time.

Leonardo was born in Vinci, Italy, in 1452. He was a brilliant inventor and engineer. Leonardo believed in using observation and experimentation to solve problems. At that time, the scientific method was almost completely unknown. Most thinkers and other <u>authorities</u> of the day had no interest in such methods. Leonardo acquired vast <u>technical</u> knowledge on his own. He used his scientific know-how to conduct experiments. When he could not get the materials he needed, Leonardo made <u>improvisations</u> with materials he was able to find.

Leonardo loved to think of new ways of doing things. Although he hated war, he designed cannons, machine guns, parachutes, and armored military vehicles that were far beyond anything that existed at the time. Leonardo loved the idea of flying and studied birds for many years to learn how they soared through the sky. He even designed a flying machine that he hoped could carry a man high into the air. The <u>contraption</u> he designed would have been too heavy to get off the ground. Nevertheless, the ideas on which it was based would later be used to develop the modern helicopter.

Leonardo's genius is <u>confirmed</u> by the many writings he left behind. He filled thousands of notebook pages with notes and drawings. They described some of the amazing projects that he never got around to completing. These notebooks have inspired generations of scientists and engineers ever since.

If any man could truly be said to have lived before his time, that man would be Leonardo da Vinci.

1. Underline the way in which the author thinks you may be <u>acquainted</u> with Leonardo. Then, tell what *acquainted* means.

2. Circle the words that identify the painting that is a major <u>attraction</u>. What *attraction* might draw you into a museum?

3. Circle the words that tell what some people's impressions of Leonardo are <u>strictly</u> based on. Tell why this is not a good idea.

4. What group of people is identified as the <u>authorities</u> of the day? How did Leonardo differ from them?

5. Underline the synonym for "<u>technical</u> knowledge." What kind of *technical* knowledge might be useful for an inventor?

6. Underline the words that tell when Leonardo had to make <u>improvisations</u>. When might *improvisations* be useful?

7. Circle the words that identify Leonardo's <u>contraption</u>. Describe a *contraption* that you might like to build.

8. Underline words that tell how Leonardo's genius is <u>confirmed</u>. What else might *confirm* someone's genius?

"Uncle Marcos" by Isabel Allende
Reading Warm-up B

Read the following passage. Pay special attention to the underlined words. Then, read it again, and complete the activities. Use a separate sheet of paper for your written answers.

At the dawn of the twentieth century, few people dared to speculate that human beings would soon be able to fly. Yet, two brothers named Orville and Wilbur Wright were about to make that dream come true.

The adventurous Wright brothers had never been afraid of a challenge. Together, as young men, they opened a bicycle shop in Dayton, Ohio. Their business was a commercial success, but simply making money was not enough to satisfy the Wright brothers. Soon, they developed an interest in flying and started building a series of gliders. Fearing that the gliders would be unable to withstand strong winds, they built a sturdier airplane powered by a lightweight gasoline engine. They took their new airplane to Kitty Hawk, North Carolina, to test it out.

On December 17, 1903, the brothers tossed a coin to see who would go up first. Orville won. He flew for 12 seconds and traveled 120 feet. Although the farthest the plane flew that day was only 825 feet, the airborne brothers were rightfully proud of their extraordinary aerial feat. They knew that aviation history had been made that day.

The Wright brothers soon began making better and better airplanes. When they offered their invention to the United States government, impassive officials showed no interest. What practical use could there be for a flying machine? It did not take very long, however, for people around the world to realize that the Wright brothers' invention could change the course of history.

Wilbur died shortly before the airplane could be used as a deadly war machine during World War I. Orville, however, lived long enough to see air travel become a reality for ordinary people.

Today, the original airplane flown by the Wright brothers at Kitty Hawk is accessible to all visitors at the National Air and Space Museum in Washington, D.C.

1. Underline the words that tell what few people dared to speculate. What future event might you *speculate* about?

2. Underline words that support the idea that the Wright brothers were adventurous. What might *adventurous* people do?

3. Circle the words that tell what commercial means. What business do you think you could make a *commercial* success?

4. Why might a glider be unable to withstand strong winds? What does *withstand* mean?

5. What is the farthest you have traveled from your home? How far away from home were you?

6. Circle the word that has a meaning similar to aerial. Why were the brothers proud of their *aerial* feat?

7. Why were the officials impassive? Explain what *impassive* means.

8. To whom is the famous airplane accessible? Give an example of when it might not be *accessible*.

"Uncle Marcos" by Isabel Allende
Writing About the Big Question

Can truth change?

Big Question Vocabulary

assumption	belief	circumstance	context	convince
credible	distort	evidence	manipulate	perceive
perspective	skeptics	speculate	truth	verify

A. *Use one or more words from the list above to complete each sentence.*

1. The most magical stories look at truth from a different _____.

2. An author may _____ reality to reveal the truth.

3. In the story, Allende's _____ is that there can be many truths.

4. Uncle Marcos trusted his _____ in flying even though it was not strongly supported by the evidence.

B. *Follow the directions in responding to each item below.*

1. What person whom you know has lived the most unusual or exciting life?
   _____

2. How is the person's perspective on life similar to or different from your own? Write three sentences explaining your answer. Use two of the Big Question vocabulary words.
   _____
   _____
   _____

C. *In "Uncle Marcos," the narrator describes the fantastic escapades of an uncle who's not satisfied with the ordinary. Complete the sentence below. Then, write a short paragraph in which you connect this experience to the Big Question.*

A person who believes strongly in impractical and impossible things _____

_____

_____

_____

_____

_____

Name _____ Date _____

"Uncle Marcos" *from* **The House of the Spirits** by Isabel Allende
Literary Analysis: Character

A **character** is a person or an animal that takes part in the action of a literary work.

- A **round character** is complex, showing many different qualities—revealing faults as well as virtues. For example, a character might be sensitive in some situations but insensitive in others. A **flat character** is one-dimensional, showing a single trait.
- A **dynamic character** develops, changes, and learns something during the course of a story, unlike a **static character**, who remains the same.

The main character of a story is almost always a round character and is usually dynamic. The main character's development and growth are often central to a story's plot and theme. As you read, consider the traits that make characters seem round or flat, dynamic or static.

A. DIRECTIONS: *For each numbered item, write a sentence telling what character trait or traits the passage reveals.*

1. After a short time, bored with having to appear at ladies' gatherings where the mistress of the house played the piano, with playing cards, and with dodging all his relatives' pressures to pull himself together and take a job as a clerk in Severo del Valle's law practice, he bought a barrel organ and took to the streets with the hope of seducing his Cousin Antonieta and entertaining the public in the bargain.

   Character traits of Uncle Marcos: _____

   _____

2. In the face of this stain to the family reputation, Marcos was forced to give up organ grinding and resort to less conspicuous ways of winning over his Cousin Antonieta, but he did not renounce his goal.

   Character traits of Uncle Marcos: _____

   _____

3. He had lost his airplane and had to return on foot, but he had not broken any bones and his adventurous spirit was intact.

   Character traits of Uncle Marcos: _____

   _____

B. DIRECTIONS: *Write a brief character analysis of Uncle Marcos. Tell whether he is flat or round and dynamic or static. Give examples from the story to support your statements.*

_____

_____

_____

_____

_____

_____

Name _____ Date _____

Reading: Reflect on Details and Events to Determine an Author's Purpose

An **author's purpose** is his or her main reason for writing. In fiction, the specific purpose is often to convey the story's theme, message, or insight. Pause periodically while reading and **reflect** on the story's details and events to determine the author's purpose. Ask questions such as, *What significance might this event have?* or *Why does the author include this detail?*

Based on your reflections, formulate ideas about what the author's purpose might be.

A. DIRECTIONS: *Write one or two sentences telling why, in your opinion, Isabel Allende might have included each of the following details or events in "Uncle Marcos."*

1. Uncle Marcos sleeps during the day, stays up all night, and performs strange experiments in the kitchen.

   _____

   _____

2. He refuses to take a job in his brother-in-law's law firm.

   _____

   _____

3. He embarrasses the family by serenading Cousin Antonieta with a barrel-organ and a parrot.

   _____

   _____

4. He builds an airplane and takes off in it.

   _____

   _____

5. He gives up the fortune-telling business when he realizes that it is affecting people's lives.

   _____

   _____

B. DIRECTIONS: *Think back over the events and details of the story and your answers to the questions above. Then, in a sentence or two, write what you think the author's purpose is in "Uncle Marcos."*

_____

_____

_____

Name _____ Date _____

"Uncle Marcos" *from* **The House of the Spirits** by Isabel Allende
Vocabulary Builder

Word List

conspicuous   disconsolately   impassive   pallid   pertinent   unrequited

A. DIRECTIONS: *Each item consists of a related pair of words in CAPITAL LETTERS followed by four pairs of words. Write the letter of the pair that best expresses a relationship similar to the one expressed by the pair in capital letters.*

____ 1. PALLID : PALE ::
    A. tense : relaxed   C. anxious : worried
    B. organized : messy   D. stubborn : mule

____ 2. JOYFULLY : DISCONSOLATELY ::
    A. methodically : carefully   C. static : unchanged
    B. overflowing : empty   D. common : familiar

____ 3. UNREQUITED : RETURNED ::
    A. tamed : wild   C. tiny : molecule
    B. wrinkled : rumpled   D. exceptional : unusual

____ 4. CONSPICUOUS : CONCEALED ::
    A. forgotten : remembered   C. preferred : practical
    B. sorrowful : sincere   D. simplified : straightforward

____ 5. PERTINENT : RELEVANT ::
    A. timely : recent   C. elegant : graceful
    B. confident : doubtful   D. determined : uncertain

____ 6. IMPASSIVE : EMOTIONAL ::
    A. willful : stubborn   C. confused : puzzled
    B. passionate : romantic   D. careful : impulsive

B. WORD STUDY The Latin suffix *-ive* means "of, belonging to, quality of." Answer each of the following questions. Add the suffix *-ive* to the underlined word and use it in your new sentence.

1. Why would someone <u>reflect</u> on a poem?

    _____

2. Why would you take a CD player back to the store if it had a <u>defect</u>?

    _____

3. Why should government leaders <u>cooperate</u>?

    _____

"Uncle Marcos" *from* **The House of the Spirits** by Isabel Allende
Enrichment: The History of Human Flight

Throughout history, humans have dreamed of following birds into flight. According to an ancient Greek myth, an inventor named Daedalus and his son, Icarus, were imprisoned on the island of Crete. King Minos kept them in the labyrinth (a maze) that Daedalus had designed and built. One day, Daedalus thought of a way to escape. He fashioned a pair of wings and used wax to attach rows of birds' feathers to them. Then, he made a harness to strap the wings to his body, and when he tested the contraption, it carried him up into the air. He could fly! Daedalus made a second pair of wings for Icarus. He warned his son not to fly too close to the sun, for the sun's heat would melt the wax and cause the wings to fall apart. The day of their escape came, and the two took flight. Icarus, who was supposed to be following his father, spiraled up close to the sun. The wax melted, the wings came apart, and Icarus drowned in the sea.

DIRECTIONS: *Create a timeline of human flight. First, using a reliable source, either online or in print, answer the following questions. For each answer, write your source of information. Then, on a separate piece of paper, use the information you have gathered to create a timeline that shows the milestones in the history of human flight. (You may add to your timeline any other events related to human flight that you come across as you do your research.)*

1. When did Leonardo da Vinci live? What contribution did he make to the study of human flight?

   _____

   _____

2. When did the Wright brothers first make a sustained flight at Kitty Hawk, North Carolina?

   _____

3. When did Charles A. Lindbergh make the first solo nonstop transatlantic flight? Where did it begin and end?

   _____

4. When was the helicopter invented and flown for the first time?

   _____

   _____

5. When and where was the first jet flight?

   _____

6. When was the first manned space flight? Who was the first man to fly into outer space?

   _____

7. When did men first walk on the moon? Who were they?

   _____

Name _____ Date _____

"The Secret Life of Walter Mitty" by James Thurber
"Uncle Marcos" *from* **The House of the Spirits** by Isabel Allende
Integrated Language Skills: Grammar

Relative, Interrogative, and Indefinite Pronouns

Pronouns are words that stand for nouns or for words that take the place of nouns. There are a number of different kinds of pronouns.

A **relative pronoun** begins a subordinate clause and connects it to another idea in the sentence. The five relative pronouns are *that, which, who, whom,* and *whose.*

Uncle Marcos is a person *who* likes adventure.

An **interrogative pronoun** begins a question. The five interrogative pronouns are *what, which, who, whom,* and *whose.*

Who is Clara?

Indefinite pronouns refer to people, places, or things, often without specifying which ones. Words that are or can function as indefinite pronouns include *anyone, everybody, nobody,* and *somebody; anything, nothing,* and *something; any, all, few, many, most, one,* and *some; little* and *much;* and *another, both,* and *either.*

Everybody came out to watch Uncle Marcos take off in the airplane.

A. PRACTICE: *Underline the relative, interrogative, or indefinite pronoun in each sentence. On the line or lines following the sentence, identify each pronoun you underlined as* relative, interrogative, *or* indefinite.

1. Trunks, animals in jars of formaldehyde, and Indian lances are some of the items that Uncle Marcos brought home from his travels. _____, _____

2. In whose house did Marcos spend his time, sleeping during the day and conducting experiments at night? _____

3. Marcos's departure by airplane was a remarkable event, which virtually everyone in town had come out to witness. _____, _____

4. Who were the explorers and mountain climbers who claimed to have found the body? _____, _____

5. Everyone was saddened when they appeared with the coffin that they claimed held Uncle Marcos's body (but which actually contained bags of sand). _____, _____, _____

B. Writing Application: *Write a paragraph that summarizes what happens when Uncle Marcos courts Cousin Antonieta. Use at least one relative pronoun, one interrogative pronoun, and one indefinite pronoun in your paragraph, and underline each.*

_____

_____

_____

_____

_____

Name _____ Date _____

"The Secret Life of Walter Mitty" by James Thurber
"Uncle Marcos" by Isabel Allende

Integrated Language Skills: Support for Writing a Character Profile

If you read "The Secret Life of Walter Mitty," choose one of the heroic characters in Mitty's daydreams (commander of a navy seaplane, famous surgeon, defendant at a trial, or captain of a bomber). If you read "Uncle Marcos," write your profile on that character. Gather ideas for your **character profile** by completing this cluster diagram.

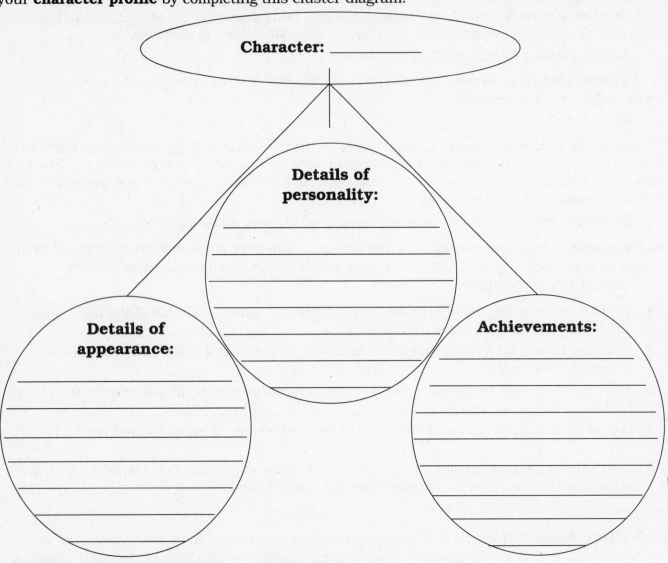

1. What single impression of the character do you want to convey?

_____

2. Place a check mark next to the details in your diagram that will help you convey that impression.

3. Briefly list ideas in the order in which you will present them in your character profile.

_____

_____

Now, use your notes to draft a character profile of the character.

"The Secret Life of Walter Mitty" by James Thurber
"Uncle Marcos" *from* **The House of the Spirits** by Isabel Allende
Integrated Language Skills: Support for Extend Your Learning

Research and Technology

If you read "The Secret Life of Walter Mitty," keep a **learning log** of the information that you gather about daydreams. If you read "Uncle Marcos," keep a **learning log** of the information that you gather about the history of human flight. Identify each source that you explore, and tell what facts you learned from each source. If you use a direct quotation from a source, enclose it in large quotation marks.

1. **Source:** _____

   What I learned: _____

   _____

   _____

2. **Source:** _____

   What I learned: _____

   _____

   _____

3. **Source:** _____

   What I learned: _____

   _____

   _____

4. **Source:** _____

   What I learned: _____

   _____

   _____

Name _____ Date _____

"Uncle Marcos" by Isabel Allende
Open-Book Test

Short Answer *Write your responses to the questions in this section on the lines provided.*

1. In "Uncle Marcos," Uncle Marcos's behavior could be described as unusual. List two examples of his unusual behavior from the story.

   _____

   _____

   _____

   _____

2. How is the relationship that Uncle Marcos has with Clara different from the relationships he has with the other characters? Use an example from the story to support your answer.

   _____

   _____

   _____

   _____

3. A dynamic character changes or learns something new in a story. In "Uncle Marcos," what event causes Uncle Marcos to change? How does he change?

   _____

   _____

4. In "Uncle Marcos," why can Uncle Marcos be considered a round character? Support your response with examples from the story.

   _____

   _____

   _____

5. Uncle Marcos's brother-in-law, Severo, is a flat character. Identify his main trait, and give an example of it from the story.

   _____

   _____

   _____

6. In your opinion, what is the author's purpose for writing "Uncle Marcos"? Provide two examples from the story that help her accomplish this purpose.

   _____

   _____

   _____

7. Cite a moment in "Uncle Marcos" when Clara behaves disconsolately. Base your answer on the definition of *disconsolately*.

_____

_____

_____

8. In "Uncle Marcos," Clara is a round character. In the diagram below, list one of her actions. Then name a character trait that the action reveals.

Action		**Character Trait**
	→	

9. Is Clara's affection for Uncle Marcos unrequited? Give two examples from the story to support your response. Base your answer on the definition of *requited*.

_____

_____

_____

_____

10. Locate the section of the story in which Uncle Marcos returns from his flight alive. What word does the author use to describe his "resurrection"? Why do you think she uses this word?

_____

_____

_____

Essay

Write an extended response to the question of your choice or to the question or questions your teacher assigns you.

11. Some characters in "Uncle Marcos" are fond of Uncle Marcos, and others are annoyed with him. Which character's feelings about Uncle Marcos most closely match your own? Explain your choice in an essay, using examples from the story to support it.

12. How a person behaves in a time of crisis reveals important information about his or her character. In an essay, identify three moments of crisis for Uncle Marcos, and explain how he responds to these crises. What inference can you make about his character, based on each response? In general, does Uncle Marcos strike you as respectable or unrespectable? Why or why not?

13. At both the beginning and the end of "Uncle Marcos," Uncle Marcos occupies a coffin. In some ways, it seems impossible that such a man would be dead. In other ways, it seems perfectly logical that he would be dead. In an essay, explain why each of these opposing ideas is valid, using evidence from the story to support your ideas.

14. **Thinking About the Big Question: Can truth change?** After Marcos's failed courtship of Cousin Antonieta, people view Uncle Marcos one way, but after he returns from his airplane flight, people view him another way. In an essay, explain why this is so. Who has actually changed: Uncle Marcos or the townspeople? Cite details from "Uncle Marcos" to support your points.

Oral Response

15. Go back to question 2, 4, 6, or 8 or to the question your teacher assigns to you. Take a few minutes to expand your answer and prepare an oral response. Find additional details in "Uncle Marcos" that will support your points. If necessary, make notes to guide your response.

"Uncle Marcos" by Isabel Allende
Selection Test A

Critical Reading *Identify the letter of the choice that best answers the question.*

_____ 1. Which phrase best describes the subject of "Uncle Marcos" by Isabel Allende?
A. the childhood of a famous explorer
B. a girl's memories of her uncle
C. the end of a love affair
D. a stranger in a small town

_____ 2. Which of Uncle Marcos's adventures leads the family to interfere?
A. his serenade of Cousin Antonieta
B. his building an airplane
C. his flying an airplane
D. his fortune-telling business

_____ 3. In Allende's story, why can Uncle Marcos be classified as a dynamic character?
A. He takes interesting trips.
B. People like him.
C. He changes after Cousin Antonieta rejects him.
D. He does not change at all.

_____ 4. What was the author's purpose for including the story of Uncle Marcos's serenading Cousin Antonieta with a barrel organ and a parrot?
A. to create suspense
B. to explain how to play a barrel organ
C. to explain how to train a parrot
D. to reveal Uncle Marcos's character

_____ 5. What is the "bird" in this sentence from "Uncle Marcos"?

Marcos spent two weeks assembling the contents according to an instruction manual written in English, which he was able to decipher thanks to his invincible imagination and a small dictionary. When the job was finished, it turned out to be a bird of prehistoric dimensions. . . .

A. a child's toy
B. a wooden eagle
C. a motorboat
D. an airplane

____ 6. In Isabel Allende's story, why can Uncle Marcos be classified as a round character?
A. He always comes home.
B. He feels at home all over the world.
C. He has sentimental feelings as well as a love of outrageous adventure.
D. He has only one main character trait.

____ 7. Uncle Marcos leaves his parrot with Clara before he goes on one of his trips. What is the author's purpose for including this detail?
A. to show that Uncle Marcos is angry with Clara
B. to show that Uncle Marcos is fond of Clara
C. to show that Clara is selfish
D. to show that Clara is angry with Uncle Marcos

____ 8. Clara waits for her uncle to come back after everyone else believes he is dead. What is the author's purpose for including this detail?
A. to show that Clara is foolish
B. to show that Uncle Marcos is a poor airplane pilot
C. to show that Uncle Marcos is hiding
D. to show that Clara has strong affection for Uncle Marcos

____ 9. Which adjective best describes the character of Severo, Uncle Marcos's brother-in-law?
A. bossy
B. mean
C. dishonest
D. conservative

____ 10. Why do Clara and Uncle Marcos close their fortune-telling business?
A. Uncle Marcos grows bored with it.
B. They were worried about the influence they were having on others.
C. Clara leaves for college.
D. They have made enough money and want to retire.

____ 11. At the end of the story, why does Uncle Marcos sail for home?
A. He is old and tired of traveling.
B. He hopes his illness will be cured.
C. He misses his sister.
D. He has a job on a ship.

_____ 12. What main impression of Uncle Marcos does Allende want the reader to have?
  A. He is foolish and selfish.
  B. He is sincere and caring.
  C. He is odd but likable.
  D. He is organized and dependable.

Vocabulary and Grammar

_____ 13. In which of the following sentences is the word *disconsolately* used most logically?
  A. Clara gazed disconsolately at her uncle's coffin.
  B. People cheered loudly and disconsolately when the plane took off.
  C. Clara and her uncle told people's fortunes disconsolately.
  D. Clara loved her uncle's stories and listened disconsolately to every detail.

_____ 14. In "Uncle Marcos," which of Marcos's feelings are *unrequited*?
  A. his affection for Clara
  B. his love for Cousin Antonieta
  C. his curiosity about faraway places
  D. his desire for adventure

_____ 15. Identify the relative pronoun in this sentence from Allende's "Uncle Marcos."
  The entire family wept as befit the occasion, except for Clara, who continued to watch the sky with the patience of an astronomer.

  A. entire   C. Clara
  B. befit   D. who

Essay

16. Choose one of the following episodes from "Uncle Marcos": his courtship of Cousin Antonieta, his building and flying an airplane, or his fortune-telling business. In a brief essay, explain what the episode reveals about Marcos's character and about the way people respond to him.

17. In a brief essay, describe the relationship between Uncle Marcos and his niece Clara. How is it different from the relationships he has with other characters in the story? Use examples from the story to support your statements.

18. **Thinking About the Big Question: Can truth change?** Near the beginning of "Uncle Marcos," Marcos fails to win the heart of Cousin Antonieta with his barrel-organ serenade. What did the townspeople think of Marcos then? After Marcos returns from his failed airplane flight, how was he thought of then? In an essay, answer these questions and tell who actually changed: Was it Uncle Marcos or the townspeople?

Name _____ Date _____

"Uncle Marcos" by Isabel Allende
Selection Test B

Critical Reading *Identify the letter of the choice that best completes the statement or answers the question.*

____ 1. What is the likeliest response of a reader to the story "Uncle Marcos"?
   A. amusement at Uncle Marcos's enthusiasm for outrageous schemes
   B. anger over the embarrassment Uncle Marcos causes the family
   C. deep sympathy for Uncle Marcos's misfortunes
   D. astonishment at Clara's continued affection for her uncle

____ 2. Which of Uncle Marcos's "adventures" does *not* draw a great deal of public attention?
   A. his alchemy experiments
   B. his courtship of Cousin Antonieta
   C. his airplane construction and flight
   D. his fortune-telling enterprise

____ 3. Which incident most clearly shows that Uncle Marcos is a dynamic character?
   A. When staying with Clara's family, he performs odd experiments.
   B. After returning from a trip, he builds a strange-looking airplane.
   C. After returning from a trip, he opens a fortune-telling business.
   D. After Cousin Antonieta rejects him, he vows never to marry.

____ 4. Uncle Marcos serenades Cousin Antonieta, unaware of the embarrassment he might cause himself or her. Given this action, which other action does he perform that most clearly shows that he is a round character?
   A. He performs alchemy experiments and makes odd noises late at night.
   B. He launches an aircraft in the town square in front of huge crowds.
   C. He closes his fortune-telling business when he realizes its effect on others' lives.
   D. He gives up experimenting with aircraft and opens a fortune-telling business.

____ 5. Clara waits for her uncle to return even after he is "buried." What is the author's purpose in including this detail?
   A. to prove that Clara is psychic, just as Uncle Marcos claims
   B. to show the strength of Clara's attachment to her uncle
   C. to reinforce the suspenseful, eerie mood of the story
   D. to emphasize the difficulties that Uncle Marcos creates for the family

____ 6. Which of Uncle Marcos's adventures embarrasses his family to the point of bringing a "stain to the family's reputation"?
   A. his expeditions in the Amazon
   B. his serenade of Cousin Antonieta
   C. his constructing an airplane
   D. his partnership in telling fortunes

____ 7. What is the author's purpose in telling the story of Uncle Marcos's building an airplane?
   A. to tell about the history of airplanes
   B. to reveal Marcos's character
   C. to explain how airplanes are built
   D. to describe an important historical event

Unit 1 Resources: Fiction and Nonfiction

_____ 8. In this sentence from Allende's story, which incident does "heroic resurrection" refer to?
Marcos's heroic resurrection made everyone forget about his barrel-organ phase.
   A. Marcos's courting of Cousin Antonieta
   B. Marcos's flight in a home-made airplane
   C. Marcos's return to town after his funeral
   D. Marcos's fortune-telling enterprise

_____ 9. Uncle Marcos's brother-in-law Severo is a flat character. Which of the following best
describes his main trait?
   A. recklessness
   B. impatience
   C. conservativeness
   D. dishonesty

_____ 10. Why does Allende choose Clara as Uncle Marcos's partner in the fortune-telling business?
   A. to show Marcos's trickiness
   B. to show Marcos's special powers
   C. to show Clara's bond with Marcos
   D. to show Clara's love for money

_____ 11. Although Uncle Marcos and Clara succeed in their fortune-telling business, they
decide to close their business. Which of Uncle Marcos's character traits helps him
make the decision?
   A. his sense of humor
   B. his need for adventure
   C. his impatience with Clara
   D. his integrity or decency

_____ 12. At the end of Allende's story, why does Uncle Marcos set out for home?
   A. He has exhausted new places to visit.
   B. He is seriously ill and hopes to be cured.
   C. He has lost all of his money.
   D. He misses his nieces and nephews.

_____ 13. By the end of Allende's story, what is the reader's main impression of Uncle Marcos?
   A. He is immature and superstitious.
   B. He is self-centered and untrustworthy.
   C. He is organized and reliable.
   D. He is unconventional and likeable.

Vocabulary and Grammar

_____ 14. In which of the following sentences is *unrequited* used correctly?
   A. Clara was the only relative who viewed Marcos in an unrequited manner.
   B. The townspeople were unrequited in their admiration of Uncle Marcos.
   C. No one in the unrequited crowd could imagine what he was planning.
   D. Despite Marcos's best efforts, his love for Cousin Antonieta was unrequited.

Name _____ Date _____

___ 15. To which of the following sentences could the word *disconsolately* logically be added?
    A. Clara gazed at her uncle's coffin.
    B. The delighted townspeople spread the story of Uncle Marcos's barrel organ.
    C. When the plane took off, people cheered.
    D. Severo laughed and felt relieved.

___ 16. If the Latin root *-vit-* means "life," what does *revitalize* mean in this sentence?
    Unfortunately, Uncle Marcos could not revitalize himself on his journey home.
    A. to make lively and energetic again
    B. to have a new and exciting adventure
    C. to collect unusual objects again
    D. to renew old friendships

___ 17. In this sentence from "Uncle Marcos," identify the relative pronoun.
    During the day, he slept in a hammock that he had strung between two columns in the hall.
    A. he   C. that
    B. hammock   D. between

___ 18. How many relative pronouns can you find in this passage from "Uncle Marcos"?
    Fortunately for Longfellow, a customs lawyer who was a friend of the del Valle family appeared and offered to take charge, placing Marcos and all his paraphernalia in a freight car, which he shipped to the capital.
    A. none   C. two
    B. one   D. three

Essay

19. The narrator of "Uncle Marcos" relates several of Uncle Marcos's "adventures": for example, his courtship of Cousin Antonieta, his building and flying an airplane, and his fortune-telling business. Choose three episodes from the story. In an essay, explain how the circumstances and outcome of each episode reveal Marcos's character and the way that people respond to him. Compare the meanings of these episodes, and explain their relationship with each other. Do the episodes reinforce each other? Does one episode add more depth to the character of Uncle Marcos? Support your points with examples and explanations.

20. Isabel Allende uses indirect characterization to reveal Uncle Marcos's character—she does not tell us directly what he is like. Instead, she shows him in action. One technique of indirect characterization she uses is showing how other characters react to Uncle Marcos. In an essay, discuss Uncle Marcos's relationships with three characters in the story. Explain what each relationship reveals about Uncle Marcos's character. Use specific examples to support your statements.

21. **Thinking About the Big Question: Can truth change?** After his failed courtship of Cousin Antonieta, people view Uncle Marcos one way; but after he returns from his airplane flight, people view him another way. In an essay, explain why this is so. Who has actually changed: Uncle Marcos or the townspeople?

Unit 1 Resources: Fiction and Nonfiction
© Pearson Education, Inc. All rights reserved.
212

"If I Forget Thee, Oh Earth . . ." by Arthur C. Clarke
from **Silent Spring** by Rachel Carson
Vocabulary Warm-up Word Lists

Study these words from the selections. Then, complete the activities.

Word List A

harmony [HAHR muh nee] *n.* cooperation; agreement
We are proud of the student-teacher <u>harmony</u> in our school.

hostile [HAHS tuhl] *adj.* unfriendly; difficult to deal with
Until you make friends, a big city can seem like a <u>hostile</u> place.

landscape [LAND skayp] *n.* view of one's natural surroundings
The <u>landscape</u> changed from very flat to hilly as we drove along.

misfortunes [mis FOR chunz] *n.* unlucky happenings
Having their money stolen was only the first of their <u>misfortunes</u>.

reminder [ri MYN der] *n.* something that makes you notice or remember
Seeing the store was a <u>reminder</u> that we had holiday gifts to buy.

stark [STAHRK] *adj.* harsh; grim; impossible to avoid
The hiker faced the <u>stark</u> truth that she was lost and alone.

unnoticed [un NOH tist] *adj.* not seen
The black cat was <u>unnoticed</u> as it moved through the dark night.

variety [vuh RY uh tee] *n.* many different kinds
We have a <u>variety</u> of different games planned for the fair.

Word List B

abundance [uh BUN duhns] *n.* very large quantity
The young dancer has an <u>abundance</u> of energy and talent.

agony [AG uh nee] *n.* severe pain or suffering
Steve was in <u>agony</u> after he broke his leg.

isolation [eye soh LAY shuhn] *n.* state of being separated from others
A patient with a disease others could catch is kept in <u>isolation</u>.

prosperous [PRAHS per us] *adj.* successful and wealthy
You can tell by their expensive car that they are <u>prosperous</u>.

radiance [RAY dee ens] *n.* soft, shining light
The moon had a <u>radiance</u> that made everything look ghostly.

residential [rez i DEN chuhl] *adj.* having to do with where people live
This is a <u>residential</u> neighborhood with very few stores or businesses.

scour [SKOW uhr] *v.* to clean by scrubbing
After art class, I had to <u>scour</u> my hands to get rid of the paint.

substantial [sub STAN chuhl] *adj.* large in amount or significance
We have a <u>substantial</u> community service program at school.

"If I Forget Thee, Oh Earth . . ." by Arthur C. Clarke
from **Silent Spring** by Rachel Carson
Vocabulary Warm-up Exercises

Exercise A *Fill in each blank in the paragraph below with an appropriate word from Word List A. Use each word only once.*

When people have troubles and [1] _____, many find it helpful to escape to nature. Some go to the mountains, where the rugged [2] _____ of tall rocks as far as the eye can see is a [3] _____ that many things are bigger than our problems. Others choose a quiet place, such as a lake, where there is a soothing [4] _____ of water and sky. Still others head for a setting as difficult as their dilemmas, such as a desert, where the [5] _____ surroundings are a challenge. The harshly [6] _____ understanding that they need to keep their wits to survive forces them to focus on something other than their troubles. Life is filled with a [7] _____ of problems. Some solutions are [8] _____ until we discover them in the wild.

Exercise B *Decide whether each statement below is true or false. Circle T or F. Then, explain your answer.*

1. A small party would have a <u>substantial</u> guest list.
   T / F _____

2. A <u>prosperous</u> business might make plans to expand.
   T / F _____

3. You might describe a pitch-black room as full of <u>radiance</u>.
   T / F _____

4. A woman who just painted her nails might not want to <u>scour</u> a pan.
   T / F _____

5. A person in <u>agony</u> is blissfully happy.
   T / F _____

6. Someone who enjoys other people would prefer to be in <u>isolation</u>.
   T / F _____

7. The dorms at a college are the <u>residential</u> part of that education community.
   T / F _____

8. You might be disappointed to receive an <u>abundance</u> of gifts on your birthday.
   T / F _____

Name _____ Date _____

Reading Warm-up A

Read the following passage. Pay special attention to the underlined words. Then, read it again, and complete the activities. Use a separate sheet of paper for your written answers.

The problem of overpopulation has long caused people to search for solutions. They have looked above to space colonies. They have also looked out on the watery landscape that is 75 percent of Earth's surface. There, it is not the view of one's surroundings that catches the imagination. It is the potential for underwater habitats.

Jacques Cousteau was one ocean explorer who believed that people could live and work underwater. In the early 1960s, he developed the "Continental Shelf Station" as a trial underwater living space. Aquanauts—deep-sea versions of astronauts—found the setting hostile and uncomfortable. Their list of complaints is a reminder of the simple things on land that we should remember and appreciate. Too often we take them for granted and they go unnoticed. For example, in the dark ocean there is no natural light. The aquanauts lost their appetite in the strange environment. They lost their privacy in the too-tight quarters.

Still, Cousteau's experiment created interest. In 1964, a popular exhibit at the World's Fair showed a variety of ways to use the underwater world. Among the different ideas were living underwater, vacationing underwater, and drilling for oil. Of these, only drilling for oil is widely done. This is evidence of the stark limitations of ocean development. Scientists found it impossible to avoid the conclusion that humans are just not at home underwater.

However, the idea of underwater vacations is not completely lost. In Key Largo, Florida, an ocean research facility called *La Chalupa* has been turned into an underwater hotel. Guests scuba dive 21 feet down to enter the hotel. There they find nothing like the hardships and misfortunes that bothered Cousteau's aquanauts. These "aqua-vacationers" enjoy private bedrooms and gourmet meals. Windows nearly four feet high help them find harmony with the creatures they view around them in the peaceful atmosphere of the sea.

1. Underline the phrase that is a clue to underlined landscape. What is the watery *landscape* described in the passage?

2. Underline the word that is a clue to underlined hostile. Give another synonym for *hostile*.

3. Circle the word that is a clue to underlined reminder. Underline what serves as a *reminder*.

4. Underline what the passage says goes underlined unnoticed. Give a synonym for *unnoticed*.

5. Circle the word that is a clue to underlined variety. Underline the *variety* of ideas in the exhibit.

6. Underline the phrase that gives a clue to underlined stark. Explain a *stark* limitation of living underwater.

7. Circle the word that is a clue to underlined misfortunes. Underline the *misfortunes* of the aquanauts in Cousteau's experiment.

8. Circle a word that is a clue to underlined harmony. Give an antonym for *harmony*.

"If I Forget Thee, Oh Earth . . ." by Arthur C. Clarke
from **Silent Spring** by Rachel Carson
Reading Warm-up B

Read the following passage. Pay special attention to the underlined words. Then, read it again, and complete the activities. Use a separate sheet of paper for your written answers.

Even as we understand the causes of pollution, it is hard to eliminate it completely. There is an <u>abundance</u> of ways that we pollute without thinking about it. For most families, this large list includes two <u>residential</u> requirements for a comfortable home. One is an oil or gas furnace for heat in winter. This emits carbon monoxide into the air. The other, an air conditioner in summer, contains chemicals that harm Earth's protective ozone layer.

In our <u>prosperous</u> country, most families have a car; some successful families have two or more. Each gasoline-burning vehicle is a source of compounds that cause acid rain. This damages crops, vegetation, soil, and lakes, as well as buildings and monuments. There is no easy way to rid its effects on nature. We may be able to scrub a building clean, but we cannot <u>scour</u> a lake or the soil.

What are people to do? We cannot live in <u>isolation</u> from nature, separated from the air, water, and land around us so that our actions do no harm. We interact with the environment all the time. Although we may live in colonies in space or underwater someday, for now the world most people know is on Earth.

Despite the ways that we all contribute to pollution, there is a <u>substantial</u> amount we can do to reduce it. If each person acts responsibly, together we can have a very significant effect.

What can *you* do? Walk or ride a bicycle whenever you can. Chances are you will not suffer any <u>agony</u> from the exercise—and neither will the globe. If there is a transit system where you live, use that, too. A full bus equals the passenger capacity of six cars, while one commuter train car equals fifteen full automobiles. Recycle if you can. Turn off unnecessary lights at home; high-polluting fossil fuels are often used to create electricity. Look at the <u>radiance</u> of the moon at night and you may not mind the softer light of a low-watt bulb.

1. Circle the word that is a clue to <u>abundance</u>. Give a synonym for *abundance*.

2. Circle the word that is a clue to <u>residential</u>. What would you see in a *residential* neighborhood where you live?

3. Circle the word that is a clue to <u>prosperous</u>. Give an antonym for *prosperous*.

4. Circle the word that is a clue to <u>scour</u>. Name something you might *scour* at home.

5. Circle the phrase that is a clue to <u>isolation</u>. Underline the reason why we cannot live in *isolation* from nature.

6. Circle the word that is a clue to <u>substantial</u>. Describe two *substantial* ways that people can reduce pollution.

7. Circle the word that is a clue to <u>agony</u>. Give a synonym for *agony* that is a form of the clue word.

8. Underline the phrase that is a clue to <u>radiance</u>. Describe a time of day when you might enjoy the *radiance* of the sun.

"If I Forget Thee, Oh Earth . . . " by Arthur C. Clarke
from **Silent Spring** by Rachel Carson
Writing About the Big Question

Can truth change?

Big Question Vocabulary

assumption	belief	circumstance	context	convince
credible	distort	evidence	manipulate	perceive
perspective	skeptics	speculate	truth	verify

A. *Use one or more words from the list above to complete each sentence.*

1. If we _____ on future events, we may see how truth changes.

2. Never make the _____ that people in the future will see the same truth we do.

3. Sometimes, it can be difficult to _____ people that the truth changes.

4. To convince someone of the truth, we must gather _____.

B. *Follow the directions in responding to each item below.*

1. What is happening in today's world that must change? List one thing.

   _____

   _____

2. What truth must change before the change you described above can happen? Use at least two of the Big Question vocabulary words.

   _____

   _____

C. *Some people feel that the condition of Earth is a constant, unchangeable truth. Complete the sentences below. Then, write a short paragraph in which you connect this experience to the Big Question.*

I speculate that in 100 years, the Earth will be _____.

My assumptions are based on _____.

"If I Forget Thee, Oh Earth . . ." by Arthur C. Clarke
from **Silent Spring** by Rachel Carson
Literary Analysis: Theme

The **theme** of a literary work is the central message or insight about life that is conveyed through the work. Sometimes, the theme is stated directly. More often, it is suggested indirectly through the words and experiences of the characters or through the events of a story.

How the theme is developed depends in part on the genre, or form, of the work. In nonfiction literature, such as essays, the theme is usually stated directly as a main idea. Then, the writer supports the idea with facts, details, and examples to prove the point.

In most fiction—short stories, novels, poetry, and plays—the theme is implied, or suggested. Readers must figure out the theme by looking at the ideas expressed through story events and character actions.

DIRECTIONS: *Read the following passages, and describe how each passage relates to the selection's theme.*

from "If I Forget Thee, Oh Earth . . ."

He was looking upon the funeral pyre of a world—upon the radioactive aftermath of Armageddon. Across a quarter of a million miles of space, the glow of dying atoms was still visible, a perennial reminder of the ruinous past. It would be centuries yet before that deadly glow died from the rocks and life could return again to fill that silent, empty world.

1. What does this passage imply about what has happened to Earth?

   _____

2. How does this passage relate to the theme of the story?

   _____

3. How would you state the theme of this story?

   _____

from Silent Spring

In the gutters under the eaves and between the shingles of the roofs, a white granular powder still showed a few patches; some weeks before it had fallen like snow upon the roofs and lawns, the fields and streams.

No witchcraft, no enemy action had silenced the rebirth of new life in this stricken world. The people had done it themselves.

1. What might the "white granular powder" be? What are the effects of the powder?

   _____

2. How does this passage relate to the theme of the selection?

   _____

3. How would you state the theme of this selection?

   _____

"If I Forget Thee, Oh Earth . . ." by Arthur C. Clarke
from **Silent Spring** by Rachel Carson
Vocabulary Builder

Word List

blight   maladies   moribund   perennial   purged

A. DIRECTIONS: *Revise each sentence so that the underlined vocabulary word is used logically. Be sure not to change the vocabulary word.*

1. I <u>purged</u> the wound on my foot, thereby increasing the chances of infection.

   _____

2. Those flowers are <u>perennials</u>, so you will need to plant them again next year.

   _____

3. Because of the <u>blight</u>, the potatoes we grew were especially fine this year.

   _____

4. Due to various <u>maladies</u>, they became more vigorous and cheerful.

   _____

5. The fact that her garden was <u>moribund</u> filled her with delight.

   _____

B. DIRECTIONS: *Write the letter of the word or phrase that is the best synonym for the Word List word.*

___ 1. perennial
    A. occasional
    B. temporary
    C. perpetual
    D. unusual

___ 2. maladies
    A. complaints
    B. diseases
    C. mistakes
    D. theories

___ 3. moribund
    A. depressing
    B. upsetting
    C. cheering
    D. dying

___ 4. purged
    A. cleansed
    B. destroyed
    C. manufactured
    D. created

Name _____ Date _____

"If I Forget Thee, Oh Earth . . ." by Arthur C. Clarke
from Silent Spring by Rachel Carson
Writing to Compare Literary Works

Use a chart like the one below to make prewriting notes for your essay of comparison and contrast. Then, answer the two questions following the chart.

Points of Comparison/Contrast	"If I Forget Thee . . ."	*from* Silent Spring
My response to each selection		
Statement of each selection's theme		
Possible reasons why author chose genre		

1. In general, do you think fiction or nonfiction is more effective in expressing a theme? Explain.

   _____

   _____

   _____

2. Which of these two selections do you think is more effective in expressing its theme? Explain.

   _____

   _____

   _____

"**'If I Forget Thee, Oh Earth . . .'**" by Arthur C. Clarke
from **Silent Spring** by Rachel Carson
Open-Book Test

Short Answer *Write your responses to the questions in this section on the lines provided.*

1. Reread the first paragraph of "If I Forget Thee, Oh Earth . . ." How would you describe the mood, or feeling, of this story opening? Cite details that help create this mood.

   _____

   _____

2. Use the graphic organizer to summarize Marvin's experience in "If I Forget Thee, Oh Earth . . ." Include significant events and moments of realization.

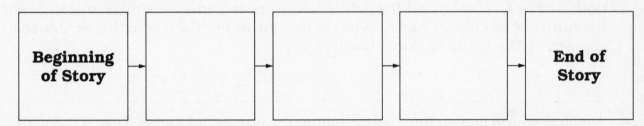

3. In "If I Forget Thee, Oh Earth . . . ," Marvin's father wants to spark a desire in his son. The author of the story also wants to spark a desire in the reader. What are these desires, and how are they related?

   _____

   _____

   _____

4. The excerpt from *Silent Spring* provides a "before" and "after" look at a typical American town. Describe the town before and after. Bring your descriptions to life with details from the essay.

   _____

   _____

   _____

   _____

5. Why might Carson want to write about an imaginary town instead of a real one? Explain, using details from *Silent Spring* to support your ideas.

   _____

   _____

   _____

6. Is Rachel Carson's theme in *Silent Spring* stated, implied, or both? Explain.

    _____

    _____

    _____

7. In both "If I Forget Thee, Oh Earth . . ." and the excerpt from *Silent Spring*, there is a blight upon the Earth. Explain what this blight is in each work. Base your answer on the definition of *blight*.

    _____

    _____

    _____

8. Both Arthur C. Clarke and Rachel Carson want to convey a similar message about the future of the planet Earth. What is this message? Complete this sentence to express it: *The future of planet Earth . . .*

    _____

    _____

9. Which scenario do you find more chilling: the one in "If I Forget Thee, Oh Earth . . ." or the one in the excerpt from *Silent Spring*? Explain, using examples from the texts.

    _____

    _____

    _____

10. Imagine that Marvin from "If I Forget Thee, Oh Earth . . ." is transported to the town described in the first part of the excerpt from *Silent Spring*. What might he feel, do, or say? What kind of a citizen would he be? Explain.

    _____

    _____

    _____

Essay

Write an extended response to the question of your choice or to the question or questions your teacher assigns you.

11. The theme of a work is its central idea or message. Choose either "If I Forget Thee, Oh Earth . . . " or the excerpt from *Silent Spring*, and write an essay explaining the author's theme. Use examples or details from the selection to explain the theme and to illustrate how the writer supports his or her appeal or warning.

12. "If I Forget Thee, Oh Earth . . ." and the excerpt from *Silent Spring* are both persuasive appeals. Decide which author is more effective in persuading you to believe his or her central message, or theme. Then, in an essay, describe how you would adapt or borrow from this work to create a TV ad that communicates the same theme. Explain whether you would express the theme directly or indirectly in your ad, and why.

13. Both "If I Forget Thee, Oh Earth . . ." and *Silent Spring* were written over thirty years ago. Were the authors optimistic about the direction in which the Earth's environment and inhabitants were headed at the time? Have circumstances today changed, or do they remain basically the same? Write an essay summarizing the authors' attitudes and your own evaluation of the present state of Earth's environment.

14. **Thinking About the Big Question: Can truth change?** In an essay, state in as few words as possible the central truth expressed by both "If I Forget Thee, Oh Earth . . ." and the excerpt from *Silent Spring*. Then explain whether you agree with this truth, and why. If you do agree, can you imagine any situation in which this truth would change?

Oral Response

15. Go back to question 2, 4, 5, or 10 or to the question your teacher assigns to you. Take a few minutes to expand your answer and prepare an oral response. Find additional details in "If I Forget Thee, Oh Earth . . .," the excerpt from *Silent Spring*, or both selections (depending on the question) that will support your points. If necessary, make notes to guide your response.

"If I Forget Thee, Oh Earth . . ." by Arthur C. Clarke
from **Silent Spring** by Rachel Carson

Selection Test A

Critical Reading *Identify the letter of the choice that best answers the question.*

____ 1. At the beginning of "If I Forget Thee, Oh Earth . . . ," how would you describe the atmosphere, or mood, when Marvin and his father travel up to the servicing chamber?
A. fearful
B. sad
C. amusing
D. suspenseful

____ 2. In Arthur C. Clarke's story, why are the people living in the Colony?
A. They lost a war on Earth.
B. They prefer the Colony to Earth.
C. They crash-landed there while they were on a mission to explore space.
D. They cannot live in the Earth's ruined environment.

____ 3. Why does Marvin's father plan the trip Outside?
A. He wants to teach Marvin about living in space.
B. He wants to pass on to Marvin the dream of returning to Earth.
C. He wants to teach Marvin more about the stars and planets.
D. He wants to give Marvin a lesson in how to drive a surface vehicle.

____ 4. Which of the following BEST defines the theme of a literary work?
A. paraphrase
B. central message
C. foreshadowing
D. tone

____ 5. Which of the following BEST states the theme of "If I Forget Thee, Oh Earth . . ."?
A. To colonize outer space is challenging.
B. Knowledge should be passed down from one generation to the next.
C. The Earth must be preserved for future generations.
D. Survival in a hostile environment is almost impossible.

____ 6. In the excerpt from *Silent Spring*, why are doctors in the town puzzled?
A. More children are being born with birth defects.
B. People are becoming sick from new kinds of illnesses.
C. People are reacting violently to bee stings.
D. People are increasingly being bitten by animals.

_____ 7. All of the following statements about theme are accurate EXCEPT one. Which statement is NOT true?

    A. Works of fiction as well as nonfiction may have a theme.

    B. In a short story, the theme is usually stated directly, not implied.

    C. The theme of an essay is often stated directly as the main idea.

    D. The theme of a literary work is not the same as the work's subject or topic.

_____ 8. What is the most likely cause of the great changes that happen to the town in *Silent Spring*?

    A. pesticides

    B. floods

    C. forest fires

    D. a nuclear bomb

_____ 9. How would you state Rachel Carson's theme in *Silent Spring*?

    A. Wildlife populations should be controlled.

    B. Tourism cannot be allowed to damage the environment.

    C. Endangered species deserve our concern.

    D. People are responsible for damaging the environment.

_____ 10. Which of the following best compares the two selections: "If I Forget Thee, Oh Earth . . ." and the excerpt from *Silent Spring*?

    A. Both works make reference to the future.

    B. Both works focus on the welfare of the Earth.

    C. The authors of both works use humor to make their central point.

    D. Both works are examples of fiction.

_____ 11. Which statement accurately compares or contrasts the themes of "If I Forget Thee, Oh Earth . . ." and the excerpt from *Silent Spring*?

    A. The two themes are totally dissimilar and have nothing in common.

    B. Both themes warn about the destruction of life on Earth.

    C. Both themes recommend that humans found colonies in space.

    D. Both themes warn of the dangers of nuclear war.

_____ 12. Which of the two selections (the Clarke short story or the Carson essay) can be viewed as a serious warning to readers?

    A. "If I Forget Thee, Oh Earth . . ." by Clarke

    B. the excerpt from *Silent Spring* by Carson

    C. both selections

    D. neither selection

Vocabulary

_____ **13.** How regularly do <u>perennial</u> flowers bloom?

    A. almost never   **C.** every year

    B. seldom   **D.** once every three years

_____ **14.** Which of the following would you feel if you had a <u>malady</u>?

    A. silly   **C.** angry

    B. embarrassed   **D.** ill

_____ **15.** If a specialist describes your favorite plant as <u>moribund</u>, which of the following would most likely be your reaction?

    A. joy   **C.** sadness

    B. puzzlement   **D.** surprise

Essay

16. Choose one of the selections ("If I Forget Thee, Oh Earth . . ." or the excerpt from *Silent Spring*) and write an essay explaining the author's theme, or central message. Use specific examples or details from the selection to explain the theme and to illustrate how the writer supports his or her appeal or warning.

17. Both of these selections were written more than twenty-five years ago. Were the writers optimistic about the direction in which the Earth's environment and inhabitants were headed at the time? How would you evaluate the state of Earth's environment today? Have circumstances changed, or do they remain basically the same? Write an essay summarizing the writers' attitudes and your evaluation of the present state of the Earth's environment. Support your views with details and examples from the selections.

18. Thinking About the Big Question: Can truth change? You might say there is a central truth or message in both "If I Forget Thee, Oh Earth . . ." and the excerpt from *Silent Spring*. This possible truth is that human beings are responsible for their own futures. In an essay, tell whether you agree or disagree with this truth and why. Use information from both selections to support your opinion.

"If I Forget Thee, Oh Earth . . ." by Arthur C. Clarke
from **Silent Spring** by Rachel Carson
Selection Test B

Critical Reading *Identify the letter of the choice that best completes the statement or answers the question.*

____ 1. In "If I Forget Thee, Oh Earth . . . ," what atmosphere, or mood, does the author create when he describes Marvin's journey up to the servicing chamber?
  A. gloom
  B. fear
  C. adventure
  D. sadness

____ 2. In Arthur C. Clarke's short story, residents of the Colony seldom go Outside because the
  A. environment is radioactive.
  B. moon's surface is too rough for travel.
  C. moon's atmosphere lacks oxygen.
  D. residents lack appropriate vehicles.

____ 3. Marvin's description of his father's reckless drive across the plain in "If I Forget Thee, Oh Earth . . ." suggests that his father finds living inside the Colony
  A. stifling.
  B. exhilarating.
  C. relaxing.
  D. terrifying.

____ 4. In "If I Forget Thee, Oh Earth . . . ," residents of the Colony live there because they
  A. lost a war on Earth.
  B. prefer the Colony to Earth.
  C. got lost while exploring outer space.
  D. cannot live in the Earth's environment.

____ 5. In "If I Forget Thee, Oh Earth . . . ," Marvin's father plans the trip Outside to
  A. give Marvin a firsthand lesson about the dangers of living in space.
  B. pass on to Marvin the dream of returning to Earth someday when it is habitable.
  C. teach Marvin that, contrary to the old nursery rhyme, real stars do not twinkle.
  D. show Marvin how to drive a surface vehicle in the event of an emergency.

____ 6. Which of the following identifies the theme of a literary work?
  A. the author's attitude toward the subject matter
  B. the subject or topic of the work
  C. the central message or insight about life that the work conveys
  D. the social and cultural context in which the work is created

____ 7. Which of the following quotations from "If I Forget Thee, Oh Earth . . ." reflects Marvin's understanding of why his father has brought him Outside?
   A. "He would never walk beside the rivers of that lost and legendary world."
   B. "It seemed so peaceful beneath those lines of marching cloud."
   C. "The sun was now low behind the hills on the right: the valley before them should be in total darkness."
   D. "And even at this distance, he could see the glitter of sunlight on the polar ice."

____ 8. Which of the following relates most closely to the theme of "If I Forget Thee, Oh Earth . . ."?
   A. the challenges of colonizing outer space
   B. the passing down of knowledge from father to son
   C. the preservation of Earth for future generations
   D. survival in a hostile environment

____ 9. In *Silent Spring,* in the town in the heart of America, the doctors are baffled by
   A. increasing numbers of children born with serious birth defects.
   B. increasing numbers of people deserting the town and the surrounding farms.
   C. people's violent reactions to an increasing number of bee stings and animal bites.
   D. people's new kinds of sicknesses and several sudden, unexplained deaths.

____ 10. Which of the following statements about the theme of a literary work is accurate?
   A. Works of fiction often have a theme, but nonfiction works seldom do.
   B. In fiction, the theme is usually directly stated, rather than implied.
   C. In essays, the theme is usually directly stated as a main idea.
   D. The theme of a work is identical to the work's topic, or subject matter.

____ 11. In *Silent Spring,* why does Rachel Carson invent a town in which so many things go wrong?
   A. Inventing an example is the only way she can make her point.
   B. The author is primarily a fiction writer.
   C. It is easier to invent a single town than to list the real towns where these things happen.
   D. The fictional town calls attention to the changes occurring in many towns across America.

____ 12. Read the closing sentence from the excerpt from *Silent Spring*:

   A grim specter has crept upon us almost unnoticed, and this imagined tragedy may easily become a stark reality we all shall know.

   Which of the following does the author most likely mean by the phrase "a grim specter"?
   A. a steep decline in the economy
   B. the refusal of the public to face scientific realities
   C. the dangers of pesticides
   D. the plight of endangered species

____ 13. What is Rachel Carson's theme in the excerpt from *Silent Spring*?
   A. Overpopulation of wildlife will result in a sudden, drastic decline.
   B. If we allow tourism to continue at such a high level, the environment will suffer.
   C. Every town in America will experience these symptoms of decline.
   D. People are responsible for causing damage to the environment and to themselves.

____ 14. In which selection (or selections) does the author warn of the dire consequences that can result from human actions?
A. in "If I Forget Thee, Oh Earth . . ."
B. in the excerpt from *Silent Spring*
C. in both selections
D. in neither selection

____ 15. Which of the following statements most accurately compares and contrasts the themes of "If I Forget Thee, Oh Earth . . ." and the excerpt from *Silent Spring*?
A. Neither theme is in any way related to the other.
B. One theme warns of the effect of pesticides; the other warns of global warming.
C. Both themes warn the reader of serious threats to all forms of life on Earth.
D. Both themes warn the reader of something that might happen far into the future.

Vocabulary

____ 16. Which of the following words would apply to a wound that has been <u>purged</u>?
A. infected   C. bandaged
B. cleansed   D. aggravated

____ 17. How regularly does a <u>perennial</u> drought occur?
A. almost never   C. over and over
B. seldom   D. once every few years

____ 18. If a person is experiencing multiple <u>maladies</u>, how does he or she feel?
A. exuberant   C. very ill
B. reflective   D. selfish

Essay

19. "If I Forget Thee, Oh Earth . . ." and the excerpt from *Silent Spring* are both persuasive appeals. Which author is more effective in convincing you to believe his or her central message, or theme? In an essay, clearly state the theme of the selection you have chosen as more persuasive. Then, explain how the author persuaded you. Cite specific facts, examples, or other details that you found most convincing.

20. Both Arthur C. Clarke and Rachel Carson create imaginary settings in order to convey their theme, or central message. In an essay, compare and contrast the atmosphere, or mood, that the authors establish in these selections. Discuss how both writers use sensory images and figurative language to create the atmosphere in their works.

21. **Thinking About the Big Question: Can truth change?** In as few words as possible, state the central truth expressed by both "If I Forget Thee, Oh Earth . . ." and the excerpt from *Silent Spring*. Then, in an essay, explain whether you agree with this truth and why. If you do agree, can you imagine any situation in which this truth would change?

Name _____ Date _____

Exposition: Problem-and-Solution Essay

Prewriting: Narrowing Your Topic

To help you focus your essay on a specific aspect of the problem, answer the questions in the following chart.

Question:	Your Answers:
What is the problem?	
Who is affected by the problem?	
What causes the problem to occur?	
What are some possible solutions to the problem?	

Drafting: Outlining the Problem

Use the following sunburst organizer to list aspects of the central problem. At the end of each ray, explore a detail or an aspect of the problem.

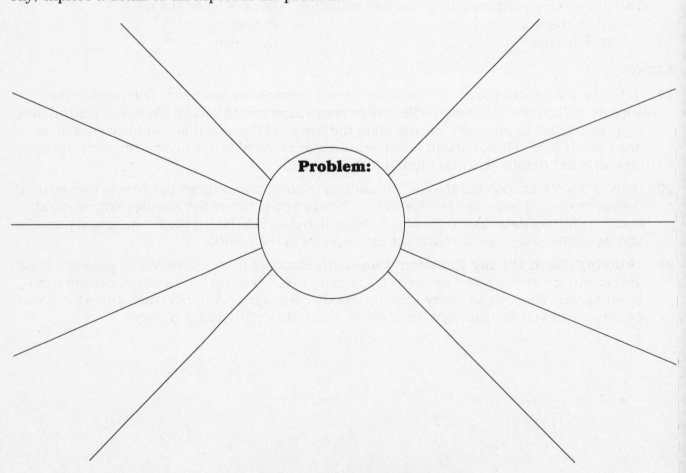

Name _____ Date _____

Writing Workshop
Revising Faulty Pronoun-Antecedent Agreement: Integrating Grammar Skills

Revising Faulty Pronoun-Antecedent Agreement

A pronoun should agree with its antecedent in person, number, and gender. The **antecedent** is the word or words to which a pronoun refers. In the following example, the pronoun *she* and its antecedent, *Laura*, are both third-person, singular, and female.

Laura arrived late because *she* missed the first bus.

Use a plural pronoun to refer to a compound antecedent joined by *and.* Use a singular pronoun to refer to singular antecedents joined by *or* or *nor.*

Neither *Laura nor Jack* arrived on time because *they* missed the first bus.

Be careful with number when the antecedent is an indefinite pronoun. The indefinite pronouns *each* and *one,* as well as those ending in *-body* and *-one,* are always singular. The indefinite pronouns *both, few, many, others,* and *several* are always plural. The indefinite pronouns *all, any, more, most, none,* and *some* may be singular or plural, depending on the nouns to which they refer.

Most of the children arrived late because *they* missed the first bus.

Identifying Correct Pronoun-Antecedent Agreement

A. DIRECTIONS: *Circle the pronoun in parentheses that correctly completes each sentence. Underline the antecedent with which the pronoun agrees.*

1. Everyone needed (his or her, their) bus pass to get on the bus.
2. Many of the students brought (his or her, their) lunch with them.
3. A few of my friends bought (his or her, their) lunch in the school cafeteria.
4. Neither Liane nor Stacy could find (her, their) bus pass.

Fixing Errors in Pronoun-Antecedent Agreement

B. DIRECTIONS: *On the lines provided, rewrite the following sentences so that they use the correct pronouns. If a sentence is correct as presented, write* correct.

1. Most of the students liked his or her trip to the planetarium.

   _____

2. Everyone on the trip had their chance to interact with the exhibits.

   _____

3. Either Juan or Nancy had their questions answered by museum guides.

   _____

4. All of the guides offered their assistance to visitors.

   _____

Unit 1 Vocabulary Workshop—1
Using a Dictionary

In a dictionary, in addition to finding the definition, pronunciation, and origin of a word, you may also be able to discover the meaning of commonly used phrases and slang.

---

heartrending [härt´ ren´ ding] *adj.* causing much grief or mental anguish
heartsick [härt´ sik´] *adj.* extremely unhappy
heartstrings [härt´ stringz´] *pl. n.* deepest feelings or affections
heartthrob [härt´ throb´] *n.* **1** the heartbeat **2** [slang] *a.* a tender emotion *b.* a sweetheart
heart-to-heart [härt´ tə härt´] *adj.* intimate and candid; *n.* an intimate conversation

---

DIRECTIONS: *Fill in each blank in the following letter with the correct "heart" word.*

Dear Abbey,

I am writing to tell you that I think it is about time we had a (1) _____

_____ about your studies. I am (2) _____ at the

thought of your neglecting your schoolwork. You are a bright girl and could be doing

very well. The "D" on your report card pulled on my (3) _____ .

What is it that is causing your distraction? Are you spending time on the telephone

with your (4) _____ instead of studying? If so, I must advise

you to focus on your schoolwork. If you do not, you will end up with the (5) _____

_____ situation of summer school.

Sincerely,

Dad

Unit 1 Vocabulary Workshop—2
Using a Thesaurus

A thesaurus comes in handy to find new and interesting words to use in writing a speech. Sometimes you will use a thesaurus in order to find the exact word that fits your intention. Other times you will use it to vary your word choice.

Abbey laughed out loud when she got her father's letter. He had used words containing "heart" five times! She picked up a thesaurus and looked up all the "heart" words and phrases in the letter. She found entries for three of the words:

> **heartrending** agonizing, distressing, excruciating, sad, tragic
> **heartsick** depressed, disappointed, sad, unhappy
> **heartstrings**
> **heartthrob**
> **heart-to-heart** conversation, rap session, talk

DIRECTIONS: *Select appropriate words from the thesaurus entries to rewrite the letter for Abbey's dad. For the words with no entries, look back at the dictionary definitions to help you find new words for Abbey's Dad's "heart" words.*

Dear Abbey,

I am writing to tell you that I think it is about time we had a (1) _____

_____ about your studies. I am (2) _____ at the

thought of your neglecting your schoolwork. You are a bright girl and could be doing

very well. The "D" on your report card pulled on my (3) _____.

What is it that is causing your distraction? Are you spending time on the telephone

with your (4) _____ instead of studying? If so, I must advise

you to focus on your schoolwork. If you do not, you will end up with the (5) _____

_____ situation of summer school.

Sincerely,

Dad

Name _____ Date _____

Analyzing Broadcast Media Presentations

After choosing your news broadcast or talk show, fill out the following chart to evaluate the content and presentation of the program.

Subject of news broadcast or talk show: _____

Describe the general purpose of the program (i.e., to inform, to entertain, etc.).
What is the main topic of the program?
What relevant and reliable information is given during the program?
What language or images might be slanted toward a particular cultural or political outlook?
What questions do you have after watching the program?

Unit 1 Resources: Fiction and Nonfiction
234

Unit 1: Fiction and Nonfiction
Benchmark Test 2

Literary Analysis: Author's Voice *Read the selection. Then, answer the questions that follow.*

I've come to terms with my dreaminess, my absent-mindedness—well, okay, my ditziness! Why do I characterize myself this way? A few examples might make this description very clear. They might include such mild eccentricities as mismatched socks and paint smudges on jeans and in hair. Or I could cite more embarrassing moments, perhaps having to do with personal hygiene or misunderstandings. But why bother with the descriptions; you've probably already grasped the idea!

1. Which of these phrases best describes the author's voice?
   A. somber and weighty
   B. driven and intense
   C. neutral and lifeless
   D. humorous and informal

2. Keeping the author's voice in mind, what is *most likely* the author's purpose for writing?
   A. to inform
   B. to persuade
   C. to explain
   D. to entertain

3. Which of the following descriptions could the author add and still maintain the same voice?
   A. a serious description of how her absent-mindedness led to an accident
   B. an emotional description about forgetting her mother's birthday
   C. a sad description of how her carelessness resulted in hurt feelings
   D. a humorous description of running out of gas in the middle of a tunnel

Literary Analysis: Character *Read the selection. Then, answer the questions that follow.*

Agnes, with whom the controversy began and around whom it continues to swirl, seems at first glance colorless, almost invisible. But if I think hard enough, I can remember every detail of her face and the way she moved. I'm not sure why she had such a great influence on me, but she did.

4. If Agnes turns out to be the main character in the story, which word pair will most likely describe her best?
   A. flat and dynamic
   B. round and dynamic
   C. round and static
   D. dynamic and static

5. Which word best describes a flat character?
   A. one-dimensional
   B. changing
   C. boring
   D. complex

6. Which word best describes a round character?
   A. fat
   B. simple
   C. changeable
   D. complex

7. Why is the main character in a selection usually dynamic?
   A. Readers usually do not like to read about complex characters.
   B. Changes in the character are central to the plot and theme.
   C. Dynamic characters are easiest to write about.
   D. There can be only one dynamic character in a story.

8. Which word pair would best describe a villain whom the author never describes in detail and whose personality never changes?
   A. flat and dynamic
   B. flat and round
   C. flat and static
   D. round and static

Literary Analysis: Theme *Read the selection. Then, answer the questions that follow.*

Franny looked at the endless rows of vegetables yet to be weeded. Her stomach turned. Why had she insisted that she could handle a two-acre vegetable garden all by herself? And why had she acted so superior about it? Asking for help wasn't going to be easy!

9. In this selection, how can you determine a possible theme?
   A. from dialogue
   B. from the setting
   C. from the sentence structure
   D. from the plot and characterization

10. What might be a likely theme for this selection?
    A. People can be stubborn.
    B. People need other people.
    C. Gardens are hard work.
    D. Gardens are more trouble than they are worth.

11. How is the theme presented by the author?
  A. directly
  B. implied
  C. A and B
  D. none of the above

Reading Skill: Author's Purpose *Read the selection. Then, answer the questions that follow.*

Helen Boer: The Greatest Teacher I Know

In her forty years in the school system, Helen has delighted students, teachers, and administrators while she has educated them. As seriously as she takes her mission, she never takes herself too seriously. I'll always remember her wit, humor, and wisdom. Indeed, this unique combination of traits is one of the reasons I would like to nominate Helen Boer for Teacher of the Year.

12. What is the best reason to reflect on the author's purpose as you read?
  A. You can refine your idea of the author's purpose.
  B. You can analyze the characters.
  C. You can restate your idea of the author's purpose.
  D. You can analyze the plot.

13. Which of the following features generally gives the clearest indication of the author's purpose?
  A. illustrations B. index   C. type size and style D. title

14. Which sentence gives the clearest indication of the author's purpose in writing this selection?
  A. sentence one B. sentence two   C. sentence three   D. sentence four

Read the selection. Then, answer the questions that follow.

The long day was passing too slowly, he thought, as he trudged up the dusty, dry road. What had begun as a nice drive in the country had turned disastrous. The car had broken down five miles back and there were no houses in sight. He only hoped that he would find something over the next hill. The perspiration made his shirt cling to his back, and his once shiny shoes were not meant for such a trek. If only he had stayed home today, this never would have happened!

15. What is the main focus of the selection?
  A. a trip by car
  B. the aftermath of a car breakdown
  C. a car breaking down
  D. inadequate clothing for a walk

16. After reflecting on the details, how would you state the author's main purpose?
  A. to describe a disastrous day
  B. to persuade the reader to buy a new car
  C. to intrigue the reader
  D. to explain what to do in an emergency

17. In nonfiction, which of the following often hints at the author's purpose?
  A. theme
  B. vocabulary
  C. organizing features
  D. dialogue

Informational Texts: Analyze Structure and Format

Warm Up Before Exercising

To enjoy the benefits of exercise, one must begin slowly. It is always wise to stretch the muscles before beginning any strenuous workout. A brisk walk warms up the muscles and jump-starts the heart as well. **Cardiovascular**—or heart strengthening—exercise, such as walking, is one of the most important activities for a healthy heart. A healthy heart keeps the body working at optimum performance.

18. What is the author's purpose?
    A. to entertain
    B. to describe
    C. to inform
    D. to persuade

19. How does the title support the author's purpose?
    A. It provides information.
    B. It advocates a point of view.
    C. It is interesting.
    D. It is amusing.

20. Why is one of the words set in boldface type?
    A. It is unimportant.
    B. It will be tested.
    C. It is a key concept that is defined.
    D. It is linked to earlier information.

Vocabulary: Word Roots, Suffixes and Prefixes

21. In the following sentence, what is the meaning of *confines*?

    Max does not own a car so he spends most of his time within the confines of the city.

    A. borders
    B. vicinity
    C. outskirts
    D. buildings

22. The root word *-term-* means "a period of time." Using this knowledge, which of the following answer choices means "endless"?
    A. exterminable
    B. determinable
    C. interminable
    D. interchangeable

23. In the following sentence, what does the word *predetermined* mean?

    After visiting the museum, the students were expected to meet at a predetermined restaurant for lunch.

    A. centrally located
    B. decided on in advance
    C. randomly selected
    D. carefully selected

24. The suffix *-able* means "capable of, susceptible of, or tending to." Using this knowledge, what is the meaning of the word *inscrutable*?
    A. can be analyzed
    B. can be understood
    C. cannot be determined
    D. cannot be analyzed

25. In the following sentence, what is the meaning of the word *impassive*?

The defendant was quiet and impassive as the guilty verdict was read.

A. nervous   C. emotionless

B. disturbed   D. alert

26. What is the meaning of the word formed by combining *assert-* and *-ive*?

A. hesitant   C. resistant

B. confident   D. calm

Grammar

27. Which of the following is a personal pronoun?

A. I   C. there

B. herself   D. myself

28. Which word in the following sentence is a reflexive pronoun?

Jorge told himself that it would be the last time.

A. Jorge   B. the   C. himself   D. it

29. Which word in the following sentence is a personal pronoun?

The football players threw their muddy uniforms way over there.

A. football

B. players

C. their

D. there

30. Which word in the following sentence is an indefinite pronoun?

Some were on that bus.

A. that   B. some   C. on   D. bus

31. What type of pronoun is the word *who* in the following sentence?

Who wrote the sonnet we read in English class?

A. relative   B. personal   C. interrogative   D. indefinite

32. Which word in the following sentence is the relative pronoun?

The girl to whom she spoke did not understand her.

A. she   B. her   C. whom   D. girl

Spelling: Content Area Words

33. Which of the following kinds of words are content area words?
    A. words that have unaccented syllables
    B. words that come from foreign languages
    C. words that are the same parts of speech
    D. words that relate to the same area of study

34. For which content area would you most likely use the words *island* and *isthmus*?
    A. chemistry
    B. geography
    C. mathematics
    D. art

35. For which content area would you most likely use the words *algebra* and *parallel*?
    A. science
    B. social studies
    C. mathematics
    D. art

ESSAY

Writing

36. What is the most exciting thing that has happened to you so far this year? On a separate piece of paper, write a journal entry that describes not only what happened but why it was exciting. Make sure the words you choose express your feelings.

37. Choose a memorable character from a favorite book. Then, on a separate sheet of paper, write a character profile. First, make some notes on the details of appearance, dress, mannerisms, and so on. Then, use those details to write a profile that captures the essence of that character.

38. What problem in your school or community has really been bothering you? What would you like to do about it? Write a problem/solution essay to describe the problem and suggest solutions. On a separate sheet of paper, describe the problem clearly in one persuasive paragraph. Then, suggest a solution in a second persuasive paragraph. End your essay with a summary and a call to action.

Vocabulary in Context 1—Part 1

Identify the answer choice that best completes the statement.

1. After forty years working as a bus driver, my father was looking forward to_____ .
   A. retiring
   B. exerting
   C. resisting
   D. referring

2. The land we want to buy is on a hillside_____ state forest lands.
   A. breeding
   B. bordering
   C. occupying
   D. billowing

3. The large puddle had decreased in size because the water was_____ quickly.
   A. ceased
   B. rippling
   C. conducted
   D. evaporating

4. At the family reunion, our whole_____ was gathered together.
   A. clan
   B. squad
   C. reception
   D. ceremonial

5. The leak under the sink was fixed, but the kitchen floor was still_____ .
   A. smudged
   B. faltered
   C. warped
   D. ominous

6. Last night's heavy rainfall formed that_____ down the ravine.
   A. gurgling
   B. cascade
   C. quench
   D. obstacle

7. I could only admire the rose's beautiful, colorful_____ .
   A. petals
   B. sunflowers
   C. tapestry
   D. lacy

8. While I am taking notes in class, I like to draw _____ .
   A. mirages
   B. abruptly
   C. doodles
   D. canvasses

9. He was a writer who _____ in writing magazine articles.
   A. specialized
   B. exhibited
   C. sustained
   D. accomplished

10. When it is built, the new hotel will be the largest and _____ in the city.
    A. massive
    B. dramatic
    C. spectacular
    D. grandest

11. This heavy cabinet was well made and _____ built.
    A. hardwood
    B. carelessly
    C. solidly
    D. accordingly

12. She really wants to go on the trip _____ the fact that she claims otherwise.
    A. stifling
    B. disarming
    C. moreover
    D. despite

13. A rope pulled by hand makes the church bells _____ several times a day.
    A. unfurl
    B. peal
    C. upturned
    D. askew

14. The diner had the loud sound of music coming from the _____ .
    A. luncheon
    B. fronds
    C. jukebox
    D. chandelier

15. Discussing the upcoming first day of school made the little girl nervous and _____ .
    A. apprehensive
    B. naive
    C. humiliating
    D. disheveled

16. So it would not rot, the Civil War flag was _____ in glass.
    A. amongst
    B. encased
    C. obscured
    D. unendurable

17. When she had finished planting the garden, she was pleased with her _____ .
    A. caliber
    B. marksmanship
    C. calculations
    D. handiwork

18. Her skin was quite pale and had a _____ tone to it.
    A. pungent
    B. dank
    C. pastel
    D. sallow

19. As the boy fell, I reached out and caught him in an _____ act.
    A. invariable
    B. elementary
    C. instinctive
    D. imperative

20. It had been years since I had been on skis, and I _____ to go skiing again.
    A. yearned
    B. restrained
    C. acclaimed
    D. prolonged

Diagnostic Tests and Vocabulary in Context
Use and Interpretation

The Diagnostic Tests and Vocabulary in Context were developed to assist teachers in making the most appropriate assignment of *Prentice Hall Literature* program selections to students. The purpose of these assessments is to indicate the degree of difficulty that students are likely to have in reading/comprehending the selections presented in the *following* unit of instruction. Tests are provided at six separate times in each grade level—a *Diagnostic Test* (to be used prior to beginning the year's instruction) and a *Vocabulary in Context,* the final segment of the Benchmark Test appearing at the end of each of the first five units of instruction. Note that the tests are intended for use not as summative assessments for the prior unit, but as guidance for assigning literature selections in the upcoming unit of instruction.

The structure of all Diagnostic Tests and Vocabulary in Context in this series is the same. All test items are four-option, multiple-choice items. The format is established to assess a student's ability to construct sufficient meaning from the context sentence to choose the only provided word that fits both the semantics (meaning) and syntax (structure) of the context sentence. All words in the context sentences are chosen to be "below-level" words that students reading at this grade level should know. All answer choices fit *either* the meaning or structure of the context sentence, but only the correct choice fits *both* semantics and syntax. All answer choices—both correct answers and incorrect options—are key words chosen from specifically taught words that will occur in the subsequent unit of program instruction. This careful restriction of the assessed words permits a sound diagnosis of students' current reading achievement and prediction of the most appropriate level of readings to assign in the upcoming unit of instruction.

The assessment of vocabulary in context skill has consistently been shown in reading research studies to correlate very highly with "reading comprehension." This is not surprising as the format essentially assesses comprehension, albeit in sentence-length "chunks." Decades of research demonstrate that vocabulary assessment provides a strong, reliable prediction of comprehension achievement—the purpose of these tests. Further, because this format demands very little testing time, these diagnoses can be made efficiently, permitting teachers to move forward with critical instructional tasks rather than devoting excessive time to assessment.

It is important to stress that while the Diagnostic Tests and Vocabulary in Context were carefully developed and will yield sound assignment decisions, they were designed to *reinforce*, not supplant, teacher judgment as to the most appropriate instructional placement for individual students. Teacher judgment should always prevail in making placement—or indeed other important instructional—decisions concerning students.

Diagnostic Tests and Vocabulary in Context
Branching Suggestions

These tests are designed to provide maximum flexibility for teachers. Your *Unit Resources* books contain the 40-question **Diagnostic Test** and 20-question **Vocabulary in Context** tests. At *PHLitOnline*, you can access the Diagnostic Test and complete 40-question Vocabulary in Context tests. Procedures for administering the tests are described below. Choose the procedure based on the time you wish to devote to the activity and your comfort with the assignment decisions relative to the individual students. Remember that your judgment of a student's reading level should always take precedence over the results of a single written test.

Feel free to use different procedures at different times of the year. For example, for early units, you may wish to be more confident in the assignments you make—thus, using the "two-stage" process below. Later, you may choose the quicker diagnosis, confirming the results with your observations of the students' performance built up throughout the year.

The **Diagnostic Test** is composed of a single 40-item assessment. Based on the results of this assessment, make the following assignment of students to the reading selections in Unit 1:

Diagnostic Test Score	Selection to Use
If the student's score is 0–25	more accessible
If the student's score is 26–40	more challenging

Outlined below are the three basic options for administering **Vocabulary in Context** and basing selection assignments on the results of these assessments.

1. For a one-stage, quicker diagnosis using the *20-item* test in the *Unit Resources:*

Vocabulary in Context Test Score	Selection to Use
If the student's score is 0–13	more accessible
If the student's score is 14–20	more challenging

2. If you wish to confirm your assignment decisions with a *two-stage* diagnosis:

Stage 1: Administer the 20-item test in the *Unit Resources*	
Vocabulary in Context Test Score	**Selection to Use**
If the student's score is 0–9	more accessible
If the student's score is 10–15	(Go to Stage 2.)
If the student's score is 16–20	more challenging

Stage 2: Administer items 21–40 from *PHLitOnline*	
Vocabulary in Context Test Score	**Selection to Use**
If the student's score is 0–12	more accessible
If the student's score is 13–20	more challenging

3. If you base your assignment decisions on the full 40-item **Vocabulary in Context** from *PHLitOnline:*

Vocabulary in Context Test Score	Selection to Use
If the student's score is 0–25	more accessible
If the student's score is 26–40	more challenging

Name _____ Date _____

Grade 9—Benchmark Test 1
Interpretation Guide

For remediation of specific skills, you may assign students the relevant Reading Kit Practice and Assess pages indicated in the far-right column of this chart. You will find rubrics for evaluating writing samples in the last section of your Professional Development Guidebook.

Skill Objective	Test Items	Number Correct	Reading Kit
Literary Analysis			
Plot and Conflict	1, 2, 3, 4		pp. 4, 5
Narrative Essay	5, 6, 7, 8		pp. 2, 3
Point of View	9, 10, 11, 12		pp. 6, 7
Reading Skill			
Make Predictions	13, 14, 15, 16, 17		pp. 8, 9
Read to Perform a Task	18, 19, 20, 21		pp. 10, 11
Vocabulary			
Prefixes and Suffixes *–fore, con–, –tion, –ate*	22, 23, 24, 25, 26, 27		pp. 12, 13
Grammar			
Common and Proper Nouns	28, 29, 30		pp. 14, 15
Abstract and Concrete Nouns	31, 32, 33		pp. 16, 17
Possessive Nouns	34, 35, 36		pp. 18, 19
Writing			
Anecdote	37	Use rubric	pp. 20, 21
Critique	38	Use rubric	pp. 22, 23
Autobiographical Narrative	39	Use rubric	pp. 24, 25

Name _____ Date _____

Grade 9—Benchmark Test 2
Interpretation Guide

For remediation of specific skills, you may assign students the relevant Reading Kit Practice and Assess pages indicated in the far-right column of this chart. You will find rubrics for evaluating writing samples in the last section of your Professional Development Guidebook.

Skill Objective	Test Items	Number Correct	Reading Kit
Literary Analysis			
Author's Voice	1, 2, 3		pp. 26, 27
Character	4, 5, 6, 7, 8		pp. 28, 29
Theme	9, 10, 11		pp. 30, 31
Reading Skill			
Author's Purpose	12, 13, 14, 15, 16, 17		pp. 32, 33
Analyze Structure and Format	18,19, 20		pp. 34, 35
Vocabulary			
Word Roots and Suffixes -fin-, -term-, -able,-ive	21, 22, 23, 24, 25, 26		pp. 36, 37
Grammar			
Personal and Reflexive Pronouns	27, 28, 29		pp. 38, 39
Relative, Interrogative, and Indefinite Pronouns	30, 31, 32		pp. 40, 41, 42, 43
Spelling			
Frequently Misspelled	33, 34, 35		pp. 44, 45
Writing			
Journal Entry	36	Use rubric	pp. 46, 47
Character Profile	37	Use rubric	pp. 48, 49
Problem-Solution Essay	38	Use rubric	pp. 50, 51

ANSWERS

Big Question Vocabulary—1, p. 1

Sample Answer

"Well, just look at the **evidence,**" Stuart said. "She crashed into a fire hydrant and now she is blaming me,"

"He is **distorting** the facts. He ran out in front of my bicycle to chase after his soccer ball," Carlotta replied. "I swerved to avoid hitting him."

Stuart's brother looked at him. "Are you trying to **manipulate** me into believing you did nothing wrong?" he asked. "Carlotta's story is **credible** to me."

"There are witnesses right over there." Stuart said. Let's see if we can **verify** what I told you."

Big Question Vocabulary—2, p. 2

Sample Answers

Mr. Langston: "There is nothing that will **convince** me that this was a good idea for a project! There was chaos in this classroom."

Ms. Grace: "It is my **belief** that teachers should be able to run their classrooms the way they please; however, the **circumstances** here led to a disruption of my class."

Mr. Tompkins: "From my **perspective**, this is just one big mess to clean up!"

Willa Burke: "I am not going to listen to you **skeptics**. This was the best project ever!"

Big Question Vocabulary—3, p. 3

Sample Answer

"Mom," Jason said. "you are making an **assumption** that I am responsible for this just because of the **context** of the situation. But please do not **speculate**. Instead, understand that the **truth** may be different from what you **perceive** it to be. Let me explain. . . ."

Diagnostic Test, p. 5

MULTIPLE CHOICE

1. ANS: A
2. ANS: D
3. ANS: B
4. ANS: D
5. ANS: B
6. ANS: B
7. ANS: C
8. ANS: A
9. ANS: C
10. ANS: A
11. ANS: D
12. ANS: C
13. ANS: A
14. ANS: C
15. ANS: A
16. ANS: B
17. ANS: C
18. ANS: C
19. ANS: A
20. ANS: A
21. ANS: A
22. ANS: B
23. ANS: C
24. ANS: B
25. ANS: B
26. ANS: D
27. ANS: A
28. ANS: D
29. ANS: D
30. ANS: D
31. ANS: A
32. ANS: B
33. ANS: D
34. ANS: B
35. ANS: D
36. ANS: A
37. ANS: C
38. ANS: D
39. ANS: A
40. ANS: B

from The Giant's House and "Desiderata"
by Elizabeth McCracken

Vocabulary Warm-up Exercises, p. 14

A.
1. assumed
2. exaggerate
3. nutrition
4. imposing
5. incomplete
6. resisting
7. previously
8. conclusions

B. Sample Answers

1. A third grader is too young to know about *adolescence*, the transition to adulthood.

2. If you *continually* fail, you should study harder or get extra help.

3. Unless you had translators, it would be difficult to exchange letters, or carry on a *correspondence*, with someone who speaks another language.

4. If you were uncertain, or *doubtful*, about someone's honesty, you probably would not trust that person to pay you back, so you would not lend him or her money.

5. Yes, a work of *fiction* can include real people, but they would be involved in made-up situations.

6. Someone who was *passionate* about baseball would probably enjoy reading about it.

7. A *persistent* headache would probably make it difficult for someone to be cheerful.

Reading Warm-up A, p. 15

Words that students are to circle appear in parentheses.

Sample Answers

1. just because she was tall; One of the *conclusions* that people might jump to is that I talk too much, but I just like to express my opinions.

2. the troubling notion that she was always going to stand out in a crowd; I have been *resisting* going to the dentist.

3. (height); My sister does not like driving across the *towering* bridge.

4. (stretching it to six feet); I *exaggerate* when I say that I can run a mile in under five minutes.

5. diet; *Nutrition* is making sure that you eat the right foods to help you grow and stay healthy.

6. that she could just keep growing forever; I *assumed* I just had a sore throat, but it turned out that I really had tonsillitis.

7. teased her about her height; *Previously*, I took piano lessons, but now I am learning to play the drums.

8. (an important part . . . had been missing); My recipe for chocolate chip cookies was *incomplete*, so they did not have any chips!

Reading Warm-up B, p. 16

Words that students are to circle appear in parentheses.

Sample Answers

1. (young people); I think *adolescence* would last from about age twelve to eighteen.

2. panning for gold; Just as a *prospector* goes looking for hidden, precious minerals, a genealogist goes looking for hidden, precious information.

3. desire to learn everything they can about their ancestors; I have a *persistent* interest in playing soccer.

4. to find out as much as they can about the people in their family; I have had a *correspondence* with a friend who moved to Nebraska last year.

5. (fact); I enjoy reading science-*fiction* novels.

6. (hesitant); They might feel *doubtful*, or uncertain, about talking about the past because they have had painful experiences that they would rather forget.

7. (excitement); I am *passionate* about trying to keep the environment safe from smoke and harmful chemicals.

8. over time; *Continually* means "going on over a long period of time."

Listening and Viewing, p. 17

Sample Answers

Segment 1. Elizabeth McCracken was inspired to write about her eccentric family, who told her very odd, interesting stories when she was growing up. Some students may suggest that they would base characters on people they know because having models would help them to develop the characters and make the characters more realistic. Students who believe it is fun to use their imagination may answer that they would invent characters.

Segment 2. Elizabeth McCracken enjoys writing fiction because she can invent most of what she writes about and likes making her own rules to follow while writing. Students may answer that it is important to research certain details and make them factually accurate so that the story has credibility, even if much of it is made up.

Segment 3. It is important for Elizabeth McCracken to develop her characters to the point where she can figure out what they will do as the plot of her book progresses; she likes getting to the point at which she no longer feels as if she is making up the characters. Students should suggest memorable characters who have stayed with them as readers.

Segment 4. She advises young people to write the kind of story they want to read and to write to entertain themselves. Students may suggest that reading fiction can inspire them to write imaginatively and to learn how to create interesting, memorable characters in stories.

Learning About Fiction and Nonfiction, p. 18

A 1. fiction; 2. nonfiction; 3. fiction; 4. nonfiction

B. 1. fiction

2. It features a character, Alicia, who can shrink herself to a size that permits her to repair a laptop computer by going inside the machine. Alicia must be an imaginary character. Therefore, the piece is fictional.

from The Giant's House
by Elizabeth McCracken

Model Selection: Fiction, p. 19

A. 1. inside; 2. first person

B. Sample Answers

Plot: James, who is exceptionally tall, wants to learn more about the factors responsible for his height. Peggy, who works at the local library, tactfully inquires into how she can help the boy. In a sympathetic spirit, she researches the topic herself after James has failed to find much information. Most of the material she uncovers about giants emphasizes their freakishness. When Peggy turns the books over to James, he tells her that they are not helpful: What he really wants is current medical information on how to cure his condition.

Theme: One possible theme is that adjustment to a physical difference may be a difficult or even heart-rending process.

"Desiderata" by Elizabeth McCracken

Model Selection: Nonfiction, p. 20

Most students will probably say that two of McCracken's purposes were to share her thoughts and experiences and to entertain. She shares her thoughts and experiences when she describes her reactions to various family documents; she entertains by relating amusing anecdotes, such as Martha's comments on the Dollies' toilet training.

from The Giant's House and "Desiderata"
by Elizabeth McCracken

Open-Book Test, p. 21

Short Answer

1. The book is a work of fiction. Even though the setting comes from real life, the main character and the central event—time travel—are invented.
   Difficulty: *Easy* **Objective:** *Literary Analysis*

2. The article is an example of narrative nonfiction. Narrative nonfiction tells stories of real-life events.
   Difficulty: *Challenging* **Objective:** *Literary Analysis*

3. The book is a novel. A novel is a long work of fiction that contains chapters, a main plot, more than one character, and sometimes subplots.
   Difficulty: *Average* **Objective:** *Literary Analysis*

4. The book is a work of nonfiction. It describes real people and events and is narrated by a real person, the author herself. It has a clear purpose—persuading readers to vote for the author—and it presents the author's own ideas.
   Difficulty: *Average* **Objective:** *Literary Analysis*

5. James's conflict is that he is too tall. He touches the walls as he walks, leaving smudges higher than other boys'. He hardly fits in the library's chairs. He feels awkward talking about his height.
   Difficulty: *Easy* **Objective:** *Literary Analysis*

6. Some students may respond that the story would be different in current times because James would most likely do his own research on the Internet. Others may say that key details such as the card catalog and the old *Medical Curiosities* book would be missing.
   Difficulty: *Average* **Objective:** *Literary Analysis*

7. Peggy feels helpless because she knows she can't help James find what he is looking for—a cure that doesn't exist.
   Difficulty: *Easy* **Objective:** *Interpretation*

8. Her family papers are important to her because they make her feel connected to her ancestors. Examples include her grandmother's letters, where she learns about her own mother's childhood, and her aunt Blanche's letters, where she learns about her aunt Elizabeth's final years.
   Difficulty: *Average* **Objective:** *Interpretation*

9. Sample answer: As a fiction writer, McCracken says she responds to and reflects on the many archived and valued family documents compiled by her grandfather.
   Difficulty: *Challenging* **Objective:** *Interpretation*

10. Sample answer: No, the author does not feel vindictive, or revengeful, toward her relatives. She feels affectionate and grateful toward them.
    Difficulty: *Average* **Objective:** *Vocabulary*

Essay

11. Students who choose *The Giant's House* may say that one important idea is that we should be sensitive to the differences of those around us. Students who choose "Desiderata" may say that one important idea is that our family heritage should be treasured. All reasonable responses should be supported with relevant evidence from the text.
    Difficulty: *Easy* **Objective:** *Essay*

12. Students' essays should demonstrate by example how two characteristics of fiction are present in *The Giant's House* and two characteristics of nonfiction are present in "Desiderata." Fiction characteristics include characters, plot, conflict, setting, point of view, and theme. Nonfiction includes real people, places, and events, a narrator who is a real person and facts, true-life experiences, and/or a discussion of ideas; nonfiction is written for a specific audience and purpose and uses a particular tone.
    Difficulty: *Average* **Objective:** *Essay*

13. Students should acknowledge that by following her own rule, Peggy discovers James's true concern—finding a cure for being tall. It also gives her the opportunity to do her own research about tall people, which in turn helps her better understand how James might feel. Students should also acknowledge that, on the other hand, Peggy's questions were painful for James. The topic of his tallness is a source of discomfort, embarrassment, and even despair for him.
    Difficulty: *Challenging* **Objective:** *Essay*

14. Students should respond that the author held one belief about her grandfather—that he was a "quiet careful man"—but that the love letter she discovered revealed that he was, in fact, a passionate, romantic soul.
    Difficulty: *Average* **Objective:** *Essay*

Oral Response

15. Oral responses should be clear, well organized, and well supported by appropriate examples from the selections.
    Difficulty: *Average* **Objective:** *Oral Interpretation*

from **The Giant's House and "Desiderata"**
by Elizabeth McCracken

Selection Test A, p. 24

Learning About Fiction and Nonfiction

1. ANS: C   DIF: Easy   OBJ: Literary Analysis
2. ANS: D   DIF: Easy   OBJ: Literary Analysis
3. ANS: C   DIF: Easy   OBJ: Literary Analysis
4. ANS: A   DIF: Easy   OBJ: Literary Analysis
5. ANS: B   DIF: Easy   OBJ: Literary Analysis

Critical Reading

6. ANS: D   DIF: Easy   OBJ: Comprehension
7. ANS: C   DIF: Easy   OBJ: Comprehension
8. ANS: B   DIF: Easy   OBJ: Interpretation
9. ANS: C   DIF: Easy   OBJ: Comprehension
10. ANS: B   DIF: Easy   OBJ: Interpretation
11. ANS: C   DIF: Easy   OBJ: Comprehension
12. ANS: D   DIF: Easy   OBJ: Comprehension
13. ANS: C   DIF: Easy   OBJ: Literary Analysis
14. ANS: C   DIF: Easy   OBJ: Interpretation
15. ANS: B   DIF: Easy   OBJ: Interpretation

Essay

16. Students should point out that James's principal conflict is his anxiety over his exceptional height. He is so concerned about his tallness that he is looking for a medical cure for it. Peggy's conflict, or difficulty, is trying to find information for James where there is none. Students should recognize that the conflicts are not resolved in this passage. Students' speculations about the future outcome for both characters will vary but should be consistent with the characters as they are portrayed in the selection.
   Difficulty: *Easy*
   Objective: *Essay*

17. Students should note that McCracken's archive offers her a fascinating window on the past. Positive aspects of keeping a family archive are learning about unexpected sides of people's personalities and showing different perspectives on a person—as is the case with Martha. A negative aspect of creating an archive includes finding out things one does not want to know, such as the lawsuit threatened by a relative. Another negative is the feeling of frustration when an archive is fragmentary and incomplete. Students' comments on whether they would like to maintain a family archive will vary but should be supported by reasons.
   Difficulty: *Easy*
   Objective: *Essay*

18. Students should respond that the love letter McCracken discovered revealed that her grandfather was, in fact, a

passionate, romantic soul, which changed her ideas about the type of man he was.
   Difficulty: *Easy*
   Objective: *Essay*

Selection Test B, p. 27

Learning About Fiction and Nonfiction

1. ANS: C   DIF: Average   OBJ: Literary Analysis
2. ANS: C   DIF: Average   OBJ: Literary Analysis
3. ANS: A   DIF: Average   OBJ: Literary Analysis
4. ANS: C   DIF: Average   OBJ: Literary Analysis
5. ANS: A   DIF: Challenging   OBJ: Literary Analysis
6. ANS: D   DIF: Challenging   OBJ: Literary Analysis

Critical Reading

7. ANS: B   DIF: Average   OBJ: Literary Analysis
8. ANS: C   DIF: Challenging   OBJ: Interpretation
9. ANS: B   DIF: Challenging   OBJ: Interpretation
10. ANS: D   DIF: Average   OBJ: Comprehension
11. ANS: B   DIF: Average   OBJ: Comprehension
12. ANS: B   DIF: Average   OBJ: Comprehension
13. ANS: A   DIF: Average   OBJ: Comprehension
14. ANS: D   DIF: Challenging   OBJ: Interpretation
15. ANS: A   DIF: Average   OBJ: Comprehension
16. ANS: B   DIF: Average   OBJ: Comprehension
17. ANS: B   DIF: Average   OBJ: Interpretation
18. ANS: D   DIF: Average   OBJ: Comprehension
19. ANS: C   DIF: Average   OBJ: Comprehension
20. ANS: D   DIF: Average   OBJ: Interpretation

Essay

21. Students should note that James faces a conflict about his exceptional height. He is confused and self-conscious. He seeks information, but, at first, he is afraid to reveal his true concerns to Peggy. Peggy faces an external conflict because she has to work hard to find information for James. She also faces an internal conflict because she feels concerned for and compassionate about James's feelings. The conflicts basically remain unresolved. Accept any reasonable response to the irresolution.
   Difficulty: *Average*
   Objective: *Essay*

22. Among the satisfactions of an archive, students should note McCracken's obvious pleasure in entertaining anecdotes and the surprising revelations that the documents occasionally offer: A good example is the love letter written by her grandfather and saved by her grandmother. Among the frustrations are the facts that sometimes one finds out things one does not want to know and

Unit 1 Resources: Fiction and Nonfiction

sometimes one feels frustrated by the incompleteness of the portraits offered by a fragmentary collection of documents. Students' evaluations of the author's opinions will vary, but they should support their opinions with reasons, examples, or other evidence.

Difficulty: *Average*

Objective: *Essay*

23. Students' evaluations of the character and analyses of an author's motivation will vary. However, most students will probably say that James's self-consciousness is a realistic portrayal of any teenager but especially one who is noticeably different. Students may suggest that making up a character rather than reporting on a real person serves at least two purposes: It protects the feelings of a living person, and it gives the author freedom to create details she or he might not be able to find out about a real person.

Difficulty: *Challenging*

Objective: *Essay*

24. Students should respond that the author held one belief about her grandfather—that he was a "quiet careful man"—but that the love letter she discovered revealed that he was, in fact, a passionate, romantic soul.

Difficulty: *Average*

Objective: *Essay*

"The Washwoman" by Isaac Bashevis Singer

Vocabulary Warm-up Exercises, p. 31

A. 1. impression
2. clotheslines
3. conceive
4. bloomers
5. endure
6. contributed
7. uttered
8. devoted

B. Sample Answers

1. False; Something *brittle* breaks easily, so it is not soft.
2. True; A person who has *collapsed* is very ill and would need a doctor.
3. True; *Accumulated* means "collected," and you can collect things you do not need or want any longer.
4. False; *Gaunt* means "sickly and pale," which are signs of illness.
5. False; An *institution* is something that people believe in and accept, so it would not be easy to change their minds about it.
6. True; *Shard* means "a broken piece."
7. False; A young tree would not be *gnarled*, which means "twisted and weathered."
8. False; If the curtains *straggled*, or hung in a messy way, the room would probably be messy in other ways.

Reading Warm-up A, p. 32

Words that students are to circle appear in parentheses.

Sample Answers

1. (long ropes); We do not have *clotheslines* at home because we always dry our laundry in a dryer.
2. a type of long pants that were gathered at the ankles, an undergarment; *Bloomers* was not a good name because that was not the name of the woman who invented them.
3. (women's rights); She worked tirelessly to help women recognize that greater equality was possible through social reform.
4. (being second-class citizens); *Endure* means "to put up with; to tolerate"
5. (wrote articles that helped unify women in the fight for the right to vote); I have *contributed* my time as a volunteer working in a soup kitchen to help the homeless.
6. (picture); *Imagine* is a synonym for *conceive*.
7. People mistakenly thought clothing was what they cared about; I would like people to have the *impression* that I am fun, loyal, and mature.
8. a word of protest; Being silent would be the opposite of *uttered* because it means "spoke or made a sound."

Reading Warm-up B, p. 33

Words that students are to circle appear in parentheses.

Sample Answers

1. collections of knick-knacks, clothes; *Accumulated* means "collected or gathered over time."
2. (broken piece); You should handle a *shard* carefully so you do not get cut.
3. looked as if he never got enough to eat; I would encourage a friend who looked *gaunt* to see a doctor.
4. marriage, motherhood; No, a laundromat is not an *institution* because the word means "established practice or custom."
5. twisted; No, something *gnarled* would not be attractive because it means "twisted and misshapen."
6. carelessly hung sheets; *Straggled neatly* would not make sense because you cannot have something that both hangs in a messy way and hangs neatly.
7. The old woman either broke or cracked a bone when she fell. *Strong* and *flexible* are antonyms for *brittle*.
8. her body simply worn out; Yes, someone who has *collapsed* can recover if he or she gets the proper care.

Writing About the Big Question, p. 34

A. 1. assumption
2. belief
3. circumstance
4. evidence

B. Sample Answers

1. In a crowded store, I watched a mother whose son was screaming and begging. Everyone was staring at

him. The mother pointed it out to her child, and he stopped.

2. My **assumption** was that the child wouldn't care, but he stopped screaming instantly. That **convinced** me that it's good to look for **evidence** before jumping to conclusions.

C. Sample Answer

is not predictable and can change as both grow older.

A mother and child probably love each other greatly when the child is young. That is a great truth for both of them. As the child grows to adulthood, though, the child changes. New experiences change what the adult thinks; his or her truth has shifted. They may or may not still love each other, but the relationship has changed because they now see different truths.

Literary Analysis: Narrative Essay, p. 35

Sample Answers

1. One winter day, the eighty-year-old Gentile washwoman takes a huge bundle of the dirty laundry. Two months later she appears, looking very ill. She returns the clean laundry and then is seen no more.

2. A. "small women, old and wrinkled," "small and thin," "narrow shoulders," "a certain pride and love of labor"

   B. "I could not rest easy in my bed because of the wash." "The wash would not let me die." "I do not want to be a burden on anyone!"

   C. At first she "swayed, as though she were about to fall under the load. . . ." "Under the bundle tottered the old woman. . . ."

3. I think he's saying that even the humblest worker can have dignity and that the washwoman was a "holy soul" because she was honest, did her work well, and had an extreme sense of duty.

Reading: Ask Questions to Make Predictions, p. 36

Sample Answers

2. **Question:** Will the washwoman complain a lot about how badly her son treats her?
   Prediction: Some students may say yes; others, no.

3. **Question:** How will she feel?
   Prediction: She will feel bad and will want to see her son get married.

4. **Question:** What will happen to her?
   Prediction: She will get sick or she will die.

5. **Question:** Did she die?
   Prediction: Most students will probably think that the washwoman died.

Vocabulary Builder, p. 37

Sample Answers

A. 1. The fight during the game showed just how much rancor there was between the teams.

2. When the two-year-old refused to eat, her obstinacy made her mother grow impatient.

3. The king inherited several castles from his forebears.

4. As atonement for littering, the boy had to spend five Saturdays helping to pick up other people's litter in the park.

5. A pious old family friend was pleased to learn that we were religious.

6. I have accumulated a large collection of stamps from around the world.

B. 1. You might feel a sense of foreboding because there is a superstition that a black cat means something bad is likely to happen.

2. I would feel very proud of myself for being at the forefront of my class.

3. A rich stranger's appearance might foreshadow the upcoming financial well-being of the main character.

Enrichment: Learning From Our Elders, p. 38

Students' answers should reflect thoughtful consideration of the questions.

Open-Book Test, p. 39

Short Answer

1. The washwoman is described as more than seventy years old, small, wrinkled, and thin, but with a strength attributed to her peasant ancestry. This description is important because it gives the reader an image of a woman who looks frail but does physically challenging work.
   Difficulty: *Average* **Objective:** *Literary Analysis*

2. Sample answer: "The old woman had no faucet where she lived but had to bring in the water from a pump."
   Difficulty: *Easy* **Objective:** *Literary Analysis*

3. The author may include this detail to show that even though they were fond of each other, the women held very different religious beliefs.
   Difficulty: *Challenging* **Objective:** *Interpretation*

4. The son is disloyal because he does not visit his mother or invite her to his wedding. When she is sick, his contribution to her well-being is not to help or visit her but to pay for a coffin and a funeral.
   Difficulty: *Easy* **Objective:** *Interpretation*

5. The washwoman lives her life and does her work without feeling bitter or angry about it.
   Difficulty: *Average* **Objective:** *Vocabulary*

6. Washwoman—works hard, takes pride in her work, does not want to be a burden on anyone; Mother—is considerate of the washwoman, appreciates her work, studies philosophic works; Both—devoted to their children, have strong religious beliefs
   Sample answer: The author strongly portrays the washwoman's devotion to hard work through his

description of how difficult it was to do laundry and her struggle to carry the bundle of laundry.

Difficulty: *Average* **Objective:** *Interpretation*

7. The washwoman stubbornly attends her son's wedding without being invited, and she stubbornly launders the family's clothes in spite of being ill almost to the point of death.

Difficulty: *Challenging* **Objective:** *Literary Analysis*

8. One possible prediction is that neither the washwoman nor the laundry will reappear. This prediction is supported by details such as the woman's age and physical condition, the exceedingly harsh winter, and the unusually large size of the load. Another possible prediction is that the washwoman will return with the laundry in due time. This prediction is supported by details relating to the woman's reliability, strength of will, and dedication.

Difficulty: *Easy* **Objective:** *Reading*

9. The washwoman's ghost like appearance and extreme ill health may have surprised those who predicted her return. Those who predicted her death may describe her return as fantastic or unbelievable.

Difficulty: *Average* **Objective:** *Reading*

10. The author's mother may agree with this statement, considering her deep concern for the washwoman's well-being and the author's mother's appreciation for hard, honest work.

Difficulty: *Average* **Objective:** *Interpretation*

Essay

11. Students' responses should recast one story incident, such as the son's wedding, from the washwoman's point of view. Students should recognize that their own version includes the inner thoughts and feelings of the washwoman—perhaps feelings of pain or despair that are difficult to see through the strong exterior presented in the essay.

Difficulty: *Easy* **Objective:** *Essay*

12. Students may respond that the author learned the value of hard work, dedication, and responsibility. As he grew up and became a professional writer, this lesson may have contributed to his success. It may also have helped him to remain strong in the face of the devastation of World War II. Other students may say that the author learned the value of importance of family, which gave him material and purpose for his writings as he preserved family and cultural history for later generations.

Difficulty: *Average* **Objective:** *Essay*

13. Students should cite two passages from the essay in which the woman is identified as a Gentile and should note that in each case, the reference is a compliment. Students should conclude that these positive references guide the reader toward and build support for the final conclusion of the essay—that virtues such as dedication, humility, and inner strength can and do appear in people of all religions.

Difficulty: *Challenging* **Objective:** *Essay*

14. Students may respond that the washwoman lives by the truth that it is better to bear a burden than to be a burden and that this truth does not change from the beginning to the end of the essay. This truth sustains her throughout her illness and motivates her to survive until her work is done.

Difficulty: *Average* **Objective:** *Essay*

Oral Response

15. Oral responses should be clear, well organized, and well supported by appropriate examples from the selection.

Difficulty: *Average* **Objective:** *Oral Interpretation*

Selection Test A, p. 42

Critical Reading

1. ANS: B	DIF: Easy	OBJ: Literary Analysis
2. ANS: C	DIF: Easy	OBJ: Interpretation
3. ANS: D	DIF: Easy	OBJ: Literary Analysis
4. ANS: B	DIF: Easy	OBJ: Literary Analysis
5. ANS: C	DIF: Easy	OBJ: Comprehension
6. ANS: C	DIF: Easy	OBJ: Reading
7. ANS: D	DIF: Easy	OBJ: Comprehension
8. ANS: C	DIF: Easy	OBJ: Comprehension
9. ANS: C	DIF: Easy	OBJ: Interpretation
10. ANS: C	DIF: Easy	OBJ: Reading
11. ANS: D	DIF: Easy	OBJ: Interpretation

Vocabulary and Grammar

12. ANS: A	DIF: Easy	OBJ: Vocabulary
13. ANS: B	DIF: Easy	OBJ: Vocabulary
14. ANS: C	DIF: Easy	OBJ: Grammar
15. ANS: D	DIF: Easy	OBJ: Grammar

Essay

16. Students will vary in the character trait they choose to mention. They may mention her sense of duty, her honesty, her physical or emotional strength, or her pride in her work. Make sure they cite one or two events from the essay that illustrate the character trait they have chosen.

Difficulty: *Easy*

Objective: *Essay*

17. In their essays, students should clearly state what their prediction was. Then, they should identify the clues that led them to their prediction. For example, they might predict that the washwoman had died because she was so reliable and had never before failed to return the family's laundry.

Difficulty: *Easy*

Objective: *Essay*

18. Students may respond that this truth about bearing a burden sustains the washwoman throughout her illness

and motivates her to survive until her work is done. This truth does not change for her between the beginning and end of the essay.

Difficulty: *Easy*

Objective: *Essay*

Selection Test B, p. 45

Critical Reading

1. ANS: D	DIF: Average	OBJ: Literary Analysis
2. ANS: B	DIF: Average	OBJ: Literary Analysis
3. ANS: A	DIF: Average	OBJ: Comprehension
4. ANS: B	DIF: Average	OBJ: Comprehension
5. ANS: C	DIF: Challenging	OBJ: Reading
6. ANS: C	DIF: Challenging	OBJ: Interpretation
7. ANS: A	DIF: Challenging	OBJ: Interpretation
8. ANS: B	DIF: Average	OBJ: Reading
9. ANS: D	DIF: Average	OBJ: Comprehension
10. ANS: C	DIF: Average	OBJ: Reading
11. ANS: D	DIF: Challenging	OBJ: Interpretation
12. ANS: D	DIF: Challenging	OBJ: Literary Analysis
13. ANS: C	DIF: Average	OBJ: Literary Analysis
14. ANS: B	DIF: Average	OBJ: Interpretation

Vocabulary and Grammar

15. ANS: C	DIF: Average	OBJ: Vocabulary
16. ANS: B	DIF: Average	OBJ: Vocabulary
17. ANS: D	DIF: Average	OBJ: Vocabulary
18. ANS: B	DIF: Average	OBJ: Grammar
19. ANS: C	DIF: Average	OBJ: Grammar

Essay

20. Students may vary in the wording of the theme, which he states directly at the end of the essay. To Singer, the washwoman represents honest, decent people who struggle throughout their lives for very little recognition. He believes that the washwoman, who had such a difficult life on earth, should be rewarded in heaven.

Difficulty: *Average*

Objective: *Essay*

21. In their essays, students may vary in the characteristics they mention. They may mention the washwoman's sense of duty, her honesty, her physical strength, her emotional strength, or her pride in her work. Make sure they cite one example from the essay to illustrate each characteristic.

Difficulty: *Average*

Objective: *Essay*

22. Students may respond that the washwoman lives by the truth that it is better to bear a burden than to be a burden, and that this truth does not change between the

beginning and end of the essay. This truth sustains her throughout her illness and motivates her to survive until her work is done.

Difficulty: *Average*

Objective: *Essay*

"New Directions" by Maya Angelou

Vocabulary Warm-up Exercises, p. 49

A. 1. aroma
2. tempted
3. responsibility
4. pastry
5. blistering
6. assess
7. balmy
8. provisions

B. Sample Answers

1. False; Someone who is *dependent* needs your help and attention.
2. False; A situation that caused *embarrassment* would make you feel shame, so you would not enjoy it or want to repeat it.
3. True; A *domestic* is a worker who helps with household chores.
4. True; *Disastrous* means "causing suffering or loss," as when a storm destroys your house or car.
5. True; *Resolve* means "determination," and since solving problems can be hard, if you lack determination, you would give up easily.
6. True; *Industry* means "hard work and great effort" and someone who works hard will get more done than someone who does not.
7. False; *Unpromising* means "not likely to go well."
8. False; *Presenting* means offering, giving, or explaining and does not imply being secretive.

Reading Warm-up A, p. 50

Words that students are to circle appear in parentheses.

Sample Answers

1. (food and anything else they needed); Other *provisions* are water and first-aid supplies.
2. (lunch); *Responsibility* means "something that is your job or duty to do."
3. (gave in); Joe was *tempted* to watch television, and he responded by watching for only an hour.
4. (smell); The *aroma* of a spicy dish might be strong with the smells of many spices and seasonings.
5. (cooling and refreshing); The sun can be *blistering* at high noon in midsummer.
6. examine; I have often had to *assess* my behavior or my grades at school.

7. They might work harder because the weather would be comfortable, and they could accomplish more. *Stormy* is an antonym for *balmy*.

8. (dough); It would not have much taste or nutritional value. A filling I would use for *pastry* is apples.

Reading Warm-up B, p. 51

Words that students are to circle appear in parentheses.

Sample Answers

1. She was the daughter of former slaves in Louisiana who both died when she was a child. She was married at age 14, a mother by age 18, and widowed at age 20. *Unpromising* means "unfavorable; not likely to go well."

2. (servant); *Maid* is a synonym for *domestic*.

3. Having *resolve* gave Sarah the determination to do things that would improve her life, like starting a business. Having *resolve* can give me the determination to set big goals for myself and to meet them.

4. She developed a scalp problem and lost patches of hair; *Disastrous* means "causing suffering or loss."

5. She was ashamed of her appearance; A scalp problem caused some of her hair to fall out, which made her ashamed, but it also made her look for a cure that led to her own line of hair-care products.

6. Hair-care products for African American women; She was visiting with women in their homes and demonstrating how to use the products and how they worked.

7. (hard work); My mother is the picture of *industry* because she works, runs a household, and volunteers in the community.

8. Madame Walker's 3,000 employees; She gave her employees good jobs, and in return her employees helped her company become successful, enabling her to become a millionaire.

Writing About the Big Question, p. 52

A. 1. circumstance
2. perceive
3. truth
4. assumption

B. Sample Answer

A man who moved in next door seemed aloof and never went out. I **assumed** he was weird or unfriendly. Then one day he got a new job. Suddenly, he was friendly and easy to talk to. Now I'm **convinced** he was just worried all the time.

C. Sample Answer

hard work and the determination to make a change. Annie found herself in a bad situation when her husband left. The truth of her life looked bleak. She had no money, no husband, and she had two small children. She thought up a plan, worked hard to make it work, and she changed her life. She earned money and fed her children and as a result changed the truth of her life.

Literary Analysis: Narrative Essay, p. 53

Sample Answers

1. When Mrs. Annie Johnson's marriage ended in 1903, she had two small sons. She built a business selling homemade meat pies to workers at the cotton gin and the lumber mill. She was successful and eventually opened a store.

2. (a). "over six feet tall, big-boned," "tall, brown-skinned woman bent over her brazier"
   (b). "I decided to step off the road and cut me a new path." "Mix groceries well enough to scare hungry away and from starving a man"
   (c). "She worked into the early hours boiling chicken and frying ham." "Annie never disappointed her customers."

3. I think she is saying that people should take charge of their lives, should try new things if they are disappointed with their lives, and should not be afraid to make changes.

Reading: Ask Questions to Make Predictions, p. 54

Sample Answers

1. **Question:** What will she do now? How will she live?
   Prediction: She will have to get a job and will probably have to leave her sons with someone else.

2. **Question:** Will she be able to earn money?
   Prediction: I think she is clever, hardworking, and not afraid. I predict she will find a way to earn money.

3. **Question:** Will she be successful and sell many meat pies?
   Prediction: Her business will be very successful, and the workers will depend on her.

4. **Question:** Will the workers want to travel far from the cotton gin and lumber mill?
   Prediction: The workers will go a long distance to buy her pies.

Vocabulary Builder, p. 55

Sample Answers

A. 1. Two people who settle an argument *amicably* settle it in a friendly way.

2. If you were to clean a kitchen *meticulously*, it would look spotless.

3. I would describe stormy weather as *ominous*.

4. The task I find most *unpalatable* is vacuuming.

5. The politician may have *conceded* the election because she saw that she wasn't going to get enough votes to win.

6. The day would be *balmy* if it were warm, sunny, and pleasant.

B. 1. Someone might *concur* with an opinion they don't agree with in order to end a conversation.

2. Three groups might *converge* on the state capitol for a political rally.

3. The best method I can *conceive* of is to do more writing.

Enrichment: Women's Work, p. 56

Sample Answers

A. 1. **Progress:** Women today have access to higher education. They can vote, hold public office, and work in a variety of fields that were previously not open to them, such as law enforcement and airplane piloting. In some families, women and men take more equal roles in domestic duties such as raising children, cooking, and cleaning.

2. **Needs improvement:** Women still struggle with issues of unequal pay, limited opportunities, and a lack of respect in certain fields and occupations.

B. Students should focus on one of the women and the unique contribution she has made to women and to their status in society. For example, a student writing to Susan B. Anthony might praise her efforts to win voting rights for women. The student might tell Anthony that women today not only vote, but they also serve in the United States Congress, head political organizations, and work as community leaders throughout the country.

"The Washwoman"
by Isaac Bashevis Singer
"New Directions" by Maya Angelou

Integrated Language Skills: Grammar, p. 57

Common and Proper Nouns

1. The only (Gentile) in the <u>building</u> was the <u>janitor</u>. (Fridays) he would come for a <u>tip</u>, his "(Friday) <u>money</u>."

2. She lived on (Krochmalna Street) too, but at the other <u>end</u>, near the (Wola) <u>section</u>.

3. My <u>mother</u> spoke a little (Polish), and the old <u>woman</u> would talk with her about many <u>things</u>.

4. The <u>son</u> had not invited the old <u>mother</u> to his <u>wedding</u>, but she went to the <u>church</u> and waited at the <u>steps</u> to see her <u>son</u> lead the "young <u>lady</u>" to the <u>altar</u>.

"New Directions" by Maya Angelou

Open-Book Test, p. 60

Short Answer

1. Some students may characterize Annie's husband as dishonest, selfish, or hypocritical, citing his secret longing to leave the marriage, his desire to preach rather than help raise his children, and his plans to seek a new romance. Others may characterize him as merely weak, uncaring, or unrealistic.

Difficulty: *Average* **Objective:** *Interpretation*

2. It means that they parted in a friendly way. This tells you that Annie was an independent woman—already focusing on the future and leaving the past behind.

Difficulty: *Challenging* **Objective:** *Vocabulary*

3. Annie "wasn't a fancy cook but she could 'mix groceries well enough.'" The author probably included this detail to show that Annie was capable of turning even an average skill into a source of great success.

Difficulty: *Average* **Objective:** *Literary Analysis*

4. She makes her plans carefully and secretly so that she won't fail. In the middle of the night, she carries buckets of stones to the cotton gin and the saw mill to make sure she is strong enough to execute her idea.

Difficulty: *Average* **Objective:** *Interpretation*

5. Students may have predicted that Annie would succeed in spite of the slow business, based on details related to her meticulous planning and determined personality.

Difficulty: *Easy* **Objective:** *Reading*

6. *Unpalatable* means "distasteful or unpleasant." The workers did not find Annie's pies unpalatable. They found them delicious and satisfying.

Difficulty: *Average* **Objective:** *Vocabulary*

7. Annie—is a determined, loving mother and is careful, patient, and hard working; William—feels called to preach, is looking for new romance; Both—are unhappy in marriage, follow a new path.

Difficulty: *Average* **Objective:** *Interpretation*

8. Annie sells her pies "on balmy spring days, blistering summer noons, and cold, wet, and wintry middays." This details gives the impression of a woman who cannot be stopped from doing what she sets out to do.

Difficulty: *Average* **Objective:** *Literary Analysis*

9. Predictions of Annie's success will be verified; predictions of her failure will not be verified. The degree of Annie's success may surprise even those who predicted it. Those who did not predict it should recognize Annie's ability to overcome every obstacle.

Difficulty: *Average* **Objective:** *Reading*

10. Sample answer: "If the future road looms ominous or unpromising, and the roads back uninviting, then we need to gather our resolve and . . . step off the road into another direction."

Difficulty: *Easy* **Objective:** *Literary Analysis*

Essay

11. Students should describe the lack of options that were available to Annie Johnson when she was looking for a way to support her family. They should note that, instead of becoming separated from her children by a traditional job, she went her own way—in a "new direction"—and opened her own business. She went in a new direction not only as a single woman, but also as a businessperson trying to support her family.

Difficulty: *Easy* **Objective:** *Essay*

12. Students may say Annie is an appropriate role model because she is brave, determined, dedicated to things that truly matter, and wise in business matters. For example, she makes choices based on her values rather than choices that might lead to an easier, more comfortable life. She also demonstrates caution and good planning, waiting to build a loyal clientele before opening a stall from which to sell her pies.

   Difficulty: *Average* **Objective:** *Essay*

13. Students should recognize that Angelou is championing an active rather than a passive kind of living: she believes we should all have the freedom, or right, to take stock of our lives, but also that it is our *job* to do this periodically. By "roads" Angelou means our life paths—the places we choose to go, the work we choose to do, and the things we choose to believe. After assessing both our past and future "roads," Angelou says, we should have the courage to change course, if necessary. Students should conclude their essay with a statement of agreement or disagreement and one or two supporting reasons.

   Difficulty: *Challenging* **Objective:** *Essay*

14. Students may respond that Annie Johnson lives by the truth that if a person isn't satisfied with life, he or she should "cut a new path," or move in a different direction. This truth does not change for Annie during the course of the essay. Rather, this truth is what sustains her and guides her toward success. Given Annie's ability to overcome the extreme challenges described in this essay, students may conclude that Annie most likely lived by this truth her entire life.

   Difficulty: *Average* **Objective:** *Essay*

Oral Response

15. Students should give an oral explanation in response to the question they choose or the one assigned to them.

   Difficulty: *Average* **Objective:** *Oral Interpretation*

"New Directions" by Maya Angelou

Selection Test A, p. 63

Critical Reading

1. ANS: A	DIF: Easy	OBJ: Literary Analysis
2. ANS: C	DIF: Easy	OBJ: Comprehension
3. ANS: D	DIF: Easy	OBJ: Comprehension
4. ANS: A	DIF: Easy	OBJ: Comprehension
5. ANS: B	DIF: Easy	OBJ: Literary Analysis
6. ANS: C	DIF: Easy	OBJ: Interpretation
7. ANS: B	DIF: Easy	OBJ: Reading
8. ANS: C	DIF: Easy	OBJ: Interpretation
9. ANS: C	DIF: Easy	OBJ: Literary Analysis
10. ANS: B	DIF: Easy	OBJ: Interpretation
11. ANS: D	DIF: Easy	OBJ: Interpretation

Vocabulary and Grammar

12. ANS: A	DIF: Easy	OBJ: Vocabulary
13. ANS: D	DIF: Easy	OBJ: Vocabulary
14. ANS: A	DIF: Easy	OBJ: Grammar
15. ANS: B	DIF: Easy	OBJ: Grammar

Essay

16. In their essays, students should note that Annie Johnson chooses a new direction when her marriage ends. The traditional choice is for her to take a job as a domestic and have someone else take care of her children. Instead, she starts a business that will allow her to keep her children with her. When her business succeeds, she expands it into a store. Operating a successful business as a single mother during that time period is an example of going in a new direction.

   Difficulty: *Easy*

   Objective: *Essay*

17. Students should note that Maya Angelou's theme is that if people are unhappy with their lives, they should not be afraid to change their lives by taking a new direction. Annie Johnson's life story illustrates that theme. Annie thinks of a new way to earn money, and when she succeeds, she dares to make changes that improve her life even more. Students may cite her selling of the meat-pies, her move to a stall, and her expanding to a store.

   Difficulty: *Easy*

   Objective: *Essay*

18. Students may respond that this truth does not change for Annie during the course of the essay. Rather, this truth sustains her and guides her toward success. She cuts a new path when she makes meat pies to sell to mill workers, then she sells from a food stall, and then expands the stall into a store with many items for sale.

   Difficulty: *Easy*

   Objective: *Essay*

Selection Test B, p. 66

Critical Reading

1. ANS: B	DIF: Average	OBJ: Literary Analysis
2. ANS: A	DIF: Average	OBJ: Interpretation
3. ANS: C	DIF: Average	OBJ: Comprehension
4. ANS: C	DIF: Average	OBJ: Interpretation
5. ANS: B	DIF: Challenging	OBJ: Literary Analysis
6. ANS: B	DIF: Average	OBJ: Reading
7. ANS: A	DIF: Challenging	OBJ: Interpretation
8. ANS: B	DIF: Average	OBJ: Reading
9. ANS: C	DIF: Average	OBJ: Interpretation
10. ANS: D	DIF: Challenging	OBJ: Reading skill
11. ANS: D	DIF: Challenging	OBJ: Interpretation
12. ANS: C	DIF: Average	OBJ: Literary Analysis

13. ANS: A	DIF: Challenging	OBJ: Reading
14. ANS: A	DIF: Challenging	OBJ: Interpretation
15. ANS: B	DIF: Average	OBJ: Comprehension

Vocabulary and Grammar

16. ANS: A	DIF: Average	OBJ: Vocabulary
17. ANS: D	DIF: Average	OBJ: Vocabulary
18. ANS: B	DIF: Challenging	OBJ: Vocabulary
19. ANS: B	DIF: Average	OBJ: Grammar
20. ANS: B	DIF: Challenging	OBJ: Grammar

Essay

21. In their essays, students may note the lack of options available to Annie Johnson when she was looking for a way to support her family. Instead of being unhappy away from her children in a traditional job as a domestic, Annie went her own way and opened her own business. She not only went a new direction as a single woman, she also took a new direction in trying to support her family.

    Difficulty: *Average*

    Objective: *Essay*

22. Students should note that Maya Angelou's message is that if people are unhappy with their lives, they should not be afraid to change their circumstances by taking a new direction. She adds that, if they fail, they should not feel embarrassed, but they should continue to try to find success or happiness. Annie Johnson's life illustrates Angelou's message. She created a new job for herself, and when she succeeded, she dared to make changes that improved her life even more. Students should cite her selling of the meat pies and her move to a store.

    Difficulty: *Average*

    Objective: *Essay*

23. Students may respond that Annie Johnson lives by the truth that if a person isn't satisfied with life, he or she should "cut a new path," or move in a different direction. This truth does not change for Annie during the course of the essay. Rather, this truth is what sustains her and guides her toward success. Given Annie's ability to overcome the extreme challenges described in this essay, students may conclude that Annie most likely lived by this truth her entire life.

    Difficulty: *Average*

    Objective: *Essay*

"Sonata for Harp and Bicycle" by Joan Aiken

Vocabulary Warm-up Exercises, p. 70

A.
1. tragic
2. director
3. employees
4. crumbling
5. corridors
6. concealed
7. doomed
8. mocked

B. Sample Answers
1. False; *Admirable* people are respected, not disliked.
2. True; It is upsetting to get too much homework.
3. False; A *distinguished* actor would be expected to perform well.
4. False; If your *intention* is to do well in school, you will study a lot.
5. False; If the value of the building rises, the price would rise as well.
6. False; *Reluctant* people would not be enthusiastic about their work.
7. True; If they struggled *vainly*, they did not achieve their goal.
8. False; A *witty* remark is one that many people would find amusing.

Reading Warm-up A, p. 71

Words that students are to circle appear in parentheses.

Sample Answers
1. (Northshore High School); As a janitor, he sweeps the corridors.
2. (students); They may have made fun of the tasks they perform. They may not appreciate how important their job is.
3. the old janitor was raging inside; *Concealed* means "hid."
4. (Ed), (Mr. Rush); School *employees* include teachers, office workers, and cafeteria workers, too.
5. He had no doubt that the unopened envelope he had stuffed into his shirt pocket contained a letter of dismissal. Someone your age might feel *doomed* because she forgot to do her homework or got caught lying to her parents.
6. No, it would not be tragic if Ed kept his job, because he does it well.
7. falling apart; *Crumbling* means "falling to pieces."
8. (Janitorial Services); He must feel very pleased to become director, because he will make more money and will have more authority. Also, he knows he is appreciated.

Reading Warm-up B, p. 72

Words that students are to circle appear in parentheses.

Sample Answers
1. (scientist), (educator); Bell is best known as the inventor of the telephone.
2. His *intention* was to become a teacher of the deaf like his father. *Intention* means "plan."
3. He wanted to help deaf people.

4. He was not eager to leave his family. *Reluctant* means "hesitant."

5. his own school for the deaf; They hoped Bell could help their deaf children to communicate more effectively.

6. (struggled); Their luck changed in 1876 when the telephone worked.

7. He spilled acid on himself. I am *agitated* when my sister borrows my clothes without asking.

8. Yes. It is *witty* because it is amusing to think that the man who invented the telephone had his work interrupted by his own invention.

Writing About the Big Question, p. 73

A. 1. distort, verify

2. convince

3. speculate

4. skeptics

B. Sample Answers

1. I thought this older student was a bully. Then one day, I saw him walk a younger student home who was afraid to go by himself.

2. I **believed** the student was a bully. When he helped the child, I **perceived** he was really considerate but didn't always show it.

C. Sample Answer

making decisions that either hurt you or help you. The characters in "Sonata for Harp and Bicycle" each made decisions that altered their fate. Heron is the most obvious example. He gave up on Daisy, thinking she had rejected him. For him, his truth was a life spent in despair because he could not be with her. So he committed suicide. Had the two of them communicated better, that truth would have been entirely different. They could have been together and lived happy lives.

Literary Analysis: Plot, Foreshadowing, and Suspense, p. 74

Sample Answers:

A. Jason was frustrated. "You'll be sorry," he said. "I shall do something desperate."

"Oh, no, you mustn't!" Her eyes were large with fright. She ran from the room and was back within a couple of moments, still drying her hands.

"If I took you out for a coffee, couldn't you give me just a tiny hint?"

Side by side Miss Golden and Mr. Ashgrove ran along the green-floored passages, battled down the white marble stairs among the hundred other employees from the tenth floor, the nine hundred from the floors below.

B. Students should mention two clues:

Clue 1: Miss Golden's exclaiming that he is doomed and telling him about the curse.

Clue 2: Jason's visit to an R.A.F. friend; the large canvas-covered bundle Jason brings along with the roses and wine.

My response to story's ending: They should also describe their response to the story's ending and tell why they responded in that way.

Reading: Read Ahead to Verify Predictions, p. 75

Sample Answers:

1. **My Prediction:** He is looking into the eyes of a ghost.

   Outcome: I was right. It was a ghost.

2. **My Prediction:** He is going to try to make the two ghosts meet each other.

   Outcome: I was right. He arranges a wake-up call for Daisy so she will meet the Wailing Watchman.

3. **My Prediction:** He and Miss Golden are going to disappear.

   Outcome: I was wrong. He and Miss Golden use a single parachute to jump off the fire escape.

Vocabulary Builder, p. 76

Sample Answers

A. 1. C; 2. B; 3. D

4. C; 5. A; 6. B

B. 1. The colorful sunset *captivates* my imagination.

2. I would find some way to *incorporate* all of these ideas in my report.

3. When I push this button, it *activates* machinery that will transport me to another dimension.

Enrichment: Sonata Form in Music, p. 77

Sample Answers:

1. The term *sonata* refers to a musical composition with three or four distinct movements. It is usually played on a keyboard instrument or on another instrument accompanied by a keyboard instrument.

2. *Sonata* comes from *sonare*, meaning "to sound."

3. A sonata consists of three or four distinct sections, or movements. The first and third movements are usually slow, and the second and fourth are fast.

4. A symphony

5. Her story has several distinct parts (the modern-day romance between Miss Golden and Mr. Ashgrove, the ghosts' romance, and Jason Ashgrove's actions to discover the mystery in the Grimes Buildings) that are resolved harmoniously at the end.

6. Miss Bell plays the harp, and Heron rings his bicycle bell.

Open-Book Test, p. 78

Short Answer

1. She begins with the statement of an unusual office policy: No one is allowed in the building after five o'clock. This makes the reader wonder *why*.

   Difficulty: *Easy*   **Objective:** *Literary Analysis*

2. Sample answer: The announcements reinforce the fact that no one is allowed to be in the building after five o'clock; the prediction based on this fact is that something will happen to one of the characters in the building after that time.
Difficulty: *Challenging* **Objective:** *Reading*

3. Ashgrove's main conflict is that he wants to know why nobody can be in the building after five o'clock. Miss Golden says that no one is given that information until being taken on the "Established Staff."
Difficulty: *Easy* **Objective:** *Literary Analysis*

4. Climax: Jason and Berenice go back into the building to reunite the ghosts. Examples of rising action should include Jason's attempts to find out the mystery, his first visit to the building after five o'clock, Berenice's revealing the doomed fate of those who encounter William Heron, and the plans they make to resolve the conflict.
Difficulty: *Average* **Objective:** *Literary Analysis*

5. *Furtive* means "sneaky." William Heron's behavior is not furtive because he makes a clamor on his bicycle and he chases people rather than sneaks up on them.
Difficulty: *Average* **Objective:** *Vocabulary*

6. Sample answers: The "well of gloom" that sinks beneath Jason foreshadows the ghost urging him to jump into the "smoky void." The "cold fingers of the wind nag[ging] and flutter[ing] at the tails of his jacket" foreshadow the invisible hands that grip him inside the building.
Difficulty: *Challenging* **Objective:** *Literary Analysis*

7. He embraces her so suddenly because if he is to die within five days, they have no time to lose. Lively details include her hair sprayed across his suit and the typewriter behind them that begins "chattering to itself in . . . enthusiasm."
Difficulty: *Average* **Objective:** *Interpretation*

8. Examples of this include the typewriter springing to life, Jason's various romantic comments to Berenice, and the couple's successful Oat Crisps copy. Students may say that the author changed the tone at this point in order to begin hinting at the story's happy ending.
Difficulty: *Average* **Objective:** *Interpretation*

9. Most predictions were probably somewhat correct. Although students may have guessed that something would happen to someone in the building after five o'clock, they probably did not guess that this something would involve two people (or four), a love story (or two), and a happy ending (or two).
Difficulty: *Average* **Objective:** *Reading*

10. Sample answer: She has them parachute off the fire escape to show that through their efforts—and their own love—they have neutralized the curse of the Wailing Watchman. The shower of bridal petals and the midair kiss also help make this point.
Difficulty: *Challenging* **Objective:** *Interpretation*

Essay

11. Jason has disregarded the instructions forbidding anyone to remain in the building after five o'clock. Therefore, he is doomed to the same fate as William Heron. If he can resolve the dilemma of Heron and Miss Bell, Jason can escape his fate and he and Berenice can be together.
Difficulty: *Easy* **Objective:** *Essay*

12. Students should respond that William and Miss Bell, once in love, were separated through a misunderstanding and have been pining for each other for fifty years. On the other hand, Jason and Berenice met only recently but are forced by strange and possibly dangerous circumstances to reveal their love for each other. The couples are similar in that both romances developed in the Grimes Buildings; both couples experience separation or the prospect of separation; and both couples end up happily together. Students should also note that if it were not for the ghost couple, Jason and Berenice would not have ended up declaring their love, exorcising the building, and pursuing a relationship. Meanwhile, if it were not for Jason and Berenice, the ghost couple would never have been reunited.
Difficulty: *Average* **Objective:** *Essay*

13. Students' essays may note the universal appeal of mysteries—the intrigue of a particular set of mysterious or unexplained circumstances, the pleasure of reading clues and making predictions about what will happen, and the unsettling yet safe sensation of following a fictional story with an unknown ending.
Difficulty: *Challenging* **Objective:** *Essay*

14. Students may respond that at first, the ghost seems menacing, dangerous, and irrational, seeking to intimidate and harm people for no reason at all, and later, when the reasons behind his actions are revealed, they better understood his distress. The author may be prompting readers not to make uninformed judgments about those who seem angry or aggressive but rather to seek to understand the source of their pain.
Difficulty: *Average* **Objective:** *Essay*

Oral Response

15. Students should give an oral explanation in response to the question they choose or the one assigned to them.
Difficulty: *Average* **Objective:** *Oral Interpretation*

Selection Test A, p. 81

Critical Reading

1. ANS: C   DIF: Easy   OBJ: Comprehension
2. ANS: C   DIF: Easy   OBJ: Interpretation
3. ANS: C   DIF: Easy   OBJ: Reading
4. ANS: D   DIF: Easy   OBJ: Comprehension

5. ANS: A	DIF: Easy	OBJ: Reading
6. ANS: A	DIF: Easy	OBJ: Comprehension
7. ANS: B	DIF: Easy	OBJ: Interpretation
8. ANS: D	DIF: Easy	OBJ: Literary Analysis
9. ANS: B	DIF: Easy	OBJ: Comprehension
10. ANS: C	DIF: Easy	OBJ: Comprehension
11. ANS: D	DIF: Easy	OBJ: Literary Analysis
12. ANS: B	DIF: Easy	OBJ: Interpretation

Vocabulary and Grammar

13. ANS: A	DIF: Easy	OBJ: Vocabulary
14. ANS: B	DIF: Easy	OBJ: Vocabulary
15. ANS: D	DIF: Easy	OBJ: Grammar

Essay

16. Most students will say that they were both frightened and amused, and their essays should mention examples of details or events that evoke the feelings they identify. Entering the dark, empty building and meeting the ghost of William Heron are the scariest parts of the story. The romance, the solution to the ghosts' problem, and the parachuting from the fire escape are light-hearted parts intended to amuse.

Difficulty: *Easy*

Objective: *Essay*

17. Students may predict that Jason will try to help the ghosts. The reader knows that Jason is very curious and likes to solve mysteries. He also displays bravery by going into the building alone at night, so he will not be scared out of seeing the ghost again. Jason probably feels sympathetic to the ghosts' tragic love because he is in love with Berenice.

Difficulty: *Easy*

Objective: *Essay*

18. Students may respond that at first, William the ghost seemed menacing, dangerous, and irrational, as he nearly pushes Jason off the platform for no reason at all. Later, when the romantic reasons behind William's actions are revealed, students might say that they better understand William's desperate distress.

Difficulty: *Easy*

Objective: *Essay*

Selection Test B, p. 84

Critical Reading

1. ANS: D	DIF: Average	OBJ: Interpretation
2. ANS: C	DIF: Average	OBJ: Reading
3. ANS: A	DIF: Challenging	OBJ: Reading
4. ANS: D	DIF: Average	OBJ: Comprehension
5. ANS: D	DIF: Challenging	OBJ: Reading
6. ANS: C	DIF: Average	OBJ: Interpretation
7. ANS: D	DIF: Average	OBJ: Comprehension

8. ANS: B	DIF: Average	OBJ: Comprehension
9. ANS: C	DIF: Average	OBJ: Literary Analysis
10. ANS: A	DIF: Challenging	OBJ: Literary Analysis
11. ANS: D	DIF: Average	OBJ: Interpretation
12. ANS: A	DIF: Average	OBJ: Interpretation
13. ANS: B	DIF: Challenging	OBJ: Interpretation
14. ANS: B	DIF: Average	OBJ: Reading

Vocabulary and Grammar

15. ANS: D	DIF: Challenging	OBJ: Vocabulary
16. ANS: C	DIF: Average	OBJ: Vocabulary
17. ANS: B	DIF: Average	OBJ: Grammar
18. ANS: C	DIF: Challenging	OBJ: Grammar

Essay

19. In their essays, students should identify three or four events in the story that create a chain of rising action (for example, the curious loudspeaker announcements; Jason's asking Miss Golden why everyone must leave at 5:00 P.M.; Miss Golden's horrified refusal to explain; Jason's entrance into the building after dark; his encounter with the ghost of William Heron; and Jason's hair turning white). As each event leads smoothly into the next, we increasingly wonder what will happen next.

Difficulty: *Average*

Objective: *Essay*

20. In their essays, students should identify three elements that suggest that the tone of the story is light. The title, the loudspeaker announcements, the romance, and the absence of any real threat are major clues. The title suggests an odd and quirky tale; the loudspeaker announcements are improbable—even ridiculous. The romance between Jason and Miss Golden is unrealistically swift. Though Jason encounters a ghost, we never fear for his life because we know that the romance that has been hinted at must grow to fruition.

Difficulty: *Average*

Objective: *Essay*

21. Students may respond that at first, the ghost seemed menacing, dangerous, and irrational, seeking to intimidate and harm people for no reason at all; and that later, when the reasons behind his actions are revealed, they better understood his distress. The author may be prompting readers not to make uninformed judgments about those who seem angry or aggressive, but rather to seek to understand the source of their pain.

Difficulty: *Average*

Objective: *Essay*

"The Cask of Amontillado" by Edgar Allan Poe

Vocabulary Warm-up Exercises, p. 88

A. 1. enthusiasm

2. ventured

Unit 1 Resources: Fiction and Nonfiction

3. perceived
4. nevertheless
5. injuries
6. unnecessarily
7. render
8. revenge

B. Sample Answers

1. The coach threw a party to celebrate the team's <u>colossal</u> *victory*.
2. She was *disappointed* by the <u>excessive</u> price of the dress that she wanted so badly.
3. I am in *a* hurry, so please give me an <u>immediate</u> reply.
4. The fact that it rained a lot last spring is *no* <u>indication</u> that it will rain a lot next spring.
5. I have had a <u>succession</u> of great teachers, so I *have* enjoyed school a lot.
6. *Despite* one <u>interruption</u> after another, the job was completed in record time.
7. After exercising <u>vigorously</u> for six months, my aunt managed to *lose* almost twenty pounds.

Reading Warm-up A, p. 89

Words that students are to circle appear in parentheses.

Sample Answers

1. <u>get even</u>; The plan for *revenge* was a "sour experience," so it must not have been successful.
2. (eating popcorn), (watching old movies); I feel *enthusiasm* for photography and stamp collecting.
3. <u>a picture of Roger in a single sentence</u>; My brother is a college freshman who loves loud music and playing football.
4. *Despite* the fact that Roger is not interested in her, she still sees Becky as a threat. Her feelings are not based on reality.
5. <u>Becky as a threat</u>; A person can sometimes imagine something is happening when it is not. Perceptions can be misleading.
6. <u>leave messages for me at home</u>; Since the narrator was avoiding her at school, she took the risk of being ignored and having her feelings hurt when she *ventured* to do this.
7. (my former best friend); With Roger out of the picture, there was no reason for the narrator to be rude to Becky.
8. (myself); Her *injuries* are emotional and social, the result of having mistreated her old friend.

Reading Warm-up B, p. 90

Words that students are to circle appear in parentheses.

Sample Answers

1. They were moving energetically. *Vigorously* means "with strength or force; energetically."
2. (largest); A battleship or a skyscraper might be described as *colossal*.

3. An *immediate* success happens right away.
4. <u>A spectacular parade</u>; An *interruption* is "a break in continuity."
5. (the highest); *Tiers* can be found in theaters and in sports arenas. They can also be found on wedding cakes.
6. <u>the noise level</u>; *Excessive* means "too much."
7. (floats, bands, and marchers); A synonym for *succession* is *series*.
8. An *indication* of trouble might be a loud argument or someone pushing someone. A synonym for *indication* is *sign*.

Writing About the Big Question, p. 91

A. 1. manipulate
2. truth
3. evidence
4. perceive

B. Sample Answers

1. I saw a TV commercial in which the announcer claimed a cell phone had crystal-clear sound. What the announcer didn't say was that it had crystal-clear sound only in certain areas.
2. People **manipulate** the truth in order to get what they want. What they say may be true, but it is distorted in order to **convince** me to buy their product.

C. Sample Answer

how he or she interprets experiences.

Montresor and Fortunato could have been great friends. They were very much alike in many ways. Montresor felt wronged by Fortunato, however, and that changed everything.

Literary Analysis: Plot, Foreshadowing, and Suspense, p. 92

Sample Answers

A. The wine sparkled in his eyes and the bells jingled. My own fancy grew warm with the Médoc. We had passed through <u>long walls of piled skeletons</u>, with casks and puncheons intermingling, into the <u>inmost recesses of the catacombs</u>. I paused again, and this time I made bold to <u>seize Fortunato by an arm</u> above the elbow.

"The niter!" I said; "see, it increases. It hangs like moss upon the vaults. <u>We are below the river's bed. The drops of moisture trickle among the bones.</u> Come, we will go back <u>ere it is too late.</u> Your cough—"

"It is nothing," he said; "let us go on. But first, another draft of the Médoc."

B. Students should identify two clues. Possible clues:

Clue 1: the narrator's making sure his servants wouldn't be at home

Clue 2: the narrator's wearing a black mask; the journey deep into the catacombs; the piles of bones that line the catacombs; the pile of bones that hides the building stone and mortar

My response to story's ending: They should also describe their response to the story's ending and tell why they responded in that way.

Reading: Read Ahead to Make and Verify Predictions, p. 93

Sample Answers

1. **My Prediction:** With his mask and cloak, he is making sure that no one can identify him walking with Fortunato.

   Outcome: I was right. It is all part of his plan to escape punishment for his revenge.

2. **My Prediction:** He has purposely made sure the servants are away so there will be no witnesses.

   Outcome: I was right. He does not want anyone to see Fortunato entering his home.

3. **My Prediction:** They are at the end of their journey. Here is where Fortunato will meet his fate.

   Outcome: I was right, but I never expected the narrator to kill Fortunato in such a horrible way.

Vocabulary Builder, p. 94

Sample Answers

A. 1. A; 2. B; 3. D
   4. A; 5. D; 6. C

B. 1. As I walked up the mountain, the trail's <u>elevation</u> increased more and more.

   2. The huge male lion provides <u>protection</u> for the rest of the group.

   3. When he could not pay his rent, the landlord threatened him with <u>eviction</u>.

   4. The coach made a <u>substitution</u> when John was injured.

Enrichment: Coats of Arms, p. 95

Sample Answers

A. 1. The nobility used coats of arms to distinguish themselves from other noble families and from the lower classes. The symbols and motto represented key qualities of their heritage.

   2. Montresor's coat of arms suggests he prizes wealth, power, aggression, and revenge.

B. You might ask students to explain their coats of arms to the class. Make sure they have included four different symbols or figures and a motto.

"Sonata for Harp and Bicycle" by Joan Aiken
"The Cask of Amontillado" by Edgar Allan Poe

Integrated Language Skills: Grammar, p. 96

Abstract and Concrete Nouns

A. Words that should be circled by students are set in parentheses.

1. The thousand (injuries) of <u>Fortunato</u> I had borne . . . but when he ventured upon (insult) I vowed (revenge).

2. <u>Jason</u> could see two long <u>passages</u> coming toward him, meeting at an acute (angle) where he stood.

3. It must be understood that neither by (word) nor (deed) had I given <u>Fortunato</u> (cause) to doubt my good (will).

4. "We must remedy the (matter), <u>Berenice</u>. We must not begrudge our new-found (happiness) to others."

B. You might have students exchange paragraphs to identify the abstract and concrete nouns.

"The Cask of Amontillado" by Edgar Allan Poe

Open-Book Test, p. 99

Short Answer

1. Montresor's attitude toward revenge is that it must be undertaken very carefully so as to avoid being caught. He says: "I must not only punish but punish with impunity."

   Difficulty: *Challenging*   **Objective:** *Interpretation*

2. Some students may say the repetition creates unease, anticipation, and tension; others may say it helps Montresor appeal to Fortunato's vanity and turn it to his own advantage.

   Difficulty: *Average*   **Objective:** *Literary Analysis*

3. No, he does not. Instead of making his plans explicit, Montresor keeps them hidden from Fortunato.

   Difficulty: *Easy*   **Objective:** *Vocabulary*

4. Students may have predicted that at that point Fortunato's fate was sealed and Montresor would have his revenge. Details that support this prediction include Fortunato's drunkenness, his ill health, and his pride—all of which are weaknesses that render him unable to perceive or divert the danger he is in.

   Difficulty: *Average*   **Objective:** *Reading*

5. Students may say the mood is eerie or suspenseful. Sounds and objects might include the flambeaux, the jingling of the bells on Fortunato's hat, Fortunato's unsteady footsteps, Fortunato's hacking cough, the niter, the wine casks, Fortunato's grotesque laughter and gestures, Montresor's trowel, the low arches, and human remains.

   Difficulty: *Average*   **Objective:** *Literary Analysis*

6. During this conversation, Montresor produces from within his cloak a trowel. The trowel foreshadows his later work erecting the stone-and-mortar wall.

   Difficulty: *Easy*   **Objective:** *Literary Analysis*

7. Students may say that Montresor's behavior suggests that he is unstable and possibly insane. This insight may have caused some students to predict momentarily that Montresor would abandon his task; other students may have grown more firmly convinced that Montresor would in fact murder Fortunato.

   Difficulty: *Challenging*   **Objective:** *Reading*

8. Climax: the final exchange between Montresor and Fortunato, in which Fortunato laughs hysterically as if the whole episode were a joke, then begs Montresor in vain to have mercy. Examples of rising action include the first conversation between the two, Fortunato's increasing ill health as they descend, and the various stages of the erection of the wall.

   Difficulty: *Average* **Objective:** *Literary Analysis*

9. Students may say that the punishment of a torturous death does not fit the crime of hurling insults and that this imbalance suggests that Montresor himself is insane.

   Difficulty: *Average* **Objective:** *Interpretation*

10. Sample answer: Montresor will not be caught because no one has entered the crypt in Fifty years and Montresor says "May he rest in peace," which implies than Fortunato's body will not be disturbed.

    Difficulty: *Challenging* **Objective:** *Interpretation*

Essay

11. Students may say that insofar as Fortunato is foolish, the motley costume, suggestive of a court jester, is appropriate. They may also point out that Montresor's black mask and cloak, suggestive of an executioner's garb, symbolize death, and that the mask itself symbolizes Montresor's duplicity as he poses as Fortunato's gullible friend.

    Difficulty: *Easy* **Objective:** *Essay*

12. Students who believe Montresor shows guilt or remorse may point to his use of the word "heart" rather than "stomach," suggesting that his emotions, rather than his body, are sickened. Students who think Montresor is actually sickened by the environment may point to his ruthless, unforgiving character or to the fact that at the time of the telling of the story, fifty years later, he is still mired in hatred for his adversary.

    Difficulty: *Average* **Objective:** *Essay*

13. Students may say that according to Montresor's description, Fortunato is a skillful wine expert who does not try to deceive others with knowledge he does not possess—but that on the other hand, he *does* pretend to know about painting and gemstones. Based on this description, Fortunato seems no better and no worse than any other person: He has both strengths and weaknesses of character. However, students may say that this portrait is unreliable because of Montresor's own dishonest and possibly insane character, or they may say that in spite of his ruthlessness, Montresor seems to have a chillingly clear view of his victim.

    Difficulty: *Challenging* **Objective:** *Essay*

14. Students should reply that based on his first conversation with Montresor, Fortunato believes that he is accompanying Montresor to his home in order to judge a cask of wine and that both Fortunato's drunkenness and his pride contribute to his inability to see the situation more clearly. Students should also note that Fortunato recognizes the real truth—that

Montresor intends to kill Fortunato—only when Montresor shackles Fortunato to the wall in a recess of the crypt. Fortunato responds with confused astonishment, which students may find appropriate given the vast difference between what he *thought* was happening and what actually *was* happening.

Difficulty: *Average* **Objective::** *Essay*

Oral Response

15. Students should give an oral explanation in response to the question they choose or the one assigned to them.

    Difficulty: *Average* **Objective::** *Oral Interpretation*

Selection Test A, p. 102

Critical Reading

1. ANS: B	DIF: Easy	OBJ: Comprehension
2. ANS: D	DIF: Easy	OBJ: Interpretation
3. ANS: B	DIF: Easy	OBJ: Literary Analysis
4. ANS: C	DIF: Easy	OBJ: Interpretation
5. ANS: C	DIF: Easy	OBJ: Reading
6. ANS: D	DIF: Easy	OBJ: Comprehension
7. ANS: A	DIF: Easy	OBJ: Interpretation
8. ANS: C	DIF: Easy	OBJ: Interpretation
9. ANS: C	DIF: Easy	OBJ: Literary Analysis
10. ANS: C	DIF: Easy	OBJ: Reading
11. ANS: A	DIF: Easy	OBJ: Interpretation

Vocabulary and Grammar

12. ANS: A	DIF: Easy	OBJ: Vocabulary
13. ANS: B	DIF: Easy	OBJ: Vocabulary
14. ANS: D	DIF: Easy	OBJ: Grammar
15. ANS: C	DIF: Easy	OBJ: Grammar

Essay

16. Students should identify one event from the rising action, climax, and resolution of "The Cask of Amontillado." Students may cite Fortunato and Montresor's entering the catacombs as an event that takes place during the rising action. During the climax, Montresor begins to wall Fortunato in. In the resolution, Montresor completes his act of revenge.

    Difficulty: *Easy*

    Objective: *Essay*

17. In their essays, students should begin by identifying a specific character trait (e.g., clever, crazy, bitter, determined, vengeful). They should support that trait with two examples from the story. For example, they can write that Montresor is clever because he makes his plans so carefully and is never found out. They might also mention how clever he is when he tricks Fortunato into entering the catacombs.

    Difficulty: *Easy*

    Objective: *Essay*

18. Students should note that Fortunato only recognizes the real truth—that Montresor intends to kill Fortunato—when Montresor shackles Fortunato to the wall in a recess of the crypt. Fortunato responds with confused astonishment.

Difficulty: *Easy*
Objective: *Essay*

Selection Test B, p. 105

Critical Reading

1. ANS: B	DIF: Average	OBJ: Comprehension
2. ANS: B	DIF: Average	OBJ: Comprehension
3. ANS: A	DIF: Average	OBJ: Literary Analysis
4. ANS: D	DIF: Challenging	OBJ: Reading
5. ANS: B	DIF: Challenging	OBJ: Interpretation
6. ANS: C	DIF: Challenging	OBJ: Interpretation
7. ANS: B	DIF: Average	OBJ: Comprehension
8. ANS: C	DIF: Average	OBJ: Comprehension
9. ANS: C	DIF: Average	OBJ: Interpretation
10. ANS: C	DIF: Average	OBJ: Interpretation
11. ANS: B	DIF: Challenging	OBJ: Interpretation
12. ANS: C	DIF: Average	OBJ: Literary Analysis
13. ANS: D	DIF: Challenging	OBJ: Literary Analysis
14. ANS: B	DIF: Challenging	OBJ: Reading
15. ANS: D	DIF: Challenging	OBJ: Reading

Vocabulary and Grammar

16. ANS: D	DIF: Average	OBJ: Vocabulary
17. ANS: A	DIF: Average	OBJ: Vocabulary
18. ANS: C	DIF: Average	OBJ: Grammar
19. ANS: C	DIF: Challenging	OBJ: Grammar

Essay

20. In their essays, students may note that descriptive details (such as the niter, glowing flambeaux, deep crypt, piles of skeletons and bones, and drops of moisture trickling among the bones) create a mood of eerie suspense. They should identify one scene, such as Fortunato and Montresor's trip through the vaults, in which this mood is strongly expressed.

Difficulty: *Average*
Objective: *Essay*

21. Students should identify one event from the rising action, climax, and resolution of "The Cask of Amontillado." Students may cite Fortunato and Montresor's entering the catacombs as an event that takes place during the rising action. During the climax, Montresor begins to wall Fortunato in. In the resolution, Montresor completes his act of revenge.

Difficulty: *Average*
Objective: *Essay*

22. Students should reply that, based on his first conversation with Montresor, Fortunato believes that he is accompanying Montresor to his home in order to judge a cask of wine; and that both Fortunato's drunkenness and his pride contribute to his inability to see the situation more clearly. Students should also note that Fortunato only recognizes the real truth—that Montresor intends to kill Fortunato—when Montresor shackles Fortunato to the wall in a recess of the crypt. Fortunato responds with confused astonishment, which students may find appropriate given the vast difference between what he *thought* was happening and what actually *was* happening.

Difficulty: *Average*
Objective: *Essay*

"Checkouts" by Cynthia Rylant
"The Girl Who Can" by Ama Ata Aidoo

Vocabulary Warm-up Exercises, p. 109

A.
1. kilometers
2. items
3. transition
4. photographs
5. approved
6. discussion
7. attractive
8. fascinating

B. Sample Answers
1. My *intuition* told me that Alice would be a good friend, and it turned out to be true because we have been friends for two years.
2. One *solitary* pursuit that I enjoy is walking on the beach early in the morning.
3. To bring out the natural *sheen* of a pet's coat, I would have to bathe the pet frequently and brush its fur.
4. No, I would not be likely to be climbing mountains in a *lowland* because the land there is lower than the surrounding area.
5. If a tornado hit my city, the *resulting* aftermath would probably be the destruction of many homes and stores.
6. I look forward to the Fourth of July with great *anticipation* because I really enjoy the fireworks displays.
7. A trait I have that I would like to *emphasize* is my sense of humor.

Reading Warm-up A, p. 110

Words that students are to circle appear in parentheses.

Sample Answers
1. (history); One topic that I find *fascinating* is the history of the Civil War.
2. you can even have photographs developed; Two of my favorite *photographs* are of my parents long ago. In the

first one, they are having a picnic. In the second one, they are admiring me when I was an infant.

3. (How did we get from small general stores to mega-supermarkets); *Transition* means "the act of changing from one form or condition to another."

4. displays; I would regard as *attractive* a store display in which mannequins appeared in natural poses, as if they were really interacting.

5. (tea, coffee, canned goods); The only *items* on the list I could not find were dill pickles and Spanish olives.

6. credit cards as a method of payment; *Approved* means "accepted as good."

7. (the history of the supermarket); The topic of a recent *discussion* I had was whether to surprise my sister with a birthday party or tell her about it ahead of time.

8. the expensive downtowns; My school is just a few *kilometers* from where I live.

Reading Warm-up B, p. 111

Words that students are to circle appear in parentheses.

Sample Answers

1. pursuit; Watching the sun come up is one of my favorite *solitary* moments in the day.

2. (hills); A *lowland* is not likely to have mountains, as the area is lower, not higher, than the surrounding area.

3. tiresome; One activity that I regard as *tedious* is folding laundry.

4. (often prevent runners from ever getting to compete in their chosen event); It took Ted two years to deal with the problem and its *resulting* costs.

5. *Anticipation* of success might cause injury because someone could take unnecessary risks in order to win. *Anticipation* means "the act of expecting something to happen."

6. that consistency is important; If I were giving training advice to a runner, I would *emphasize* the importance of drinking enough water during workouts.

7. (to take an extra day off); Carla relied on *intuition* when choosing her friends.

8. gold medal; Another item that might have a *sheen* is a silver bracelet.

Writing About the Big Question, p. 112

A. 1. convince
2. Skeptics
3. verify
4. distort

B. Sample Answers

1. I didn't think I could possibly do well on a math exam. I actually did pretty well.

2. Because I **assumed** it would be hard, I didn't think I would do well and I didn't study very hard. When I did better than I expected, it changed my

perspective. I knew I could do well if I **believed** in myself and studied harder.

C. Sample Answer

People may have assumptions about others or themselves based on what they have heard from others. Those beliefs can be changed when they see things for themselves. The truths that people believe can change as they experience more.

Literary Analysis: Point of View, p. 113

Sample Answers

1. If the girl were the first-person narrator in "Checkouts," we would learn the girl's thoughts and feelings, but not the boy's. Some important parts of the narrative would be left out: for example, the humor of the boy's comparing himself to the cocky cashier, the grim store manager, the bland butcher, and the brazen bag boys.

2. If the scene were narrated in the third-person omniscient point of view, the humor that the perspective of a young child provides would be lost. The ending might seem more sharply ironic. However, we would be able to know exactly what Nana thinks and feels.

Vocabulary Builder, p. 114

Sample Answers

A. 1. Sunk in reverie, the six-year-old twins had dreamy expressions on their faces.

2. She downplays her accomplishments in a humble manner.

3. Rushing directly from work to the party resulted in Sam's state of dishevelment.

4. May's sister took a perverse pleasure in making her cry.

5. The soil is so extremely fertile that it yields bountiful harvests.

B. 1. A person with a humble attitude might behave in a shy manner.

2. A fertile piece of land might look very green with a good crop growing on it.

3. You would be satisfied because you would understand the topic thoroughly.

Open-Book Test, p. 116

Short Answer

1. The girl feels depressed and lonely because she has been forced to leave her childhood town. She sits for a month and looks at photos of her old life.

   Difficulty: *Average*   **Objective:** *Interpretation*

2. Sample answer: Boy's Behavior—does not look at the girl; Girl's Behavior—looks straight ahead; My Behavior—smile and say "hi." Students may say the two act childishly when they refuse to acknowledge each other.

   Difficulty: *Average*   **Objective:** *Interpretation*

3. Sample answer: The author writes that the girl "had never told [her parents] how much she loved grocery shopping" and that the boy "believed he must have looked the fool in her eyes."
   Difficulty: *Easy* **Objective:** *Literary Analysis*

4. Nana believes that women's main role in the world is to have babies. She believes that Adjoa's legs are too thin to support the heavy hips of a pregnant woman.
   Difficulty: *Average* **Objective:** *Interpretation*

5. Sample answer: Adjoa says that "about almost everything else apart from my legs, Nana is such a good grown-up."
   Difficulty: *Easy* **Objective:** *Interpretation*

6. At the end of "The Girl Who Can," Nana no longer feels that Adjoa's legs are perverse; instead, she sees that they are perfect legs for running.
   Difficulty: *Average* **Objective:** *Vocabulary*

7. "Checkouts" is told in the third-person point of view. The narrator refers to the girl as "she" and the boy as "he." "The Girl Who Can" is told in the first-person point of view. The narrator refers to herself as "I."
   Difficulty: *Average* **Objective:** *Literary Analysis*

8. The reader learns what Nana thinks and feels through Nana's actions and words, as reported by Adjoa. For example, Adjoa says that when she tells Nana something, Nana either stops and stares or bursts out laughing.
   Difficulty: *Challenging* **Objective:** *Literary Analysis*

9. Students may say that they get to know Adjoa better than they do the girl in "Checkouts." "The Girl Who Can" is told in the first-person point of view, which makes the reader feel as if Adjoa were speaking directly to him or her.
   Difficulty: *Challenging* **Objective:** *Literary Analysis*

10. Sample response: Both girls find it difficult to share their thoughts and feelings with adults. The girl in "Checkouts" does not feel that it is "safe" to tell her parents that she loves grocery shopping, and Adjoa finds it "risky" to say something serious to grown-ups.
    Difficulty: *Challenging* **Objective:** *Interpretation*

Essay

11. Students may speculate that the girl from "Checkouts" adapted to Cincinnati and stayed there and that she probably married, had children, and lived a conventional domestic life. They may also speculate that Adjoa went on to become an accomplished runner, perhaps leaving her small African village for a university and life in a larger city. Students' descriptions should correspond logically to the characters' backgrounds and traits as revealed in the stories.
    Difficulty: *Easy* **Objective:** *Essay*

12. Students should identify the story and the new point of view and should provide examples of how the new point of view would change the story. For example, with the bag boy as first-person narrator in "Checkouts," we

would know nothing about the girl's background, we would not understand why she snubbed the boy, and we would know a lot more about the bag boy. Students should identify and explain their preference for one or the other point of view.
Difficulty: *Average* **Objective:** *Essay*

13. Students may respond that the girl in "Checkouts" faces the challenge of adapting to a new home, which she eventually does, or the challenge of getting to know the bag boy, which she does not. They may also respond that Adjoa faces the challenge of communicating important ideas to the grown-ups or that she pursues the goal of winning the district games—both of which she succeeds in doing. Students should offer logical reasons why each girl does or does not meet with success in pursuing these goals.
    Difficulty: *Challenging* **Objective:** *Essay*

14. Students should respond that at first Nana believes women should have thick, sturdy legs and solid hips to support the weight of pregnancy but that by the end of the story she realizes that thin legs can also be useful. This change may cause Nana to realize that people have different goals, purposes, and talents in life and that every body is beautiful and useful in its own way.
    Difficulty: *Average* **Objective:** *Essay*

Oral Response

15. Students should give oral explanations in response to the question they choose or the one assigned to them.
    Difficulty: *Average* **Objective:** *Oral Interpretation*

Selection Test A, p. 119

Critical Reading

1. ANS: D	DIF: Easy	OBJ: Comprehension
2. ANS: A	DIF: Easy	OBJ: Literary Analysis
3. ANS: C	DIF: Easy	OBJ: Interpretation
4. ANS: B	DIF: Easy	OBJ: Literary Analysis
5. ANS: D	DIF: Easy	OBJ: Interpretation
6. ANS: A	DIF: Easy	OBJ: Comprehension
7. ANS: A	DIF: Easy	OBJ: Literary Analysis
8. ANS: C	DIF: Easy	OBJ: Comprehension
9. ANS: A	DIF: Easy	OBJ: Comprehension
10. ANS: A	DIF: Easy	OBJ: Interpretation
11. ANS: C	DIF: Easy	OBJ: Interpretation
12. ANS: C	DIF: Easy	OBJ: Literary Analysis

Vocabulary

13. ANS: D	DIF: Easy	OBJ: Vocabulary
14. ANS: B	DIF: Easy	OBJ: Vocabulary
15. ANS: B	DIF: Easy	OBJ: Vocabulary

Essay

16. Students should note that "Checkouts" is written in the third-person omniscient point of view. That point of view enables the writer to reveal all of the characters' thoughts and feelings. "The Girl Who Can," in contrast, is written in the first-person point of view, which means we can know only what the narrator thinks and feels. Make sure students provide examples from the stories to support their points.
    Difficulty: *Easy*
    Objective: *Essay*

17. In their essays, students should list some characteristics for each girl and note that the authors reveal their characteristics indirectly. Instead of telling us that the girl in "Checkouts" is impulsive, for example, the author shows us what she does, says, and thinks—falling in love immediately with the bag boy. We learn more about Adjoa than we do about the girl in "Checkouts" because the first-person point of view lets us view all of the other characters and events through Adjoa's eyes.
    Difficulty: *Easy*
    Objective: *Essay*

18. Students should respond that by the end of the story, Nana realizes that thin legs can also be useful. This change may cause Nana to realize that people have different goals, purposes, and talents in life, and that all people are beautiful and useful in their own way.
    Difficulty: *Easy*
    Objective: *Essay*

Selection Test B, p 122

Critical Reading

1.	ANS: D	DIF: Average	OBJ:	Comprehension
2.	ANS: A	DIF: Average	OBJ:	Literary Analysis
3.	ANS: C	DIF: Challenging	OBJ:	Interpretation
4.	ANS: A	DIF: Average	OBJ:	Comprehension
5.	ANS: B	DIF: Challenging	OBJ:	Interpretation
6.	ANS: C	DIF: Average	OBJ:	Literary Analysis
7.	ANS: B	DIF: Average	OBJ:	Comprehension
8.	ANS: C	DIF: Average	OBJ:	Comprehension
9.	ANS: A	DIF: Average	OBJ:	Literary Analysis
10.	ANS: C	DIF: Average	OBJ:	Comprehension
11.	ANS: B	DIF: Challenging	OBJ:	Interpretation
12.	ANS: A	DIF: Average	OBJ:	Comprehension
13.	ANS: A	DIF: Average	OBJ:	Interpretation
14.	ANS: A	DIF: Average	OBJ:	Literary Analysis
15.	ANS: B	DIF: Challenging	OBJ:	Interpretation
16.	ANS: C	DIF: Challenging	OBJ:	Literary Analysis
17.	ANS: B	DIF: Average	OBJ:	Interpretation

Vocabulary

18.	ANS: B	DIF: Average	OBJ:	Vocabulary
19.	ANS: B	DIF: Average	OBJ:	Vocabulary
20.	ANS: A	DIF: Challenging	OBJ:	Vocabulary

Essay

21. Students should identify the story and new point of view. Look for three examples of how the story would change with its new point of view. For example, with the bag boy as first-person narrator in "Checkouts," we would know nothing about the girl's background, we would not understand why she snubbed the boy, and we would know a lot more about the bag boy. Make sure students state which point of view (the new one or original) they prefer and why.
    Difficulty: *Average*
    Objective: *Essay*

22. Students should identify the stories' different points of view and give examples to discuss their effect. For example, in "Checkouts," the fact that we know what both the girl and the bag boy really think and feel (third-person omniscient) adds to the humor and irony of the ending. In "The Girl Who Can," the first-person point of view contributes to the story's humor and causes us to sympathize with the narrator's predicament and triumph.
    Difficulty: *Challenging*
    Objective: *Essay*

23. Students should respond that at first, Nana believes women should have thick, sturdy legs and solid hips to support the weight of pregnancy, but that by the end of the story, she realizes that thin legs can also be useful. This change may cause Nana to realize that people have different goals, purposes, and talents in life, and that all people are beautiful and useful in their own way.

Writing Workshop

Autobiographical Narrative: Integrating Grammar Skills, p. 126

A. 1. Parsons'; 2. men's; 3. Los Angeles'; 4. brother-in-law's

B. 1. Years ago, I read a children's book about the world's mysteries.

2. The book's first chapter was about Loch Ness' famous monster.

3. correct

4. The two monsters' origins are a mystery.

Benchmark Test 1, p. 127

MULTIPLE CHOICE

1. ANS: D
2. ANS: D
3. ANS: D
4. ANS: B
5. ANS: C
6. ANS: A
7. ANS: B
8. ANS: D
9. ANS: C

10. ANS: B
11. ANS: C
12. ANS: A
13. ANS: B
14. ANS: D
15. ANS: A
16. ANS: B
17. ANS: A
18. ANS: C
19. ANS: B
20. ANS: D
21. ANS: B
22. ANS: B
23. ANS: A
24. ANS: C
25. ANS: D
26. ANS: B
27. ANS: D
28. ANS: D
29. ANS: B
30. ANS: D
31. ANS: D
32. ANS: A
33. ANS: A
34. ANS: B
35. ANS: C
36. ANS: B

ESSAY

37. Students' anecdotes should contain a clear conflict and present events in a logical order that leads to a clear resolution.
38. Students' critiques should provide clear and sufficient background information about the work. Students should clearly state their own judgments, supporting each point with examples from the work.
39. The essay should be focused on one specific task. Events should be in chronological or logical order.

from **A White House Diary**
by Lady Bird Johnson

Vocabulary Warm-up Exercises, p. 136

A. 1. composed
2. departure
3. compassion
4. dignified
5. federal
6. rapid
7. element
8. enormity

B. Sample Answers

1. A *presidential aide* might gather information, provide advice, and assist with planning meetings and trips.
2. No, an *agonizing* problem would not be easy to solve because it would involve something painful or difficult to deal with.
3. You might help by giving her a hug, listening to her, or suggesting she talk with a counselor.
4. In a parade, you might see floats, marching bands, clowns, and people who belong to special groups following one after the other.
5. The seats are in front of you because *onward* means "going forward."
6. It would mean that an important person had been killed and the killer escaped.

Reading Warm-up A, p. 137

Words that students are to circle appear in parentheses.

Sample Answers

1. quick; I would make a *rapid* response if someone yelled "Fire!" or was threatening me.
2. (calm); Someone who is *composed* is not excited and acts normally.
3. She had seen her husband killed, the children would grow up without their father; A synonym for *compassion* is *concern.*
4. If she could behave well at such a time, people wanted to do the same; *Dignified* means "acting in a proper or honorable way."
5. Mrs. Kennedy brought an *element* of history to the President's funeral by following traditions from Lincoln's funeral and using the same catafalque; *Aspect* is a synonym for *element.*
6. (the White House); *Arrival* is an antonym for *departure.*
7. (tragedy), (sorrow); Another event that would have *enormity* is war or a natural disaster.
8. Americans get off from school and work; Two *federal* holidays my school observes are Presidents' Day and Memorial Day.

Reading Warm-up B, p. 138

Words that students are to circle appear in parentheses.

Sample Answers

1. Zachary Taylor took ill after attending a dedication ceremony for the new Washington Monument in 1850; *Presidential* means "having to do with a president or the presidency."
2. extraordinarily painful; I think the shock of a president being murdered makes an assassination *agonizing.*
3. John Wilkes Booth shot and killed Abraham Lincoln because Booth sided with the South in the Civil War; A synonym for *assassin* is *murderer.*
4. In their deep sadness, people must have questioned if there was hope for America; People may have been *desolate* because there had been three assassinations in less than 40 years.

5. (unbroken); I follow a schedule of classes in *succession*.

6. The vice president is immediately sworn in after the president dies, and that act moves the country *onward* by providing a new leader who sets new goals.

7. president riding in an open car; A president who is *insulated* is protected, but an open car makes the president vulnerable to being shot or otherwise injured.

8. The passage indicates that a person who is an *aide* to the president would be on the president's staff.

Writing About the Big Question, p. 139

A. 1. circumstance, perspective
2. distort, verify
3. perceive
4. credible

B. Sample Answers

1. I came home from school, and Mom told me that my grandmother was very sick. I was surprised because just the day before she had seemed completely healthy.

2. When it happened, I felt shock and fear. Later, I **perceived** that I shouldn't have been surprised. There was **evidence** of her illness long before—if I had only looked for it.

C. Sample Answer

make someone aware of how fragile life can be.

For Lady Bird Johnson, life must have seemed satisfying and complete. Then suddenly, it all changed. What a shock that must have been to her. It made her husband president, and she became First Lady. It also must have shown her how vulnerable everyone is. Life could never again have been as satisfying.

Literary Analysis: Autobiographical Writing and Author's Voice, p. 140

Sample Answers

1. **Words that reveal feelings:** enormity, struck

Writer's attitude: She sounds as if she is in shock and very sad.

Syntax: The first three sentences are very short, as if she is in shock. Two longer sentences reveal her feelings.

2. **Words that reveal feelings:** repetition of the word *blood* four times, *caked* twice; *poignant*; *exquisitely*

Writer's attitude: She feels extremely sorry for Mrs. Kennedy.

Syntax: Again, there is one short sentence. The paragraph ends with two long sentences in which she interrupts herself.

Reading: Preview the Text to Identify an Author's Purpose, p. 141

Sample Answers

1. The author's purpose is to inform.

2. The main subjects are Abigail Adams and Eleanor Roosevelt.

3. The author will discuss Eleanor Roosevelt's life, childhood, education, and major accomplishments.

4. The author admires his subjects very much.

Vocabulary Builder, p. 142

Sample Answers

A. 1. B; 2. D; 3. C
4. B; 5. D; 6. A

B. 1. Scientists might use the word *infinity* to describe space because space seems endless.

2. A writer might want to *refine* his writing before submitting his work to a publisher because he wants it in the most polished, final condition possible.

3. You would *definitely* want to impress your teacher when you take a test.

Enrichment: An Orderly Succession, p. 143

1. the Vice President
2. the Speaker of the House
3. A Vice President is nominated by the President and confirmed by Congress.
4. Sample answer: An orderly chain of succession prevents power struggles and lets the government continue to function normally.

Open-Book Test, p. 144

Short Answer

1. The heading reveals that the author's purpose was to describe events that occurred on November 22, 1963. Students who study the accompanying photograph's will realize that the major event she is writing about is the assassination of John F. Kennedy.

   Difficulty: *Easy* **Objective:** *Reading*

2. Yes, the events of the day were tumultuous, which means "greatly disturbed" or "in an uproar." On that day a well-loved president was shot and killed. The event threw the entire country into a state of chaos.

   Difficulty: *Average* **Objective:** *Vocabulary*

3. Mrs. Johnson's relationship with Mrs. Kennedy is polite and somewhat formal, while her relationship with Mrs. Connally is intimate and familiar. Mrs. Johnson has trouble finding the right words to say to Mrs. Kennedy but she feels free to cry with and console Mrs. Connelly.

   Difficulty: *Average* **Objective:** *Interpretation*

4. Many of the sentences in these paragraphs are short and direct. These kinds of sentences help convey the feeling of shock and the hectic unfolding of events.

   Difficulty: *Challenging* **Objective:** *Literary Analysis*

5. The mood was subdued and mournful. Johnson writes that each passenger sat "with his own thoughts." The casket was placed in the corridor of the plane, and Mrs. Kennedy was alone in a small room, still wearing blood-caked clothes.

   Difficulty: *Average* **Objective:** *Interpretation*

6. Students may say that Johnson's voice is sympathetic or anguished. Words and phrases that help create this voice include: "one of the most poignant sights"; "I tried to express how we felt"; and "I would have done anything to help her".
   Difficulty: *Challenging* **Objective:** *Literary Analysis*

7. Sample answer: Mrs. Johnson sees in the president's car "a bundle of pink, just like a drift of blossoms, lying on the back seat." This reveals her gentle, sympathetic feelings toward Mrs. Kennedy.
   Difficulty: *Average* **Objective:** *Literary Analysis*

8. Sample answer: She says that "through it all Lyndon was remarkably calm and quiet," that "he is a good man in a tight spot," and that at the Washington airport he "made a very simple, very brief, and I think, strong statement."
   Difficulty: *Easy* **Objective:** *Interpretation*

9. Students may identify the secondary purpose of expressing her own feelings about what was happening on this tragic day. Examples include her confusion at the moment of the shooting, her tumultuous feelings for Mrs. Kennedy, the grief she shared with her friend Nellie, her compassion for the Secret Service men, and her pride in her husband.
   Difficulty: *Average* **Objective:** *Reading*

10. Students may say the image of Jackie Kennedy caked with blood made the strongest impression on them, and that Johnson most likely included it to fulfill Mrs. Kennedy's own wish—that people would know what the assassins had done to her husband.
    Difficulty: *Easy* **Objective:** *Interpretation*

Essay

11. Students' diary entries may include watching the president's car drive by, hearing the shots seeing the car drive away rapidly, and learning that the president had died and that Johnson had been sworn in as president on *Air Force One*.
    Difficulty: *Easy* **Objective:** *Essay*

12. Students may say that Johnson chose this title because the book gives personal insights into historic public events and that for this reason the title is apt. Other students may respond that a diary by nature is not meant for an audience other than the writer and so this work does not qualify as such.
    Difficulty: *Average* **Objective:** *Essay*

13. Students may say that Mrs. Johnson would have made a good president. They may base their opinion on her sharp observational skills, her compassion, and her poise. Opinions should be supported with examples and details from the text.
    Difficulty: *Challenging* **Objective:** *Essay*

14. Students should reply that on the morning of November 22, 1963, Lady Bird Johnson was the vice president's wife and later that day she became the First Lady of the United States. Students should note that as a result,

Lady Bird was thrust suddenly into the public spotlight and was called on to advise and support the president. Students may say that based on evidence of her intelligence and sensitivity, Mrs. Johnson seems to have been well prepared to assume these new responsibilities.
Difficulty: *Average* **Objective:** *Essay*

Oral Response

15. Students should give oral explanations in response to the question they choose or the one assigned to them.
    Difficulty: *Average* **Objective:** *Oral Interpretation*

Selection Test A, p. 147

Critical Reading

1. **ANS:** A	**DIF:** Easy	**OBJ:** Literary Analysis
2. **ANS:** C	**DIF:** Easy	**OBJ:** Comprehension
3. **ANS:** D	**DIF:** Easy	**OBJ:** Reading
4. **ANS:** D	**DIF:** Easy	**OBJ:** Reading
5. **ANS:** B	**DIF:** Easy	**OBJ:** Reading
6. **ANS:** C	**DIF:** Easy	**OBJ:** Comprehension
7. **ANS:** D	**DIF:** Easy	**OBJ:** Literary Analysis
8. **ANS:** C	**DIF:** Easy	**OBJ:** Literary Analysis
9. **ANS:** D	**DIF:** Easy	**OBJ:** Interpretation
10. **ANS:** B	**DIF:** Easy	**OBJ:** Interpretation

Vocabulary and Grammar

11. **ANS:** C	**DIF:** Easy	**OBJ:** Vocabulary
12. **ANS:** A	**DIF:** Easy	**OBJ:** Vocabulary
13. **ANS:** D	**DIF:** Easy	**OBJ:** Grammar
14. **ANS:** C	**DIF:** Easy	**OBJ:** Grammar

Essay

15. Students' essays should identify two of Mrs. Johnson's character traits and support each one with examples. They may mention her kindness (to Mrs. Kennedy, Nellie, the Secret Service men, the President's assistant), her calm self-control (she does not go to pieces), and her ability to observe and remember details.
    Difficulty: *Easy*
    Objective: *Essay*

16. Students' reports should identify the place and date. The major events students should mention include the gunshots, President Kennedy's death, Lyndon B. Johnson's being sworn in as President, and the fact that a suspect has been arrested.
    Difficulty: *Easy*
    Objective: *Essay*

17. Students should note that Lady Bird was thrust suddenly into the public spotlight, and she was called upon to advise and support her husband, now the President. Students may say that based upon evidence in the diary

that shows her intelligence and sensitivity, Mrs. Johnson seems to have been well-prepared to assume these new responsibilities.

Difficulty: *Average*

Objective: *Essay*

Selection Test B, p. 150

Critical Reading

1. ANS: D	DIF: Challenging	OBJ: Literary Analysis
2. ANS: D	DIF: Challenging	OBJ: Reading
3. ANS: A	DIF: Challenging	OBJ: Literary Analysis
4. ANS: D	DIF: Average	OBJ: Literary Analysis
5. ANS: B	DIF: Average	OBJ: Literary Analysis
6. ANS: B	DIF: Average	OBJ: Comprehension
7. ANS: C	DIF: Challenging	OBJ: Interpretation
8. ANS: B	DIF: Challenging	OBJ: Reading
9. ANS: D	DIF: Average	OBJ: Interpretation
10. ANS: A	DIF: Average	OBJ: Interpretation
11. ANS: D	DIF: Challenging	OBJ: Interpretation
12. ANS: B	DIF: Challenging	OBJ: Reading

Vocabulary and Grammar

13. ANS: D	DIF: Average	OBJ: Vocabulary
14. ANS: B	DIF: Average	OBJ: Grammar
15. ANS: B	DIF: Average	OBJ: Grammar
16. ANS: C	DIF: Challenging	OBJ: Vocabulary

Essay

17. Students' essays should mention the date, the place, and the major events told in chronological order: the gunshot, ride to the hospital, President Kennedy's death, President Johnson being sworn in aboard Air Force One, and the fact that the police are holding a suspect. Check to see that the reports are objective—that is, they state the facts without revealing the writer's feelings or opinions.

Difficulty: *Average*

Objective: *Essay*

18. Students' essays should note that as an eyewitness to some of the events surrounding President Kennedy's assassination, her book should be a reliable source of information for the events she describes. The student might quote passages from her book. However, Mrs. Johnson does not deal with the whole incident. Some of the things she does not touch on are the extent of the President's wounds, what happened in the operating room, when President Kennedy died, the identity of the suspect, and the suspect's motive for shooting the President. To obtain information on these aspects of the incident, students would have to consult other sources.

Difficulty: *Challenging*

Objective: *Essay*

19. Students should reply that on the morning of November 22, 1963, Lady Bird Johnson was the Vice President's wife, and that later that day she became the First Lady of the United States. Students should note that as a result, Lady Bird was thrust suddenly into the public spotlight and was called upon to advise and support her husband, now the President. Students may say that, based upon evidence in the diary of her intelligence and sensitivity, Mrs. Johnson seems to have been well-prepared to assume these new responsibilities.

Difficulty: *Average*

Objective: *Essay*

"My English" by Julia Alvarez

Vocabulary Warm-up Exercises, p. 154

A. 1. childhood
2. acquired
3. particularly
4. necessarily
5. superior
6. anxiety
7. enlisted
8. referring

B. Sample Answers
1. You can make bland food tastier by adding salt.
2. Giving someone flowers would be a demonstration of affection.
3. My family observes the tradition of lighting Kwanzaa candles.
4. My little sister has the most expressive face in my family.
5. World War I drastically changed world history.
6. I would enjoy hearing an animated debate on the need for homework.
7. Yes, it is common to have more than one version of a folk tale.

Reading Warm-up A, p. 155

Words that students are to circle appear in parentheses.

Sample Answers
1. before I could read; A love of language began in the author's childhood.
2. a love of picture books; Her parents read the picture books over and over.
3. our dog chewed up one of my favorite books; I might experience *anxiety* if I forget to bring my sneakers to track practice.
4. the one the dog chewed up; *Necessarily* means "definitely."
5. (evening reader); A babysitter might be *enlisted* to prepare a meal.
6. my early fascination with words; The author won many contests and awards.

7. <u>writing poetry</u>; I *particularly* enjoy reading romance novels.

8. <u>an autumn sunrise, a pack of chewing gum</u>; *Referring* means "directing attention to."

Reading Warm-up B, p. 156

Words that students are to circle appear in parentheses.

Sample Answers

1. <u>half a dozen languages</u>; She has brought her ideas about love and social equality to the people of many different lands.

2. <u>on television and at live performances</u>; An *expressive* reading reveals the reader's feelings and emotions.

3. You could use gestures and facial expressions to make a reading *animated*. Cartoons are called *animated* films because the drawings move.

4. It is a *demonstration* of Angelou's devotion to making the world a better place. The poet wants Americans to work together to build a more loving nation.

5. (storytelling); I enjoyed the *tradition* of sharing Thanksgiving dinner with my favorite cousins.

6. She refused to speak for five years. An antonym of *drastically* is *mildly*.

7. An autobiography is the author's own *version* of his or her life. Angelou's mother's *version* would not include Angelou's private thoughts or firsthand descriptions of things that happened to her.

8. <u>Her poems are filled to overflowing with strong emotions and powerful images</u>. A poem might be *bland* if the topic were uninteresting or if the poet used dull words and imagery.

Writing About the Big Question, p. 157

A. 1. truth
2. verify, evidence
3. circumstance
4. perspective

B. Sample Answers

1. I thought my friend told me she didn't want to go to the movies with me. What she meant was that she had seen the movie already and didn't want to go again.

2. I was **convinced** my friend meant she didn't want to go with me, and my feelings were hurt. What I thought she meant **distorted** the **truth**, and I suffered for it.

C. Sample Answer

entire understanding of people and the world around us.

Language gives us our means to describe the world around us and to communicate with people. When we learn a new language, it changes how we describe things and how we communicate. It forces us to talk differently about things, and that makes us see them differently. Truth can't be the same as it was.

Literary Analysis: Autobiographical Writing and Author's Voice, p. 158

Sample Answers

1. **Word choice:** *yakked*; *storytold*; *teeny, teeny*; all the Spanish names for the songs
Writer's attitude: She's remembering her subject fondly. The "rain, wind, stars, child" part seems poetic.
Syntax: She uses long, poetic-sounding sentences.

2. **Word choice:** Repetition of *butter*; *Mami, mantequilla, scowl*. She sprinkles Spanish words in her paragraphs.
Writer's attitude: She gives a detailed example of her mix-up of Spanish and English. She's enjoying the anecdote she tells.
Syntax: The *butter* fragment really illustrates her experience. Other sentences are long; she uses dialogue.

Reading: Preview the Text to Identify an Author's Purpose, p. 159

Sample Answers

1. The author's purpose is to inform.
2. The main subject is four of the ways in which English changes.
3. borrowed words

Vocabulary Builder, p. 160

Sample Answers

A. 1. C; 2. A; 3. D
4. B; 5. A; 6. C

B. 1. A football player might be very *determined* in the final minutes of a game if he thought his team still had a chance to win.

2. You might call an *exterminator* in order to put an end to all the roaches.

3. You might have felt every minute seemed *interminable* when you had to listen to a long, boring speech.

Enrichment: Take a Survey, p. 161

Survey results should demonstrate students' efforts to learn about languages spoken by their fellow students.

from **A White House Diary**
by Lady Bird Johnson
"My English" by Julia Alvarez

Integrated Language Skills: Personal Pronouns, p. 162

A. 1. Why <u>my</u> parents didn't first educate <u>us</u> in <u>our</u> native language by enrolling <u>us</u> in a Dominican school, <u>I</u> don't know. Part of <u>it</u> was that Mami's family had a tradition of sending the boys to the States to boarding school and college, and <u>she</u> had been one of the first girls to be allowed to join <u>her</u> brothers.

2. There was also a neat little trick <u>I</u> wanted to try on an English-speaking adult at home. <u>I</u> had learned <u>it</u> from Elizabeth, <u>my</u> smart-alecky friend in fourth grade, whom <u>I</u> alternately worshiped and resented.

B. Students' descriptions should correctly use and identify personal, reflexive, and intensive pronouns.

"My English" by Julia Alvarez

Open-Book Test, p. 165

Short Answer

1. Sample answer: A reader can predict that the essay will describe how Alvarez came to learn English. The first sentence suggests that Alvarez did not know English as a child, but the title suggests that she eventually thought of it as her own.
   Difficulty: *Challenging*   **Objective:** *Reading*

2. The details in the opening paragraphs suggest that Alvarez wrote the essay to record facts about her life. Students should cite any one of the many biographical details to support their answer.
   Difficulty: *Average*   **Objective:** *Reading*

3. Sample answer: Julia can learn what her mother is thinking and feeling from looking at her countenance, or face. For example, when the corners of her eyes crinkle, her mother is amused.
   Difficulty: *Average*   **Objective:** *Vocabulary*

4. The author compares the Spanish words that slip into her English to someone butting into line and to illegal immigrants trying to cross a border. Her attitude toward Spanish is that it is an annoyance, intrusion, and embarrassment.
   Difficulty: *Challenging*   **Objective:** *Interpretation*

5. Sample answer: Detail—Her teacher at Carol Morgan would scowl. This detail shows that Julia felt insecure about learning English.
   Difficulty: *Average*   **Objective:** *Literary Analysis*

6. Sample answer: "See you later, alligator." This idiom is another way of saying good-bye.
   Difficulty: *Easy*   **Objective:** *Interpretation*

7. The attitude is respectful. For example, Alvarez writes that her grandfather was a Cornell man and a United Nations representative, and he spoke perfect English.
   Difficulty: *Challenging*   **Objective:** *Literary Analysis*

8. Sample answer: This is a good comparison because English was sometimes challenging and intimidating for Alvarez, but like skyscrapers, it was also beautiful and exhilarating.
   Difficulty: *Easy*   **Objective:** *Interpretation*

9. Sister Maria's chalkboard writing is white like snow, the sound of tapping chalk is like the tapping of snow on tree branches, her scribbling is like a snowfall, and her writing starts out slowly and builds, filling the chalkboard like snow filling a town.
   Difficulty: *Easy*   **Objective:** *Literary Analysis*

10. Sample response: The image of the "snowy print" of Sister Maria's words on the chalkboard makes a strong impression. Alvarez may have included this image because it shows in a poetic way how Sister Maria helped her fall in love with English.
    Difficulty: *Average*   **Objective:** *Interpretation*

Essay

11. Students may show that Alvarez accomplishes the purpose of entertaining by citing amusing or captivating moments in the essay; she accomplishes the purpose of inspiring by citing poetic, life-changing moments in the essay; and she expresses gratitude by citing moments in which she learned something important from a beloved adult.
    Difficulty: *Easy*   **Objective:** *Essay*

12. Students should respond that Julia first met English as a small child, listening to her parents speak it when they wanted to communicate in secret. Later, she got to know English by learning it at the Carol Morgan School. When the family moved to New York City and she immersed herself in the language—with the help of great teachers like Sister Maria—Alvarez fell in love with English. Today, by writing in English, she continues to live "happily ever after" with it.
    Difficulty: *Average*   **Objective:** *Essay*

13. Students may respond that autobiography is nonfiction; that it tells the story of the author's own life; details show what the writer notices, thinks, and feels; and it is written using first-person pronouns. Students should illustrate each element they identify with a quotation or an example from the essay.
    Difficulty: *Challenging*   **Objective:** *Essay*

14. Students should reply that when she arrived in the United States, Alvarez believed that English-speakers were smarter than non-English-speakers because the language was so difficult and yet people of all kinds spoke it with ease. This belief begins to change when her mother explains that English-speakers learn the language from infancy, just as Julia has learned Spanish. The belief continues to change as Julia herself grows comfortable with the language and ceases to be intimidated by it.
    Difficulty: *Average*   **Objective:** *Essay*

Oral Response

15. Oral responses should be clear, well organized, and well supported by appropriate examples from the essay.
    Difficulty: *Average*   **Objective:** *Oral Interpretation*

"My English" by Julia Alvarez

Selection Test A, p. 168

Critical Reading

1. ANS: B	DIF: Easy	OBJ: Comprehension
2. ANS: C	DIF: Easy	OBJ: Reading
3. ANS: B	DIF: Easy	OBJ: Reading

4. ANS: C	DIF: Easy	OBJ: Literary Analysis
5. ANS: B	DIF: Easy	OBJ: Comprehension
6. ANS: D	DIF: Easy	OBJ: Literary Analysis
7. ANS: D	DIF: Easy	OBJ: Interpretation
8. ANS: A	DIF: Easy	OBJ: Comprehension
9. ANS: D	DIF: Easy	OBJ: Interpretation
10. ANS: A	DIF: Easy	OBJ: Reading
11. ANS: D	DIF: Easy	OBJ: Interpretation

Vocabulary and Grammar

12. ANS: A	DIF: Easy	OBJ: Vocabulary
13. ANS: D	DIF: Easy	OBJ: Vocabulary
14. ANS: B	DIF: Easy	OBJ: Grammar
15. ANS: C	DIF: Easy	OBJ: Grammar

Essay

16. Students' essays should note that Alvarez's purpose is to narrate an important part of her life and also to entertain the reader. Most will say that she succeeds. They may use examples of anecdotes, figures of speech, and word choice to support their views.
    Difficulty: *Easy*
    Objective: *Essay*

17. Students may say that Alvarez's teacher made language come alive and encouraged her students' imaginations. Students should then identify the teacher and grade, and tell what was special about the teacher's class. They should give some specific examples. Look for a statement summarizing why the teacher was important.
    Difficulty: *Easy*
    Objective: *Essay*

18. Alvarez's belief begins to change when her mother explains that English-speakers learn the language from infancy, just as Julia has learned Spanish. The belief continues to change as Julia herself grows comfortable with the language and ceases to be intimidated by it.
    Difficulty: *Easy*
    Objective: *Essay*

Selection Test B, p. 171

Critical Reading

1. ANS: B	DIF: Average	OBJ: Reading
2. ANS: A	DIF: Average	OBJ: Reading
3. ANS: C	DIF: Challenging	OBJ: Literary Analysis
4. ANS: C	DIF: Challenging	OBJ: Interpretation
5. ANS: D	DIF: Average	OBJ: Interpretation
6. ANS: B	DIF: Average	OBJ: Interpretation
7. ANS: C	DIF: Challenging	OBJ: Interpretation
8. ANS: B	DIF: Challenging	OBJ: Interpretation
9. ANS: C	DIF: Average	OBJ: Comprehension

10. ANS: B	DIF: Average	OBJ: Comprehension
11. ANS: D	DIF: Challenging	OBJ: Literary Analysis
12. ANS: D	DIF: Average	OBJ: Reading
13. ANS: D	DIF: Average	OBJ: Literary Analysis

Vocabulary and Grammar

14. ANS: B	DIF: Average	OBJ: Vocabulary
15. ANS: C	DIF: Challenging	OBJ: Vocabulary
16. ANS: B	DIF: Average	OBJ: Grammar
17. ANS: D	DIF: Average	OBJ: Grammar

Essay

18. In their essays, students should clearly identify a word, phrase, idiom, or writer to which they have responded in some strong fashion. They should coherently explain their experience with the word, phrase, or writer. They should also make clear connections between their own experience and one or more of Alvarez's experiences.
    Difficulty: *Average*
    Objective: *Essay*

19. Students should note that her voice is breezy or conversational and informal; some may say that her voice is poetic at points. She achieves her voice by sprinkling many Spanish words in the essay, listing English idioms that delight her, anecdotes and figures of speech, and using slang and made-up words. She is clearly delighted by her subject. Some of her sentences are very long, rolling on like great waves.
    Difficulty: *Challenging*
    Objective: *Essay*

20. Students should reply that when she arrived in the United States, Alvarez believed that English-speakers were smarter than non-English-speakers because the language was so difficult and yet people of all kinds spoke it with ease. This belief begins to change when her mother explains that English-speakers learn the language from infancy, just as Julia has learned Spanish. The belief continues to change as Julia herself grows comfortable with the language and ceases to be intimidated by it.
    Difficulty: *Average*
    Objective: *Essay*

"The Secret Life of Walter Mitty"
by James Thurber

Vocabulary Warm-up Exercises, p. 175

A. 1. specialists
2. performance
3. occur
4. complicated
5. menacing

6. objection
7. delicately
8. misty

B. Sample Answers

1. No, a person who wanders *aimlessly* has no specific purpose or direction.
2. You might think that two people who *bicker* a lot have different points of view.
3. No, *careless* driving is more likely to cause an accident.
4. No, a *fleeting* glance is very brief and would not give you enough time to learn a poem by heart.
5. Yes, an *initiative* allows voters to decide about new laws that are proposed by citizens.
6. No, *scornful* looks are reserved for things that people do not approve of.
7. No, a *squad* could not consist of just one person because it refers to a small group of people.

Reading Warm-up A, p. 176

Words that students are to circle appear in parentheses.

Sample Answers

1. simple; Computer programming is *complicated*.
2. (expert); A cartographer is a *specialist* in mapmaking.
3. awaken their subjects; I would handle an expensive vase *delicately*.
4. (vague); Dreams are like out-of-focus events that are hard to remember.
5. threatens their safety; A person or an animal that is *menacing* could frighten or injure someone.
6. (play); A band *performance* could go wrong if the musicians play out of tune.
7. Can eating spicy food late at night cause bad dreams? Can I learn to remember my dreams?
8. dreams reveal secret feelings that we cannot express in our waking hours; I think that some dreams may occasionally reflect hidden thoughts and emotions.

Reading Warm-up B, p. 177

Words that students are to circle appear in parentheses.

Sample Answers

1. the first puzzle piece; *Inserted* means "put into."
2. with no apparent direction; Wandering through a park might be done *aimlessly*.
3. (doodling); He is not very interested in what he is doing. He is bored.
4. never lasted long enough; Our memory of dreams is *fleeting*.
5. fearless soldiers; I would enjoy leading the cheerleading *squad*.
6. She is annoyed that Billy is daydreaming. She could have said, "I need your full attention, Billy."
7. (argued)(raised their voices); He daydreams about a world in which people do not bicker.

8. school enrichment; The initiative helped pay for special programs in school, like the literary magazine that Billy would be working on.

Writing About the Big Question, p. 178

A. 1. truth
2. perspective, credibility
3. manipulate
4. perceives

B. Sample Answers

1. I sometimes dream I'm a rock star and perform before huge audiences. My music is brilliant.
2. My daydream helps me feel better about my singing. It changes my **perspective** and makes me **believe** that just maybe I'll get better if I work at it.

C. Sample Answer

rich and entertaining.

In our imaginations, we can change the world any way we want. We can change ourselves. Anything is possible. The truth is whatever we want it to be.

Literary Analysis: Character, p. 179

Sample Answers

1. Mrs. Mitty is bossy and nagging. She treats her husband as if he were a child.
2. Walter Mitty is timid and incompetent. He does not like anyone to laugh at him—he is embarrassed by his incompetence.
3. Walter Mitty has a vivid imagination. In his imagination, he is attractive, assertive, and capable of violence.
4. Mrs. Mitty is nosy, meddlesome, and bossy. Walter Mitty stands up to her—maybe for the first time. She is surprised and thinks he must be sick.

Reading: Reflect on Details and Events to Determine an Author's Purpose, p. 180

Sample Answers

1. Thurber is showing how bossy Mrs. Mitty is. He also shows that Walter Mitty follows her orders without questioning her or saying anything.
2. Thurber shows that in his imagination, Walter Mitty is famous, respected, competent, and heroic—the opposite of who he is in real life.
3. Thurber provides another example of Walter Mitty obeying his wife. This time Mitty offers an argument but still obeys his wife's instructions.
4. Thurber provides another example of Walter Mitty's rich fantasy life. In his daydream, Mitty is courageous and competent.
5. Thurber shows Mitty imagining himself bravely facing a firing squad. The firing squad may represent Mrs. Mitty, showing how Mitty feels about her. Both the firing squad and Mrs. Mitty are powerful forces attacking

Mitty. Mitty is "inscrutable to the end," though. He does not give the firing squad or Mrs. Mitty the satisfaction of knowing what he thinks and feels.

Vocabulary Builder, p. 181

Sample Answers

A. 1. B; 2. C; 3. D
   4. A; 5. C; 6. D

B. 1. Because he was running too fast, the runner's pace was not *sustainable*.
   2. The end of this story is not *predictable*.
   3. Getting his college degree and then starting his own business is *attainable*.

Enrichment: Fine Arts, p. 182

Sample Answers

1. ***The Man With Three Masks:*** The overall mood is mysterious. It is not clear whether the man or the mask he holds is smiling. The red seems cheerful, but it fades to brown, which is sad, and the tie is businesslike.
   New Orleans Fantasy: The overall mood is cheerful and carefree, but there is also a hint of mystery. The figure might be a performer or someone in search of something.

2. ***The Man With Three Masks:*** I like the painting because it suggests the way people hide their true selves behind masks. I do not think the painting is pleasant, however. It is sad.
   New Orleans Fantasy: I like the colors in this painting, especially the stripes on the figure's arms and legs. It is lively and imaginative, and it makes me wonder what the figure is doing.

3. ***The Man With Three Masks:*** There is a little sadness in the painting, and Walter Mitty is sad in the way he does not stand up for himself. The figure in the painting is young, handsome, and graceful. I picture Walter Mitty as older and slouched over. Walter Mitty hides his true feelings from his wife, though, just as the man in the painting hides behind a mask. This man might resemble one of the characters Walter Mitty imagines being in his daydreams.
   New Orleans Fantasy: The feeling in the painting is humorous, just as the story is comical. The main figure looks like a comical circus performer and not like Mitty, who is meek and insecure. The figure does not look like any of the characters Mitty imagines being. These characters are serious and dignified. The figure is flying or swinging through a dreamy world, though, as if anything might be possible for him or her. In this way, the figure is like Mitty's imagination, which makes anything possible for him.

Open-Book Test, p. 183

Short Answer

1. Mrs. Mitty thinks of Walter as a child who needs to be taken care of. She nags him to buy overshoes and to wear his gloves.
   Difficulty: *Average*   **Objective:** *Interpretation*

2. Sample answer: Fault—Has trouble remembering details; Example—It takes him a while to remember the dog biscuits. Strength—He has a vivid imagination; Example—He imagines he is a heroic war commander.
   Difficulty: *Average*   **Objective:** *Literary Analysis*

3. The characters in Mitty's daydreams treat him with respect and admiration. Examples include the hydroplane crew's trusting his skill, the medical specialist's deferring to him to perform the surgery, and the army sergeant's being impressed by his bravado.
   Difficulty: *Average*   **Objective:** *Interpretation*

4. Students may quote the following passages: "'Why don't you wear your gloves? Have you lost your gloves?'" or "In a way he hated these weekly trips to town—he was always getting something wrong. . . . But she would remember it. 'Where's the what's-its-name?' she would ask. 'Don't tell me you forgot the what's-its-name.'"
   Difficulty: *Easy*   **Objective:** *Interpretation*

5. Mrs. Mitty is a flat character. She shows a single trait: impatience with her husband.
   Difficulty: *Easy*   **Objective:** *Literary Analysis*

6. Students may say that the author includes this memory to show that Mitty has a hard time operating in the real world or to contrast his real-life inabilities with his imagined heroism.
   Difficulty: *Challenging*   **Objective:** *Reading*

7. Sample answer: Walter Mitty feels distraught when he can't remember the second item his wife has told him to get.
   Difficulty: *Average*   **Objective:** *Vocabulary*

8. Walter Mitty is a man who uses his imagination to escape reality. Students may cite any one of Mitty's daydreams as support.
   Difficulty: *Average*   **Objective:** *Literary Analysis*

9. Students may say the story ends on a comic note, because the daydream of facing a firing squad with a smile on one's face is so fantastic, or they may say the story ends on a tragic note, because the firing squad daydream suggests that Mitty is in a state of despair.
   Difficulty: *Average*   **Objective:** *Interpretation*

10. Students may say that Walter Mitty is not inscrutable because, given the unfulfilling nature of his daily life, it is no mystery why he indulges in extreme flights of fancy.
    Difficulty: *Average*   **Objective:** *Vocabulary*

Essay

11. Students' essays should suggest that in real life, Mrs. Mitty, the cop, and the parking attendant all treat Mitty with impatience, even disrespect and disdain. They do this because he appears to be distracted and does not pay attention to what he is doing or to what they are saying. In his daydreams, Walter Mitty is an important or courageous person (commander, doctor, crack shot, captain, convicted criminal) who is admired and respected by those around him. Students may conclude

that Mitty's daydreams are a direct result of his unhappy life and marriage.

Difficulty: *Easy*   **Objective:** *Essay*

12. Students should acknowledge that the sights and sounds around him trigger the details in Mitty's daydreams. For example, he is driving through traffic when he has his opening daydream, in which he is flying a Navy hydroplane in bad weather. His second daydream, in which he is an accomplished and talented doctor, is triggered by the sight of the hospital parking lot. His third daydream, in which he is a "crack shot with any sort of firearms," is triggered by a newsboy who is shouting something about a trial. That dream ends with the phrase "You miserable cur," which reminds Mitty that he has to pick up puppy biscuits. His fourth daydream, in which he is a flying ace, is triggered by a magazine article with pictures of bombers and ruined streets.

Difficulty: *Average*   **Objective:** *Essay*

13. Students should indicate that by using limited third-person point of view, Thurber allows the reader to get to know Mrs. Mitty only through her interaction with Walter, which in turn creates a comically one-dimensional image of her. Limited third-person point of view also enables Thurber to weave in and out of Walter's daydreams just as Walter does. Finally, it creates suspense and surprise for readers as they leap back and forth with Walter from one world to the other.

Difficulty: *Challenging*   **Objective:** *Essay*

14. Students should reply that when Mrs. Mitty complains that he is hard to find in the hotel lobby and nags him about the overshoes, Walter stands up for himself by saying "'I was thinking. . . . Does it ever occur to you that I am sometimes thinking?'" This attempt to get his wife to see him differently does not succeed; Mrs. Mitty merely responds that she will have to take his temperature when they get home. Students may say that Mrs. Mitty's unwillingness to see him differently throws Mitty into a state of despair that is akin to standing before a firing squad.

Difficulty: *Average*   **Objective:** *Essay*

Oral Response

15. Students should give oral explanations in response to the question they choose or the one assigned to them.

Difficulty: *Average*   **Objective:** *Oral Interpretation*

Selection Test A, p. 186

Critical Reading

1. ANS: A	DIF: Easy	OBJ: Comprehension
2. ANS: C	DIF: Easy	OBJ: Interpretation
3. ANS: D	DIF: Easy	OBJ: Literary Analysis
4. ANS: C	DIF: Easy	OBJ: Comprehension
5. ANS: B	DIF: Easy	OBJ: Literary Analysis
6. ANS: C	DIF: Easy	OBJ: Reading

7. ANS: C	DIF: Easy	OBJ: Reading
8. ANS: B	DIF: Easy	OBJ: Interpretation
9. ANS: D	DIF: Easy	OBJ: Reading
10. ANS: C	DIF: Easy	OBJ: Interpretation
11. ANS: A	DIF: Easy	OBJ: Literary Analysis

Vocabulary and Grammar

12. ANS: A	DIF: Easy	OBJ: Vocabulary
13. ANS: C	DIF: Easy	OBJ: Vocabulary
14. ANS: B	DIF: Easy	OBJ: Grammar
15. ANS: D	DIF: Easy	OBJ: Grammar

Essay

16. Students may mention Mitty's timidity (his relationship with his wife), his lack of self-esteem (the incident with the garageman), his absentmindedness (his difficulty remembering errands), and his constant daydreaming. Each trait should be supported with an example.

Difficulty: *Easy*

Objective: *Essay*

17. Students should note that in real life, Mrs. Mitty and others treat Mitty with impatience, disrespect, and scorn. They make fun of him because he is incompetent and absentminded. In his fantasy life, he is an important and courageous person, and people treat him with respect. Students should support their points with specific examples from the story. They may conclude that the author shows us both lives to give us a fuller picture of Mitty's character and also to amuse us with the contrast.

Difficulty: *Easy*

Objective: *Essay*

18. Students should reply that Mrs. Mitty sees Mr. Mitty as an incompetent daydreamer. She complains that he is hard to find in the hotel lobby and nags him about the overshoes. After Walter stands up for himself, Mrs. Mitty responds that she will have to take his temperature when they get home, indicating that she still does not see him differently.

Difficulty: *Easy*

Objective: *Essay*

Selection Test B, p. 189

Critical Reading

1. ANS: C	DIF: Average	OBJ: Comprehension
2. ANS: B	DIF: Average	OBJ: Reading
3. ANS: C	DIF: Challenging	OBJ: Reading
4. ANS: D	DIF: Average	OBJ: Literary Analysis
5. ANS: D	DIF: Challenging	OBJ: Literary Analysis
6. ANS: B	DIF: Challenging	OBJ: Reading
7. ANS: A	DIF: Challenging	OBJ: Interpretation
8. ANS: D	DIF: Average	OBJ: Interpretation

9. ANS: A   DIF: Average   OBJ: Interpretation
10. ANS: D   DIF: Average   OBJ: Literary Analysis
11. ANS: D   DIF: Average   OBJ: Reading
12. ANS: B   DIF: Challenging   OBJ: Interpretation

Vocabulary and Grammar

13. ANS: A   DIF: Average   OBJ: Vocabulary
14. ANS: A   DIF: Challenging   OBJ: Vocabulary
15. ANS: A   DIF: Average   OBJ: Vocabulary
16. ANS: C   DIF: Average   OBJ: Grammar
17. ANS: C   DIF: Challenging   OBJ: Grammar

Essay

18. Students may note that Mitty's fantasies are often triggered by something in the real world. For example, he fantasizes about being a surgeon when he passes a hospital; he fantasizes about being in court when he hears a newsboy yelling news about a trial. Students should note that in real life, Mrs. Mitty, the cop, and the parking attendant all treat Mitty with impatience, even disrespect and scorn. In his fantasy life, Mitty ignores and even "erases" this treatment. He is an important and courageous person (commander, doctor, captain) who is admired and respected by those around him. Students may note that Mitty creates his daydreams to make up for the disrespect he gets in real life.

    Difficulty: *Average*

    Objective: *Essay*

19. Students will have varying interpretations. Some may suggest that despite the fact that Mitty stands up to his wife, his real life will not change. He is far too timid and too dominated by his wife to acquire a new real-life personality. The firing-squad daydream illustrates the hopelessness of his life. Others may suggest that Mitty does change—a little—at the story's end and that the firing-squad daydream is just another illustration of his heroic, carefree fantasy life.

    Difficulty: *Challenging*

    Objective: *Essay*

20. Students should reply that when Mrs. Mitty complains that he is hard to find in the hotel lobby and nags him about the overshoes, Walter stands up for himself by saying "'I was thinking. . . . Does it ever occur to you that I am sometimes thinking?'" This attempt to get his wife to see him differently does not succeed; Mrs. Mitty merely responds that she will have to take his temperature when they get home. Students may say that Mrs. Mitty's unwillingness to see him differently throws Mitty into a state of despair that is akin to standing before a firing squad.

    Difficulty: *Average*

    Objective: *Essay*

"Uncle Marcos" *from* The House of the Spirits
by Isabel Allende

Vocabulary Warm-up Exercises, p. 193

A. 1. attraction
2. confirmed
3. contraption
4. technical
5. acquainted
6. improvisations
7. strictly
8. authorities

B. Sample Answers

(Students should write two sentences. These samples include one with the optional alternative form of the vocabulary word.)

1. A. The area where the artifacts had been found was not <u>accessible</u>.
   B. I tried to <u>access</u> the data I needed at the library.
2. A. The main character was daring and <u>adventurous</u>.
   B. The novel described his many exciting <u>adventures</u>.
3. A. I plan to work on a <u>commercial</u> project after I graduate.
   B. In my opinion, religious holidays should not be <u>commercialized</u>.
4. A. Are the <u>farthest</u> stars from us also the oldest?
   B. Saturn is much <u>farther</u> from Earth than Mars.
5. A. He seemed <u>impassive</u> when he learned of the accident.
   B. His apparent <u>passivity</u> was actually his response to the shocking news.
6. A. We could only <u>speculate</u> on her reasons for rushing out like that.
   B. The project was too <u>speculative</u> for us to make firm predictions.
7. A. I cannot <u>withstand</u> pain for too long.
   B. She <u>withstood</u> her discomfort for a long time before asking for medicine.

Reading Warm-up A, p. 194

Words that students are to circle appear in parentheses.

Sample Answers

1. <u>as the artist who painted the *Mona Lisa*</u>; *Acquainted* means "aware of or familiar with."
2. (*Mona Lisa*); One *attraction* that might draw me in to a museum would be a painting by Van Gogh.
3. (his paintings); Leonardo was also a great scientist and inventor.
4. (thinkers); Unlike those *authorities*, Leonardo believed in using observation and experimentation to solve problems.
5. <u>scientific know-how</u>; An inventor might need to know about electricity and mechanical engineering.

6. When he could not get the materials he needed; If I forget to bring my music to band practice, *improvisations* might be useful.

7. (a flying machine); I would like to build a *contraption* that would keep my little brother from bothering me when I am talking on the phone.

8. by the many writings he left behind; Genius might be *confirmed* by the works of art or music a person creates.

Reading Warm-up B, p. 195

Words that students are to circle appear in parentheses.

Sample Answers

1. that human beings would soon be able to fly; I might *speculate* about the possibility of intelligent life on another planet.

2. had never been afraid of a challenge; *Adventurous* people might climb a mountain.

3. (making money); I think I could make a *commercial* success of a babysitting service.

4. A glider might be too fragile or flimsy to *withstand* strong winds. *Withstand* means "endure, or put up with."

5. The *farthest* I have been from home is Chicago. It was 500 miles away.

6. (airborne); No one had ever built a successful manned flying machine before.

7. They were *impassive* because they were not interested in the airplane. *Impassive* means "not showing emotion."

8. The airplane is accessible to all visitors at the National Air and Space Museum. It might not be *accessible* if the museum were closed.

Writing About the Big Question, p. 196

A. 1. perspective
2. manipulate, distort
3. assumption
4. belief

B. Sample Answers

1. My Aunt Lizzy has lived the most exciting life of anyone I know.

2. Aunt Lizzy's **perspective** on life is different from mine because she is eager to take chances and experiment. She's **convinced** that things will all work out in the end. I'm just the opposite; I'm **convinced** that things will all end up for the worse.

C. Sample Answer

may enjoy life more than someone whose expectations are more limited.

Uncle Marcos didn't seem to recognize the limits in life that most people around him did. The most amazing things, like human flight, seemed within reach. Maybe he failed at many things, but he also succeeded at things many people thought were impossible. He proved that in at least some situations, the truth that people perceive can change when someone with an imagination tries something and does it.

Literary Analysis: Character, p. 197

Sample Answers

A. 1. Uncle Marcos is adventurous, eccentric or unconventional, and theatrical. He refuses to commit himself to a responsible job and an ordinary life.

2. Marcos is persistent and not always sensitive to or perceptive about others.

3. Marcos recovers his spirit easily and, despite his crash, remains ready for adventure.

B. Students should provide examples from the selection to support their analysis. Students who argue that Uncle Marcos is a flat and static character should note that each episode illustrates a single main character trait: a spirit of adventure with no concern for what others expect. Students who argue that he is a round character may support their evaluation with details such as his fondness for Clara, his decision to close the fortune-telling business, or his desire to return to the family when ill. Students who argue that Uncle Marcos is dynamic should note that his rejection by Cousin Antonieta causes him to vow never to marry.

Reading: Reflect on Details and Events to Determine an Author's Purpose, p. 198

Sample Answers

A. 1. Allende wishes to show that Uncle Marcos is curious and unconventional (he does not live by the same rules as others).

2. Allende is showing that Marcos does not want to make a long-term commitment or do something that might be boring.

3. Allende shows that Marcos is not ashamed to show his love of Antonieta in front of everyone. His ideas about what is acceptable behavior differ from those of the townspeople.

4. Allende shows that Marcos is clever and daring.

5. Allende shows that Marcos is basically a decent person.

B. The author wants to paint a detailed picture of a highly unusual man who brings adventure and new ideas to a quiet town.

Vocabulary Builder, p. 199

Sample Answers

A. 1. C; 2. B; 3. A
4. A; 5. C; 6. D

B. 1. The ideas and feelings generated in a poem might make someone *reflective*.

2. If the CD player were *defective*, I'd take it back to get it fixed or replaced.

3. Only by being *cooperative* will government leaders accomplish anything.

Enrichment: The History of Human Flight, p. 200

Some answers will vary depending on the sources students consult.

Sample Answers

1. 1452–1519; Leonardo made the first recorded drawings of a human-powered aircraft.
2. December 17, 1903
3. May 20–21, 1927; Lindbergh flew from Roosevelt Field, New York, to Paris.
4. Experiments with helicopters began in 1906; between 1907 and about 1922, various inventors built helicopters that achieved an altitude of up to 12 feet and flew a couple of miles. The first commercially successful helicopter, the Bell 47, was prototyped in 1942 and certified in 1946.
5. 1939, in Germany
6. April 12, 1961; Yuri Gagarin of the Soviet Union
7. July 20, 1969; Neil Armstrong and Buzz Aldrin of the United States

"The Secret Life of Walter Mitty"
by James Thurber
"Uncle Marcos" *from* The House of the Spirits by Isabel Allende

Integrated Language Skills: Grammar, p. 201

A.
1. some—indefinite; that—relative
2. whose—interrogative
3. which—relative; everyone—indefinite
4. Who—interrogative; who—relative
5. Everyone—indefinite; that—relative; which—relative

B. Students should compose cohesive and grammatically correct paragraphs in which they demonstrate an ability to use and identify relative, interrogative, and indefinite pronouns.

Open-Book Test, p. 204

Short Answer

1. Examples of Uncle Marcos's behavior include bringing home an assortment of odd things from his travels, having manners like those of a cannibal, performing alchemy experiments, teaching Spanish to a parrot whose native language was an Amazon dialect, buying a barrel organ to entertain the public, building the first airplane in the community.

   Difficulty: *Easy* **Objective:** *Interpretation*

2. Uncle Marcos is closer to Clara than to anyone else. She enjoys his visits while the other family members seem to tolerate them; he leaves her his parrot; the two go into the fortune-telling business together; after Uncle Marcos takes off in his airplane, Clara watches longer than anyone else; she knows all of his stories by heart; after Uncle Marcos leaves, Clara is very upset.

   Difficulty: *Average* **Objective:** *Interpretation*

3. When Cousin Antonieta rejects him, Uncle Marcos falls into a deep depression and embarks on a journey around the world.

   Difficulty: *Easy* **Objective:** *Literary Analysis*

4. Uncle Marcos can be considered a round character because he has both faults and virtues. For example, he is kind to Clara, but he also disrupts his sister's household and has a hard time taking no for an answer.

   Difficulty: *Challenging* **Objective:** *Literary Analysis*

5. Severo's main trait is impatience with Uncle Marcos. For example, seeing Uncle Marcos sleeping in only a loincloth "put Severo in a terrible mood."

   Difficulty: *Easy* **Objective:** *Literary Analysis*

6. Students may say that the author's purpose is to entertain readers with Uncle Marcos's outrageous actions and adventures. Two entertaining episodes include his serenade of Cousin Antonieta and his fortune-telling with a fake crystal ball.

   Difficulty: *Average* **Objective:** *Reading*

7. Sample answer: Clara behaves disconsolately when Uncle Marcos leaves suddenly: She sleepwalks and sucks her thumb.

   Difficulty: *Average* **Objective:** *Vocabulary*

8. Sample answer: Action—Clara refuses to weep at her uncle's farewell; Character Trait—faith in her uncle's ability to servive.

   Difficulty: *Average* **Objective:** *Literary Analysis*

9. No, Clara's affection for Uncle Marcos is not unrequited; it is returned. Uncle Marcos tells Clara stories, goes into business with her, and leaves her his parrot when he goes traveling.

   Difficulty: *Average* **Objective:** *Vocabulary*

10. Sample answer: Allende refers to his "resurrection" as "heroic." She may do so because he seems to come back from the dead or because he has, in fact, survived a dangerous adventure.

    Difficulty: *Challenging* **Objective:** *Interpretation*

Essay

11. Students who have affection for Uncle Marcos may say Clara's feelings most match their own; students who feel impatience with him may say Severo's or Nivea's feelings most match their own. Essays should include relevant examples from the text.

    Difficulty: *Easy* **Objective:** *Essay*

12. Students may identify the following moments of crisis: Uncle Marcos's rejection by Cousin Antonieta; his failed airplane flight; the stresses brought on by his fortune-telling business; and his final illness. Students should acknowledge that in each case, Uncle Marcos maintains his sense of humor and optimism and looks immediately for another project to occupy his mind. Some students may find this eternal optimism respectable, while others may view it as an inability to deal constructively with the pressures of real life.

    Difficulty: *Average* **Objective:** *Essay*

13. Students should note that on the one hand, Uncle Marcos is utterly vibrant and adventuresome; on the other hand, his restlessness and wanderlust put him in

some very dangerous situations. Students should provide relevant support for each idea.

Difficulty: *Challenging* **Objective:** *Essay*

14. Students should respond that the townspeople's *perception* of Uncle Marcos has changed: After the courtship, they view him as a pathetic romantic who will not take no for an answer, but after his attempted flight across the mountains, they view him as an adventurer who will take great risks to do great things.

Difficulty: *Average* **Objective:** *Essay*

Oral Response

15. Students should give oral explanations in response to the question they choose or the one assigned to them.

Difficulty: *Average* **Objective:** *Oral Interpretation*

"Uncle Marcos" *from* The House of the Spirits by Isabel Allende

Selection Test A, p. 207

Critical Reading

1. ANS: B	DIF: Easy	OBJ: Interpretation
2. ANS: A	DIF: Easy	OBJ: Comprehension
3. ANS: C	DIF: Easy	OBJ: Literary Analysis
4. ANS: D	DIF: Easy	OBJ: Reading
5. ANS: D	DIF: Easy	OBJ: Comprehension
6. ANS: C	DIF: Easy	OBJ: Literary Analysis
7. ANS: B	DIF: Easy	OBJ: Reading
8. ANS: D	DIF: Easy	OBJ: Reading
9. ANS: D	DIF: Easy	OBJ: Interpretation
10. ANS: B	DIF: Easy	OBJ: Comprehension
11. ANS: B	DIF: Easy	OBJ: Comprehension
12. ANS: C	DIF: Easy	OBJ: Literary Analysis

Vocabulary and Grammar

13. ANS: A	DIF: Easy	OBJ: Vocabulary
14. ANS: B	DIF: Easy	OBJ: Vocabulary
15. ANS: D	DIF: Easy	OBJ: Grammar

Essay

16. Students' essays should identify the episode and explain two things: (1) what the episode reveals about Marcos's character and (2) how people respond to him in the episode. For example, his building and flying the airplane reveal Marcos's daring and sense of adventure as well as his ability to stick to a long, complicated project. The townspeople's joyful celebration shows that they are awed by his accomplishment and realize its importance.

Difficulty: *Easy*
Objective: *Essay*

17. Uncle Marcos is closer to Clara than to anyone else, and she is fonder of him than any of the other characters are. Examples students might mention: She listens to and remembers his stories more carefully than anyone else. She watches for his return longer than anyone else—even after he is supposedly buried. He leaves his parrot to Clara. The two work together in the fortune-telling business.

Difficulty: *Easy*

Objective: *Essay*

18. Students should respond that the townspeople changed, because they changed their perception of Uncle Marcos. After the courtship, they view him as a pathetic romantic who will not take "no" for an answer. After his attempted flight across the mountains, they view him as a hero and adventurer who will take great risks to do great things.

Difficulty: *Easy*

Objective: *Essay*

Selection Test B, p. 210

Critical Reading

1. ANS: A	DIF: Average	OBJ: Interpretation
2. ANS: A	DIF: Average	OBJ: Comprehension
3. ANS: D	DIF: Average	OBJ: Literary Analysis
4. ANS: C	DIF: Average	OBJ: Literary Analysis
5. ANS: B	DIF: Average	OBJ: Reading
6. ANS: B	DIF: Average	OBJ: Comprehension
7. ANS: B	DIF: Average	OBJ: Reading
8. ANS: C	DIF: Average	OBJ: Interpretation
9. ANS: C	DIF: Average	OBJ: Literary Analysis
10. ANS: C	DIF: Challenging	OBJ: Reading
11. ANS: D	DIF: Challenging	OBJ: Literary Analysis
12. ANS: B	DIF: Average	OBJ: Comprehension
13. ANS: D	DIF: Average	OBJ: Literary Analysis

Vocabulary and Grammar

14. ANS: D	DIF: Average	OBJ: Vocabulary
15. ANS: A	DIF: Challenging	OBJ: Vocabulary
16. ANS: A	DIF: Average	OBJ: Vocabulary
17. ANS: C	DIF: Average	OBJ: Grammar
18. ANS: C	DIF: Average	OBJ: Grammar

Essay

19. Students' essays should briefly summarize three episodes and explain what each reveals about Marcos's character and about how others respond to him. For example, his building and flying the airplane reveal Marcos's daring and sense of adventure as well as his ability to stick to a long, demanding project. The

townspeople's joyful celebration of his flight shows that they are awed by his accomplishment and realize its importance. Students should note whether the episodes they discuss show only a single characteristic of Marcos or whether they show different sides of him.
Difficulty: *Average*
Objective: *Essay*

20. Students might choose his relationship with Cousin Antonieta (she is not interested, but that does not stop him from pursuing her); he is stubbornly persistent. They might write about his brother-in-law Severo (Severo tolerates Marcos's visits, but is appalled at his eccentric behavior); Marcos does not care what others think of him. They might write about his relationship with Clara (Clara adores her uncle and has great faith in his abilities); he is loveable and has affection for others.
Difficulty: *Challenging*
Objective: *Essay*

21. Students should respond that the townspeople's *perception* of Uncle Marcos has changed: After the courtship, they view him as a pathetic romantic who will not take "no" for an answer; but after his attempted flight across the mountains, they view him as an adventurer who will take great risks to do great things.
Difficulty: *Average*
Objective: *Essay*

"If I Forget Thee, Oh Earth . . ."
by Arthur C. Clarke
from Silent Spring by Rachel Carson

Vocabulary Warm-up Exercises, p. 214

A. 1. misfortunes
2. landscape
3. reminder
4. harmony
5. hostile
6. stark
7. variety
8. unnoticed

B. Sample Answers
1. F; *Substantial* means a large amount, and a small party would not have a large guest list.
2. T; *Prosperous* means successful and a successful business might expand operations.
3. F; A pitch-black room has no light in it, and *radiance* describes a soft, shining light.
4. T; To *scour* means to scrub and that might ruin a woman's freshly painted nails.
5. F; *Agony* describes intense pain or suffering, which would create the opposite feeling from being very happy.
6. F; Someone who enjoys being around people would not prefer to be separated from others, which is what happens when one is in *isolation*.

7. T; Dorms are where students live on a college campus, so they are *residential*.
8. F; *Abundance* means a great deal of something, and most people would not be disappointed to receive a large number of gifts on their birthday.

Reading Warm-up A, p. 215

Words that students are to circle appear in parentheses.
Sample Answers
1. the view of one's surroundings; The *watery landscape* is the ocean.
2. uncomfortable; *Harsh* is a synonym for *hostile*.
3. (remember); their list of complaints
4. simple things on land; *Overlooked* is a synonym for *unnoticed*.
5. (different); living underwater, vacationing underwater, and drilling for oil
6. impossible to avoid the conclusion; One *stark limitation* of living underwater would be the lack of oxygen.
7. (hardships); in the dark ocean there is no natural light. The aquanauts lost their appetite in the strange environment. They lost their privacy in the too-tight quarters.
8. (peaceful); *Conflict* is an antonym for *harmony*.

Reading Warm-up B, p. 216

Words that students are to circle appear in parentheses.
Sample Answers
1. (large); *Plenty* is a synonym for *abundance*.
2. (home); I live in a large city, so you would see mainly apartment buildings in a *residential* neighborhood.
3. (successful); *Poor* is an antonym for *prosperous*.
4. (scrub); You might *scour* dirty pans when you do the dishes at home.
5. (separated from); We interact with the environment all the time.
6. (significant); Two *substantial* ways that people can reduce pollution is by riding a bike or taking public transportation and by turning off unnecessary lights to use less electricity.
7. (suffer); *Suffering* is a synonym for *agony*.
8. softer light; Dawn is a time when you might enjoy the *radiance* of the sun because it often has a soft shining light when it first appears.

Writing About the Big Question, p. 217

A. 1. speculate
2. assumption
3. convince
4. evidence

B. Sample Answers
1. People must change the way they live in order to stop global warming.

2. People will have to **perceive** that we must reduce our need for energy, even if it costs money or is inconvenient. They must realize the **truth** that people cannot go on living as they have in the past.

C. Sample Answer

I speculate that in 100 years, the Earth will be very different from now. My assumptions are based on the fact that so much has changed in the last 100 years. The truths that people believed 100 years ago have changed and they will probably change in 100 years.

Literary Analysis: Theme, p. 218

Sample Answers

"If I Forget Thee, Oh Earth . . ."

1. The passage reveals that all life on Earth has been destroyed, probably as a result of a nuclear war.

2. The passage suggests that human beings have, some time in the story's past, engaged in a nuclear war that brought life on Earth to an end.

3. Human beings have the capacity to destroy all life on Earth and make the planet uninhabitable.

from Silent Spring

1. The white granular powder may represent pesticides. The powder has killed birds and fish, killed vegetation, and prevented livestock from breeding and trees from fruiting.

2. The passage emphasizes that human beings are responsible for greatly damaging the planet on which we live.

3. Human beings have greatly damaged Earth through the use of pesticides, endangering all species—including our own.

Vocabulary Builder, p. 219

Sample Answers

A. 1. I purged the wound on my foot, thereby decreasing the chances of infection.

2. Those flowers are perennials, so you will not need to plant them again next year.

3. Because of the blight, the potatoes we grew were damaged this year.

4. Due to various maladies, they became weaker and more depressed.

5. The fact that her garden was moribund filled her with sadness.

B. 1. C; 2. B; 3. D; 4. A

Open-Book Test, p. 221

Short Answer

1. Sample answer: The story opens with a feeling of adventure and suspense. Details such as the corridors leading upward through the ground and Marvin's goal of going "Outside" help create this mood.

   Difficulty: *Challenging* **Objective:** *Interpretation*

2. Sample answer: Marvin goes "Outside"; Marvin sees Earth hanging in the sky; Marvin realizes why his father brought him to see Earth.

Difficulty: *Average* **Objective:** *Interpretation*

3. Marvin's father wants to spark in Marvin the desire to survive and help later generations one day return to Earth. The author wants to spark in the reader the desire to keep Earth healthy. If the reader succeeds, Marvin and other humans can avoid being homeless in the future.

   Difficulty: *Average* **Objective:** *Literary Analysis*

4. Sample answer: The town was formerly alive and healthy; now it is sick and dying. Students should include some of Carson's descriptive details in their responses.

   Difficulty: *Easy* **Objective:** *Interpretation*

5. Sample answer: By using an imaginary town, Carson can show changes in the environment happening suddenly and drastically. The stark contrast between "before" and "after" strengthens the impact of her message on the reader.

   Difficulty: *Challenging* **Objective:** *Literary Analysis*

6. Carson's theme is implied in the description of the town's deterioration and stated in the essay's final paragraph.

   Difficulty: *Average* **Objective:** *Literary Analysis*

7. In "If I Forget Thee, Oh Earth . . ." the blight is nuclear radioactivity. In the excerpt from *Silent Spring*, the blight is caused by pesticides.

   Difficulty: *Average* **Objective:** *Vocabulary*

8. Sample answer: The future of planet Earth may be grim if human beings do not choose to take better care of it.

   Difficulty: *Easy* **Objective:** *Literary Analysis*

9. Students may say that the scenario in "If I Forget Thee" is more chilling because life on the moon seems desolate and lonely and because the idea of an empty, toxic Earth is frightening; or they may say that the scenario in *Silent Spring* is more chilling because it is more recognizable and therefore seems more possible. Students should support their opinions with relevant examples from the texts.

   Difficulty: *Average* **Objective:** *Interpretation*

10. Sample response: Marvin would feel overwhelmed and overjoyed by the beauty of Earth. He would warn others of the possible long-term consequences of their actions. He would make a great citizen because he would take good care of the land and its inhabitants.

    Difficulty: *Average* **Objective:** *Literary Analysis*

Essay

11. Students should clearly state the theme of the selection they have chosen. In general, they should point out that Clarke's theme concerns the danger of nuclear war and its likely devastation of Earth, or they should note that Carson focuses on the use of pesticides and the danger posed by those chemicals. Students should use examples and details from the text to support their statement of the theme.

Difficulty: *Easy* Objective: *Essay*

12. Students should describe a TV ad that borrows from or recasts one of the works in order to warn viewers about a particular environmental hazard. Students should also state the theme of the ad and explain how they would communicate it and why.

Difficulty: *Average* Objective: *Essay*

13. Students should address the fact that both writers felt that there was potential for some level of destruction if human beings did not change their ways. In their essays, students should also include a well-supported opinion about whether that is still true and whether the concerns are the same or different.

Difficulty: *Challenging* Objective: *Essay*

14. The central truth of both works is that human beings are responsible for their own future. Students may agree or disagree but should appropriately and adequately support their opinions.

Difficulty: *Average* Objective: *Essay*

Oral Response

15. Students should give oral explanations in response to the question they choose or the one assigned to them.

Difficulty: *Average* Objective: *Oral Interpretation*

Selection Test A, p. 224

Critical Reading

1. ANS: D	DIF: Easy	OBJ: Interpretation
2. ANS: D	DIF: Easy	OBJ: Comprehension
3. ANS: B	DIF: Easy	OBJ: Interpretation
4. ANS: B	DIF: Easy	OBJ: Literary Analysis
5. ANS: C	DIF: Easy	OBJ: Literary Analysis
6. ANS: B	DIF: Easy	OBJ: Comprehension
7. ANS: B	DIF: Easy	OBJ: Literary Analysis
8. ANS: A	DIF: Easy	OBJ: Interpretation
9. ANS: D	DIF: Easy	OBJ: Interpretation
10. ANS: B	DIF: Easy	OBJ: Interpretation
11. ANS: B	DIF: Easy	OBJ: Literary Analysis
12. ANS: C	DIF: Easy	OBJ: Literary Analysis

Vocabulary

13. ANS: C	DIF: Easy	OBJ: Vocabulary
14. ANS: D	DIF: Easy	OBJ: Vocabulary
15. ANS: C	DIF: Easy	OBJ: Vocabulary

Essay

16. In their essays, students should clearly state the theme of the selection they have chosen. They should use examples and details from the selection to support their statement of the theme. In general, students should point out that Clarke's theme concerns the danger of

nuclear war and its devastation of the Earth, while Carson focuses on the use of pesticides and the danger posed by these chemicals to the environment.

Difficulty: *Easy*

Objective: *Essay*

17. Students should address the fact that both writers felt that there was potential for some level of destruction if people did not change their ways. In their essays, students should include a well-supported opinion about whether that is still true and whether the concerns are the same or different. Look for examples and details to support their opinion.

Difficulty: *Easy*

Objective: *Essay*

18. Students may agree or disagree, but opinions should be appropriately and adequately supported with information from the selections.

Difficulty: *Easy*

Objective: *Essay*

Selection Test B, p. 227

Critical Reading

1. ANS: C	DIF: Average	OBJ: Interpretation
2. ANS: C	DIF: Average	OBJ: Comprehension
3. ANS: A	DIF: Challenging	OBJ: Interpretation
4. ANS: D	DIF: Average	OBJ: Comprehension
5. ANS: B	DIF: Average	OBJ: Interpretation
6. ANS: C	DIF: Average	OBJ: Literary Analysis
7. ANS: A	DIF: Challenging	OBJ: Interpretation
8. ANS: C	DIF: Average	OBJ: Literary Analysis
9. ANS: D	DIF: Average	OBJ: Comprehension
10. ANS: C	DIF: Average	OBJ: Literary Analysis
11. ANS: D	DIF: Challenging	OBJ: Interpretation
12. ANS: C	DIF: Average	OBJ: Interpretation
13. ANS: D	DIF: Average	OBJ: Literary Analysis
14. ANS: C	DIF: Challenging	OBJ: Literary Analysis
15. ANS: C	DIF: Challenging	OBJ: Interpretation

Vocabulary

16. ANS: B	DIF: Average	OBJ: Vocabulary
17. ANS: C	DIF: Average	OBJ: Vocabulary
18. ANS: C	DIF: Average	OBJ: Vocabulary

Essay

19. Students should clearly state the selection's theme. Look for examples and details to support their choice of the more persuasive selection. Students who choose Clarke's story may note these powerful, persuasive images: the stark details of life on the moon, the wonder and beauty of the view of Earth, and the sickly glow of the radioactive Earth. Students who choose Carson's essay may note the powerful images of deaths and ill-

nesses in the entire community, specific examples of the destruction of plants and animals, and Carson's statement that "The people had done it themselves."

Difficulty: *Average*

Objective: *Essay*

20. Students should note that the atmosphere, or overall mood, of both settings is somber. For example, Clarke contrasts the challenging, strictly ordered life of exile in the Colony with romantic vistas of possibilities on Earth—possibilities that now lie in ruins but may be restored once again in the future. Carson contrasts a flourishing past era of natural diversity and vigor with a devastated present, in which nature is moribund. In their essays, students should identify examples of sensory imagery and figurative language in both selections and tell how these relate to the overall mood of each work.

Difficulty: *Average*

Objective: *Essay*

21. The central truth of both works is that human beings are responsible for their own futures. Students may agree or disagree, but opinions should be appropriately and adequately supported.

Difficulty: *Average*

Objective: *Essay*

Writing Workshop

Problem-and-Solution Essay: Integrating Grammar Skills, p. 231

A. 1. his or her; *everyone*; 2. their; *many*; 3. their; *few*; 4. her; *neither*

B. 1. Most of the students liked <u>their</u> trip to the planetarium.
2. Everyone on the trip had <u>his or her</u> chance to interact with the exhibits.
3. Either Juan or Nancy had <u>his or her</u> questions answered by museum guides.
4. correct

Vocabulary Workshop 1, p. 232

Sample Answers

1. heart-to-heart
2. heartsick
3. heartstrings
4. heartthrob
5. heartrending

Vocabulary Workshop 2, p. 233

Sample Answers

Answers will vary. Samples follow:

1. conversation/talk
2. disappointed/sad/unhappy
3. hurt me/caused me deep feelings
4. boyfriend

5. sad/distressing

Benchmark Test 2, p. 235

MULTIPLE CHOICE

1. ANS: D
2. ANS: D
3. ANS: D
4. ANS: B
5. ANS: A
6. ANS: D
7. ANS: B
8. ANS: C
9. ANS: D
10. ANS: B
11. ANS: B
12. ANS: A
13. ANS: D
14. ANS: D
15. ANS: B
16. ANS: A
17. ANS: C
18. ANS: C
19. ANS: A
20. ANS: C
21. ANS: A
22. ANS: C
23. ANS: B
24. ANS: D
25. ANS: C
26. ANS: B
27. ANS: A
28. ANS: C
29. ANS: C
30. ANS: B
31. ANS: C
32. ANS: C
33. ANS: D
34. ANS: B
35. ANS: C

ESSAY

36. Journal entries should describe an exciting event using expressive language.
37. Details in the character profile should be organized to support an overall impression.

38. Essays should comprise two or three paragraphs that state a problem, suggest a solution, and sum up the most persuasive arguments.

Vocabulary in Context 1, p. 241

MULTIPLE CHOICE

1. ANS: A
2. ANS: B
3. ANS: D
4. ANS: A
5. ANS: C
6. ANS: B
7. ANS: A
8. ANS: C
9. ANS: A
10. ANS: D
11. ANS: C
12. ANS: D
13. ANS: B
14. ANS: C
15. ANS: A
16. ANS: B
17. ANS: D
18. ANS: D
19. ANS: C
20. ANS: A